Making Educational Decisions

Making Educational Decisions

An Introduction to Philosophy of Education

ROBERT E. FITZGIBBONS

Bridgewater State College

HARCOURT BRACE JOVANOVICH, INC.

New York   San Diego   Chicago   San Francisco   Atlanta
London   Sydney   Toronto

For Linda
and
Our Children

ISBN: 0-15-554621-X

Library of Congress Catalog Card Number: 80-84725

Printed in the United States of America

Cover photo by George Zimbel, courtesy of
Educational Facilities Laboratories

Preface

Making Educational Decisions, a textbook on how to think clearly and intelligently about education, is designed for use in introductory education courses, particularly courses in philosophy of education. The essentials of such studies are important for anyone who wants to be able to make educational decisions intelligently—or who needs to determine how intelligently these decisions have been made by others. Throughout the book I have attempted to answer two basic questions: What does a person need to know in order to increase his or her ability to make educational decisions intelligently? And what general strategies can be employed in gathering evidence and coming to reasonable conclusions concerning what should be taught, how it should be taught, and what the outcomes of education ought to be? It is my hope that mastering these fundamentals will help future teachers and administrators make their educational decisions intelligently, and thereby improve the education most people receive and, consequently, the quality of their lives.

In a broad sense, this book is an introduction to philosophy of education. It is especially concerned with showing the beginning student of education where, why, and how philosophy of education is relevant to—and indeed critical for—the practical business of teaching. It seems regrettable that in recent years there has been a growing tendency to denigrate the importance of philosophy of education. The course has ceased to be a requirement in certain teacher education programs and, in some areas, is no longer necessary for teacher certification. These omissions can only abet a general decline in the quality of education and the quality of teacher preparation programs. If in some way this book contributes to an increased understanding of the significance of philosophy of education and helps improve the degree to which people make educational decisions intelligently, I will be more than pleased.

The book contains sufficient material for a full semester course, but it may be abridged or supplemented in any number of ways. For review at the end of each chapter, the student is asked to define the new terms used in the chapter and to demonstrate an understanding of its central concepts. Some instructors may wish to use some or all of these sections as written homework assignments or as test items; others may prefer to use them as the basis for in-class discussions.

Interspersed throughout the text are questions that relate to the proximate textual material; in most instances, they follow quotations from a current source. Answering these questions as they arise will give the student immediate practice in applying understanding gained from the main discussion. However, like the review sections, these questions can also be used apart from the reading assignment as test items.

At the end of each Part, there is a list of books for further reading. Students who consult even a few of these books will deepen and extend their working knowledge of the major topics included in the text. But perhaps the most significant way in which the student can augment the text material is by continually relating it to his or her *own* educational beliefs and decisions and to the beliefs and decisions of others.

I should like to acknowledge the many helpful suggestions I received on this project from former students and from several colleagues who commented on early drafts of the manuscript: Emily E. Haynes Robertson, Syracuse University; Jane R. Martin, University of Massachusetts; Philip G. Smith, Indiana University; and especially, Gerald M. Reagan, Ohio State University. I am particularly grateful for the invaluable, expert editorial assistance of Carolyn Johnson of Harcourt Brace Jovanovich. And, finally, as with many of us, my greatest indebtedness is to my parents, for they guided my earliest and most crucial education.

Robert E. Fitzgibbons

Contents

PART TWO

Logic: The Basis for Making Rational
Educational Decisions   51

PART THREE

Ethics and Educational Decision-Making   133

CHAPTER **10**   Selecting a Reasonable Ethical Theory   157

PART FOUR

Educational Decisions   179

CHAPTER **11**   The Matter and Manner of Education   181

CHAPTER **12**   The Outcomes of Education   197

CHAPTER **13**   Making Intelligent Decisions Concerning
the Outcomes of Education   209

CHAPTER **14**   Making Intelligent Decisions Concerning
the Matter of Education   223

CHAPTER **15**   Making Intelligent Decisions Concerning
the Manner of Education   239

PART ONE

How Philosophy of Education Is Necessary for Making Intelligent Educational Decisions

No aspect of education is to be disparaged; it is the highest blessing bestowed on mankind, and it is the best of them on whom it is most fully bestowed. When it takes a false turn which permits of correction, we should, one and all, devote the energy of a lifetime to its amendment.

—*Plato*

CHAPTER

1

Introduction

During the 1930s, several films were made depicting the struggles of early aviators and the birth of the aviation industry. Classic scenes showed the hero flying through storm and fog to deliver the mail or to save the life of a friend. Whatever the circumstances, the essence of these scenes was the same. The pilot, flying "by the seat of his pants," did the seemingly impossible and saved the day. Flying by the seat of his pants meant flying without instruments, radio, or radar—these being either unknown or suddenly inoperative. Often visibility was zero due to the fog, and mountains surrounded the landing field; still the hero (possibly because he was the hero) sensed the field there below him. Unable to see and with no firm guide at all, he pushed the stick forward and the plane began its descent. Relaxing their grips on the armrests of their seats, the members of the audience breathed a collective sigh of relief when, miraculously, the landing field suddenly appeared and the plane was safely down.

Fortunately, modern pilots seldom fly airplanes by the seats of their pants. Since the Wright brothers first flew at Kittyhawk, we have learned a great deal about flight and airplane safety. We now have radar and radios, altimeters and ground control stations. Today, flying is not a matter of guesswork or luck; it is a serious, scientific business based upon considerable knowledge and skill.

This knowledge and skill developed because people saw a need to take flying out of the realm of the indeterminate and uncertain. Safety and reliability in air travel became accepted goals. But achieving them was not to be an easy task. The thousands of men and women committed to it had to pursue arduous intellectual paths. And those paths led them directly to some of the most significant discoveries of modern science. To these pioneers, it was obvious that their goals would be realized only through substantial increases in their knowledge.

For centuries people have conducted the education of children as if flying by the seats of their pants. However, the real world does not operate like a Hollywood sound stage: the fog of ignorance cannot be blown away at the last minute by giant fans. The Hollywood pilot can miraculously escape disaster. But in the real world, poorly educated children grow into poorly educated adults.

In making the educational decisions that so profoundly affect the destinies of children, educators need to be guided by more than mere "hunches"; that is, they must rise above primitive, unsophisticated modes of decision-making. In order to have even a moderate probability of functioning to the advantage of children, educational decisions must be based upon a knowledge and understanding of what that advantage actually is, what is necessary to effect it, and what can be done to maximize it.

This book is about education. It deals with the very practical decisions that educators, parents, government officials, and students themselves must make regarding who should be taught, what should be taught, and how it should be taught. Yet, unlike other works on the subject, this book will not attempt to tell you what you should believe concerning any of these matters, nor will it attempt to tell you specifically what you should do about them. Rather, it will explore the basic knowledge and understanding you will need in order to intelligently come to your own conclusions and to intelligently make your own decisions.

EDUCATIONAL DECISIONS AND THE NEED FOR KNOWLEDGE

Educational decisions are in certain respects very much like the decisions that modern pilots must make. Flying by the seat of one's pants is not an adequate approach in piloting jetliners or in making successful educational decisions. We can raise educational decision-making above the level of mere guesswork only by increasing our knowledge and understanding of how to make those decisions rationally. Yet the task of acquiring this knowledge is not one that can be handled cavalierly. Sustained, systematic study is necessary in order to come to a significant understanding of what needs to be known.

This, of course, is not to say that having more knowledge will guarantee that educational decisions will be made intelligently. Rather, the point here is that in most cases possessing certain knowledge is *necessary* for making sound decisions. Clearly, some very poor decisions have been made by people who possessed a great deal of knowledge. Nevertheless, without a specific body of knowledge, many problems could not be solved. For instance, consider the impossibility of landing a person on the moon if we did not possess significant knowledge of propulsion and gravitational forces. Knowledge may not be sufficient for solving problems, but in most cases it is necessary.

Knowledge, however, seldom comes easily. Each major advance in human knowledge is a victory dearly won. Hours, indeed years, of painstaking study are frequently necessary. For in order to penetrate the frontiers of knowledge, one often needs to know first what has already been determined. Sir Isaac Newton, the great physicist, once said that he stood on the shoulders of giants. By this he meant that it was only through discoveries made by others that he was able to formulate and defend his own scientific principles, principles that opened the door to the modern technological age.

That the development of our knowledge of education has lagged behind progress in the natural sciences hardly needs emphasis. Yet the beginning student of education does need to be aware of the fundamental reason for this poor showing. Whereas people working in the natural sciences had determined the methods of investigation and justification appropriate to their field, those concerned with education had not. Without a determination of such methods, no sure achievement of educational knowledge is possible. And the less we know of education, the less are our chances of making sound educational decisions.

At the same time it must be recognized that, with or without the appropriate knowledge, educational decisions must be made. They cannot be avoided. By the very nature of the world and children's part in it, the adult members of any human society are forced to make certain educational decisions. They must decide what their children should learn— what of the accumulated knowledge of the group is worth passing on to the next generations. They must also decide how to pass on this knowledge. Indeed, *not* deciding these matters is in a sense an educational decision. It is the decision to leave the choice to other individuals or groups, or else to the uncontrolled influences of the natural environment.

Just as these decisions cannot be avoided, they must be made more or less intelligently. Educational decisions that are based upon sound, relevant evidence are made more intelligently than those based upon weak or irrelevant evidence. In other words, educational decision-making can be viewed as ranging over a continuum. At one end of the continuum are those decisions made on the basis of virtually no evidence at all—"irrational" or "uninformed" decisions; at the other end are "intelligent," "fully informed" decisions. The important point to recognize here is that, since educational decisions can be made more or less intelligently, *how* intelligently they are made depends upon a person's knowledge and how it is used. The more intelligently a decision has been made, the greater has been the consideration of that which is relevant. And this, of course, requires that the person making the decision actually knows what is relevant.

When making decisions regarding how to build an airplane, the aeronautical engineer needs to possess a considerable body of knowledge. The engineer needs this knowledge in order to be able to make decisions intelligently and hence maximize the probabilities that the plane being designed will fly safely. Clearly, no sane person would want to fly in an airplane designed and built by someone who knew practically nothing about aeronautical design and construction. Similarly, no one who truly cares about the welfare of children should want to send them into an educational situation designed and implemented by someone who knows nothing or very little about education.

FOR THOSE WHO CARE ABOUT EDUCATION

This book is intended for anyone who cares about the education of children. It is designed to provide the basic knowledge necessary for making intelligent educational decisions. Thus it is meant for anyone concerned with such questions as: What kind of textbooks should be used in schools? Should children be granted certain rights in determining what they will learn? How should schools be structured? Is censorship desirable? Is developing a positive self-concept more important than mastering subject matter? This book is intended for anyone who wants or needs to learn how to arrive at sound, rational beliefs and decisions about education.

In western society, teachers and school administrators make the most immediate decisions regarding the education of children. By the very nature of their roles, they are the ones who must decide how students will be taught, how classrooms will be organized, what kind of discipline will be demanded and how much, and what kinds of subject matter will be emphasized. Teachers and administrators cannot avoid making educational decisions that will have far-reaching consequences for children. And in each case, the question must be whether the decision was better or worse than others that could have been made.

For instance, suppose that through ignorance an elementary-school teacher makes inappropriate decisions regarding the teaching of mathematics. Should the students of such a teacher be assigned in the next school year to another teacher who makes poor or inappropriate decisions regarding the teaching of mathematics, their problems are compounded. If these students are unlucky enough to be taught mathematics by incompetent teachers for two or three consecutive years, their fates are fairly well sealed. For given the school system as presently structured, students with poor beginnings in mathematics are placed in lower-level mathematics classes when they get to high school. They are not given algebra and trigonometry; and without a knowledge of these subjects, advanced courses in physics, chemistry, biology, and so on become incomprehensible.

Thus the wrong or inappropriate decisions made by elementary-school teachers can, in great measure, prevent their students from becoming physicians or scientists. Indeed, the probability is that such mistaught students will not be able to enter any occupation that requires a sophisticated knowledge of mathematics or science. Nor will they be likely to achieve the lifestyles typically associated with those occupations. The point here is that the educational decisions of teachers can, and almost always do, significantly affect the future lives of their students and, consequently, the lives of others.

Teachers do not make educational decisions in a vacuum. School administrators contribute in many ways to establishing the context in which a teacher works. For example, principals who decide that elementary schools will be graded have already established parameters within which the decisions of teachers must be made. How to teach reading to a group of third graders is a problem for the teacher in a graded school. The problem does not arise if the school is nongraded. Is such an administrative decision a good one? What decisions should administrators make, thus establishing parameters for teachers? How can we determine whether administrative decisions are good ones?

In summary, this book is intended primarily for the student who is preparing to be a teacher or school administrator. Yet it is generally appropriate for anyone who is concerned about the welfare of children and who wants to increase his or her abilities to make sound, rational educational decisions.

A PREVIEW

Intelligently made decisions are always based upon beliefs. Educational decisions are no different. How intelligently we make our educational decisions will in large measure depend upon what we believe about education and how we base our decisions on those beliefs. Part One of this book will begin with an examination of how the rationality of educational decisions is based upon and otherwise related to the beliefs of the people who make them. This study will be followed by an analysis of some of the different kinds of beliefs people have about education. In the broadest sense of the phrase these beliefs comprise what is often called a "philosophy of education."

Part Two will identify the fundamentals of rational, intelligent decision-making. It will consist for the most part in an introduction to logic, since it is only through a knowledge of logic that we can check the rationality and reasonableness of our decision-making. Part Two, then, will provide a grounding in that formal knowledge necessary for making intelligent educational decisions and for determining how intelligently others have made their decisions.

Part Three will deal with one of the most misunderstood aspects of educational decision-making—moral judgments. It will examine why and how ethics is critical to making intelligent decisions and confirm the need for a coherent, reasonable ethical theory.

Part Four will examine the kinds of practical educational decisions that teachers, school administrators, and others must make. No attempt will be made to tell you what you should decide on educational issues. Rather the objective will be to identify a method of investigation and mode of justification appropriate for making educational decisions more intelligently.

CHAPTER

2

Educational Decisions
and Beliefs

In any society, three basic educational issues must be confronted: What should the outcomes of education be? What should be taught? How should it be taught? The ways in which these issues are resolved determine the educational complex of the society. Even a cursory consideration of education in the modern world is sufficient to show that decisions on such matters are unavoidable. In the United States, for instance, it has been decided that all children should be given the same opportunity to a free and equal education. Indeed, children are required to avail themselves of this education. Certainly, things could be otherwise. Different decisions could have been made. But decisions of some kind were necessary.

Educational decisions are made by parents, politicians, and the electorate, but those most visible as educational decision-makers are teachers and school administrators. For the most part, teachers make the first-line decisions regarding how they will teach and what content they will emphasize. Of course, these decisions are usually conditioned by many factors. They may be directly influenced by tradition, or they may be a reaction to tradition. Yet whatever the context and whatever the influences, it is clear that in fact teachers do make such decisions. It is equally obvious that many other kinds of educational decisions are made by school administrators. It is primarily they who decide who will be hired to teach, and how their particular schools will be structured. In general, administrators play a significant role in setting the immediate conditions within which teachers must work and make their decisions.

But these are comments on who makes educational decisions in a modern society. In this chapter, we will not be so much concerned with *who* makes such decisions but rather with acquiring an initial understanding of the different kinds of educational decisions and of how those decisions are related to the beliefs of the person who makes them. For it is only on the basis of such understandings that we can determine whether particular decisions are made more or less intelligently.

MAJOR TYPES OF EDUCATIONAL DECISIONS

As suggested earlier, the first type of educational decision deals with *educational outcomes,* that is, with what the goals or results of education ought to be. In contemporary America, for example, some of the decisions regarding the outcomes of education are that we should strive to:

> develop the whole child
> prepare people for a useful job
> produce persons able to speak and write clearly
> develop in people an understanding of history
> produce good democratic citizens
> bring about a better society
> produce people who have learned how to learn
> develop a positive self-concept in the child

In general, decisions regarding the outcomes of education have to do with the point of education. They function to direct our actions by giving them focus as we engage in the process of education. In ancient Sparta, for instance, one of the desired outcomes of education was a ruling class of physically powerful soldier-administrators devoted to the Spartan state. In the monastic education of the Middle Ages, one outcome striven for was the salvation of souls. While in more recent times, the Nazis decided that one of the more important outcomes of education should be the maintenance of a fascist state wherein Aryans reigned supreme.

In each case, decisions regarding outcomes established the framework for subsequent decisions concerning what to teach and how to teach. Spartan education was heavily weighted in the direction of the development of the body, that is, toward physical education. For a strong emphasis on physical education was judged necessary, given what the Spartans had decided the outcomes of education ought to be. Similarly, monastic education was almost exclusively devoted to the study of theology as the

During recent years, there has been growing discontent with the matter taught in American schools. Critics argue that while the cost of public education in the United States has risen to nearly 100 billion dollars annually, the quality of that education has steadily declined. To rectify what these critics see as a most undesirable situation, many have proposed that schools eliminate the "frills" added to the curriculum in recent decades and return to an emphasis on the "basics":

> ... all [the money spent on public education] hasn't bought much. In the crudest cost-benefit terms, the more parents have spent on schools, the less their children have learned. Scores on academic achievement tests, administered to all grades in most states, reveal that academic ability of school children declined almost unremittingly in the second half of the 1960's and the first half of the 1970's. ... Many high-school graduates entering college these days cannot understand the textbooks that high school graduates used to be able to read. Textbooks are now being scaled down to this lower capability. ...

One of the major causes of the recent academic decline, many contend, is that during the 1960s a group of educational innovators

> began to argue . . . that the school system was incapable of teaching the fundamentals to America's poor children. . . . [As a result, educators] opened the schoolyard gate to the language, grammar, habits, dress and values of the slums. Middle-class values, correct grammar and word usage, careful, meticulous arithmetical operations, even the banning of gutter language, were no longer stressed as much as they once were. . . .

One proposed remedy calls for the elimination of

> many "specialized" courses in elementary schools [which] are of light academic content, of little proven value, and take up a significant part of the school day. . . . At the high-school level, pupils must know the history of our civilization and great literature of our language. They should be exposed to some higher mathematics, some real science and to at least one of the major foreign languages. . . . If they can't pass such courses, they should not receive a high-school diploma. . . .
>
> It is true that, in many ways, this means returning to a system we had about 20 years and three-quarters of a trillion tax dollars ago. This is certainly a bitter pill for us to swallow, but with the welfare of a generation of youngsters at stake, we may have no other choice. (Frank E. Armbruster, "The More We Spend, the Less Children Learn," *New York Times Magazine,* 28 August 1977, pp. 9, 11, 56, 60.)

Do you agree that the matter of education should be primarily (if not exclusively) comprised of the "basics" as outlined above? What reasons do you have for your position? What educational outcomes might one reasonably expect to occur as a result of teaching only the "basics"?

way to gain eternal salvation. And Nazi education concentrated on a version of history that would implant the notion of Aryan supremacy.

A second type of educational decision is concerned with the *matter of education,* that is, what is or could be taught. Once we have decided what the outcomes of education ought to be, we have to determine what should be taught in order to achieve those outcomes. For example, suppose it has been decided that one outcome of education should be people prepared for useful jobs. We are immediately faced with having to decide what students should be taught so that each can one day perform a useful job. If we have in mind jobs in electronics, then we will have to teach students some mathematics. For without a basic knowledge of mathematics, a person will not be prepared for a career in electronics.

The third major type of educational decision concerns the *manner of education,* the way in which some matter is or could be taught. If we have decided that the matter of education should include a certain amount of mathematics, we must next determine *how* this mathematics should be taught. There are obviously many possibilities. We could decide to teach mathematics by the discovery method, by the lecture method, by using programmed instruction, by individualized instruction, and so on.

Decisions concerning the manner of education include all of those decisions we make regarding teaching methods. They also include decisions about the overall structure of education. The decision to have public schools is a decision concerning the manner of education, since it is a decision about *how* some matter is taught. Other decisions concerning the manner of education are to have formal schools as opposed to informal learning situations, graded as opposed to ungraded schools, and so on. In general, any decision concerning how some matter is to be taught is a decision concerning the manner of education.

All of the very practical educational decisions that people must make fall into one or another of the three categories identified above. The issues decided may range from the mundane or inconsequential to the spectacular or deeply significant. The seemingly inconsequential could include such issues as whether students should be required to have a pass to go to the lavatory and whether gum-chewing in class is to be prohibited. Among the significant issues are those concerning the purposes, content, structure, and control of education. And somewhere between the inconsequential and the spectacular are most of the everyday issues and decisions of the average teacher—decisions concerning what to teach, how to teach, and what the outcomes ought to be.

ALTERNATIVES

In understanding decision-making, it is important to note that a decision can be made only if there are alternatives open. The existence of alternatives is a necessary condition for making a decision. For example, as long as you are on this planet, you cannot *decide* to be subject to the law of gravity; there are no alternatives possible for you. Of course, this is not to say that in the future an alternative might not present itself. But, for the time being, you have no decision to make on the matter. You can, however, decide to be subject to the laws of the United States, because there are alternatives open to you. For instance, you could become a citizen of another country.

In general, we make decisions more intelligently by examining as many alternatives as is reasonable and then deciding on the best of them. For example, suppose that you want to teach your students how to read. You consider only two alternative teaching strategies, namely, the sight method and the linguistic method. You decide to use the sight method. If, however, a third strategy is available to you, for example, the phonics method, and it is a strategy that would be much more effective than either the sight method or the linguistic method, then your decision was not the best decision you could have made. That is, given that your intention was to select the most effective strategy for teaching reading to your students, not identifying and examining more alternatives was not a very intelligent way to proceed. Rather than making your decision based upon such incomplete knowledge, you would have been wiser to have first identified and examined as many of the alternatives as you reasonably could and then to have made your decision. The more alternatives you identified, the greater would have been your chances of including the best choice.

Ancient Sparta provides a classic example of the role of education in a reactionary society. By 800 B.C., Sparta had conquered almost all of southern Greece, subjugating a population nearly twenty times the size of its own. Soon the Spartan ruling class came to face challenges to its power and to its institutions. To meet these threats, a harsh, regimented, repressive educational system was instituted. No longer was education to result in the cultured citizenry for which Sparta was known. The appreciation of art and poetry and the possession of theoretical knowledge were educational outcomes no longer considered "useful" to the state. Spartan education was to produce soldiers and defenders of the *status quo,* citizens who would place the welfare of the state above their own.

Were the Spartans wise in their decision to make a soldier class devoted to the state the primary outcome of education? What other alternative outcomes might they have considered? What other decisions do you believe would have been better? What reasons do you have for your beliefs?

RATIONAL VERSUS IRRATIONAL EDUCATIONAL DECISIONS

Once you are aware of most of the alternatives open to you, making a decision intelligently requires that you have some sound reasons for choosing one of the alternatives over the others. Consider, for instance, a teacher who has been using certain techniques, say, those associated with the "open classroom." If you were to ask him why he is employing those techniques as opposed to others, there are basically two ways in which he could respond. He might say that experimentation has shown that open-classroom techniques promote personalized teaching; or that they allow for truly democratic participation by students in their education; or he might offer any number of other reasons. In each instance he would be responding to your question by giving reasons, considerations that can be understood and judged by others. Whatever merit you found in those reasons, you would at least have grounds for thinking that his choice of teaching techniques was a rational one. If, on the other hand, his response to your question were something like "I don't know why I chose this approach," or "I don't have any reasons; I just did it," then you would be justified in considering his choice an instance of irrational decision-making. Rational decision-making entails having good reasons for choosing a particular alternative.

Making a decision rationally is not an all or nothing affair, however. For as we will see later, in any decision, certain reasons are better than others. A decision may be rational to varying degrees. Having absolutely no reasons for your decision means that you have made it completely irrationally. But there is also irrationality in your decision-making if you have only irrelevant reasons. In Part Two we will consider in some depth the question of how some reasons are better than others. We will also examine in more detail how it is that a decision can be made more or less rationally. For the present, we will employ this rough distinction between "having good reasons" and "having no reasons" for differentiating between rational and irrational decisions.

Given this understanding of the difference between rational and irrational decision-making, it is important to recognize that a rational decision is not necessarily a good decision. For instance, consider the following situation. You are a teacher and have met your class for the first time. No sooner have you introduced yourself than one of your students greets you with an obscene word. What should you do? You have to make a decision. You could leave the room, order the student from the room, ignore the incident, say the same word right back to the student, or take any number of other actions. Your problem is to decide upon an appropriate response from among the alternatives open to you. Suppose that a good decision here is one that results in no additional disruption. An inappropriate one would increase disruption, for example, by promoting more obscene words, physical attack, or the like. You search for options and reasons for choosing one option over the rest. Finally, you settle on a course of action: ignore the incident. You reason that to do anything else would antagonize the student who spoke and possibly other members of the class; and that if antagonized, they will be more disruptive. Best to leave them alone. So you proceed to ignore the remark. Yet within two minutes, five or six students are all yelling obscene words and your classroom is chaotic.

Did you make a very good decision? Obviously not. Clearly, had you chosen another alternative, you could have made a better decision. Nevertheless, given our definition of rational decision-making, you did make a rational decision—that is, you had some fairly good reasons for choosing the course of action you chose. The point here, then, is that although a decision is a rational one, it is not necessarily a good one.

Psychological theories concerning how people learn have a great import for teaching. Many psychologists hold the behaviorist theory of learning. They maintain that learning is a process of operant conditioning. That is, factors in a person's environment reward or punish certain behaviors: behaviors that are rewarded will be more likely to occur in the future; those that are punished will be less likely to occur. In other words, all learning involves increasing the probability that certain behaviors will occur.

According to this theory, only those manners of education that reward desirable behavior (and punish undesirable behavior) can be successful. Two current approaches to teaching that attempt to be consistent with this theory of learning are Programmed Instruction and Computer Assisted Instruction. With regard to such manners of education, B. F. Skinner, the noted Harvard psychologist, has said,

"The whole process of becoming competent in any field must be divided into a very large number of very small steps, and reinforcement [i.e., rewards] must be contingent upon the accomplishment of each step. . . . By making each successive step as small as possible, the frequency of reinforcement can be raised to a maximum, while the possibly aversive consequences of being wrong are reduced to a minimum." (B. F. Skinner, *The Technology of Teaching* [New York: Appleton-Century-Crofts, 1968], p. 21.)

How can a psychological theory be used to supply good reasons for choosing a manner of education? Are you aware of any theory of learning other than behaviorism? What manners of teaching would be considered successful according to that theory but unsuccessful according to behaviorism?

What are some of your beliefs about how people learn? How rationally do you think you hold those beliefs? Identify some teaching manners that would be consistent with your beliefs and some that would not.

But, you might ask, if making a decision rationally does not guarantee that it will be a good one, why should we worry about rationality when we make decisions? The answer is simply that although rationality is no guarantee of the appropriateness of a decision, it is only through making decisions more rationally that we can increase the *probability* that we will make good, or appropriate, decisions.

BELIEFS AS THE BASIS FOR MAKING RATIONAL EDUCATIONAL DECISIONS

In at least three respects, any rational decision has a base in the beliefs of the person who makes the decision. First, since any decision involves deliberation about alternatives, the decision-maker must believe that certain alternatives exist. For obviously, no one could seriously deliberate which alternative to pursue unless he or she believed that there were indeed at least two alternatives. If, for example, you are a teacher who has just decided to employ the discovery method to teach science, you must believe that this method is open to you and that there is at least one other method that you could have chosen.

The second way in which beliefs form the basis for rational decisions has to do with the "rationality" of the decisions. As we have seen, in order for you to make a decision rationally you must have some reasons for it. Any reasons that you have, however, must also be beliefs of yours. For if you did not believe them, you would not count them as reasons for your decision. That is, they could not be *your* reasons unless you believed them. By way of example, again suppose that you have rationally decided to employ the discovery method in teaching science. Your reasons might be that scientific laws are more meaningful to students if they have discovered them for themselves and that students will understand such laws better and remember them longer through discovery than they would through dictation. Since these are *your* reasons and hence *your* rational grounds for *your* decision, *you* must believe them. *You* must believe that scientific laws are more meaningful to students if they have discovered them for themselves. And *you* must believe that students will understand such laws better and remember them longer through discovery than they would through dictation. If these were not your beliefs, you certainly would not accept them as reasons for your decisions. It would make no sense for you to say, "These are my reasons, but I don't believe them." If *you* do not believe them, they cannot be *your* reasons.

The third way in which beliefs are fundamental to making rational decisions involves the relevance of the reasons given for each decision. In addition to having reasons for your decision, you must also believe that those reasons support your decision. That is, offering reasons in this context would be pointless unless you believed that they in some way or other supported your decision. In fact, it would be contradictory to sincerely say that you had certain reasons for your decision but that they did not in any way at all support that decision.

In summary, making educational decisions is unavoidable. Parents, politicians, teachers, and school administrators are each in their own way regularly called upon to make such decisions. With regard to these decisions, there are three major types: those concerning the outcomes of education, those concerning the matter of education, and those concerning the manner of education. In order for you to make an educational decision intelligently, you need to examine various alternatives and choose one of them rationally. And to make an educational decision rationally, you must have some reasons for deciding upon a particular alternative. But rationality in making a decision does not guarantee that the decision will be a good one or that it is better than some other decision you could have made. It does, however, increase the probability that it will be a good one.

If we are to seriously entertain any hope of improving education, the very practical educational decisions that confront us must be made rationally. How rationally and intelligently those decisions are made, in turn, depends upon the beliefs of the people who make them; for beliefs form the basis of any attempt to make rational educational decisions.

Review

1. Define each of the following terms used in this chapter:

   Decision-making   Educational outcome
   Rational decision   The matter of education
   Irrational decision   The manner of education

2. Explain why educational decisions are unavoidable.
3. Discuss how decisions concerning educational outcomes, matter, and manner are related.
4. Describe the function of alternatives in decision-making.
5. Explain how making a decision rationally increases the probability of making a good decision.
6. Identify and explain three ways in which beliefs form the basis of any rational educational decision.

The Role of Philosophy of Education in Making Educational Decisions

I n Chapter 2, we saw that if a decision is to be made rationally, it must be based on the decision-maker's beliefs. This chapter will examine some of the different kinds of beliefs people have about education, beliefs that usually function as the basis of their attempts at rational educational decision-making. Such beliefs constitute the individual's philosophy of education.

CONFUSION CONCERNING THE STUDY OF PHILOSOPHY OF EDUCATION

Discussions about the subject known as philosophy of education frequently strike many people as somewhat odd and possibly even useless.

This view is typical among students who are just beginning their study of education, and there the causes are not difficult to find.

Anyone encountering philosophy of education for the first time is confronted with a rather strange paradox. On the one hand, the study of philosophy of education appears to be quite important. Many colleges with a primary interest in the preparation of teachers prescribe a course in it, and various state boards require such a course for teacher certification. Indeed, in order to be recognized by some of the established accrediting agencies, schools must often have a written philosophy of education. On the other hand, however, many teachers and school administrators seem to have an especially low regard for the study of philosophy of education. The prescribed course, the certification requirement, and the written statement, though viewed as perhaps necessary, are thought by these educators to be ultimately irrelevant to the practical business of teaching. The paradox of philosophy of education is this disparity between the official recognition of the importance of its study and its systematic disparagement by some teachers and administrators.

Another source of this confusion is found in the fact that people have different philosophies of education. Ask any teacher or school administrator, "What is your philosophy of education?" and answers will be readily forthcoming. Typical responses include the following:

> Children learn when behavior is positively reinforced.
>
> Schools should be used to bring about the racial integration of society.
>
> Open-classroom methodologies would be better than the rigid, traditional teaching practices.
>
> Schools should stress the basics in subject matter.
>
> Teachers ought to meet the individual learning needs of their students.
>
> The aim of education ought to be the development of the whole person.

Yet as easy as it is to elicit responses to this question, it is difficult to achieve agreement with regard to them. This difficulty is one of the major impediments to a concensus on the importance of studying philosophy of education.

Certainly, more than any other single factor, the seeming impossibility of rationally resolving disagreements among supporters of different philosophies of education lies at the foundation of most negative views of the importance of the study of philosophy of education.

Nevertheless, having a philosophy of education and studying philosophy of education are both important. For, as we will see, each is necessary for increasing the degree of rationality with which educational decisions are made. But before this can be done, we need a deeper understanding of what a person's philosophy of education is.

PHILOSOPHY OF EDUCATION AS A SET OF BELIEFS

As mentioned earlier, a philosophy of education is a set of beliefs about education. Asking someone, "What's your philosophy of education?" is thus equivalent to asking, "What are your beliefs concerning education?" In this respect, most people obviously have a philosophy of education, because they have *some* beliefs about education. Having a philosophy of education is in itself neither esoteric nor particularly remarkable.

It is from your set of beliefs about education—your philosophy of education—that you draw your reasons in any attempt at making a rational educational decision. And since this is the case, it is important to recognize that you *must have* a philosophy of education, if you are to make your educational decisions rationally.

A person's philosophy of education, however, is not comprised of just *any* beliefs the person possesses. Rather, *a philosophy of education* is the set of beliefs a person has regarding what should (and should not) be

---

Ivan Illich, director of the Center for Intercultural Documentation in Mexico, is one of the more strident critics of the ways children are educated in modern industrial societies. Indeed, included in his philosophy of education is the belief that we ought to "de-school" society, that is, we ought to do away with schools. He argues that

> schools are designed on the assumption that there is a secret to everything in life; that the quality of life depends on knowing that secret; that secrets can be known only in orderly successions; and that only teachers can properly reveal these secrets. An individual with a schooled mind conceives of the world as a pyramid of classified packages accessible only to those who carry the proper tags. New educational institutions would break apart this pyramid. . . . A good educational system should have three purposes: it should provide all who want to learn with access to available resources at any time in their lives; empower all who want to share what they know to find those who want to learn it from them; and finally, furnish all who want to present an issue to the public with the opportunity to make their challenge known. . . . (Ivan Illich, *Deschooling Society* [New York: Harper & Row, 1972], pp. 108–09.)

Do you agree or disagree with this part of Illich's philosophy of education? What reasons do you have for your agreement (or disagreement)? How does answering these questions tell you something about *your* philosophy of education?

done in education and what the outcomes of education should (and should not) be, together with any other beliefs he takes as reasons supporting these beliefs. In other words, a person's philosophy of education is a specific subset of the set of all of that individual's beliefs.

Now, to see how a person's philosophy of education is involved with actual cases of educational decision-making, consider the following. Suppose that you are a history teacher and that you make a decision to use role-playing in teaching about the American Revolution. Your reasons for this decision might include the following:

1. History is more meaningful to students and they remember it longer if they learn it through role-playing.
2. Children learn better if they are actively involved in what they learn.
3. It is important for children to learn about the American Revolution.
4. Role-playing is one of the best methods for me to use in teaching about the American Revolution.

As we saw in Chapter 2, if these are your reasons for this decision, they must be your beliefs. It is in this way that your reasons for your educational decisions are included in your philosophy of education.

In general, there are two basic (but not infallible) ways to determine what beliefs are included in a person's philosophy of education. The first is to identify the educational decisions he makes and ask him what reasons he has to support those decisions. Assuming that he can and will answer truthfully, the reasons he gives will be part of his philosophy of education. The second way is to just ask him what he believes should be done in education and what he believes the outcomes of education ought to be. Then, ask him what reasons he has for these beliefs. All of these beliefs together will be included in his philosophy of education.

EMPIRICAL BELIEFS

A person's philosophy of education usually contains two distinct *kinds* of beliefs: empirical beliefs and philosophical beliefs. As an initial attempt at definition, we can say that an empirical belief is a belief that in principle can be confirmed by reference to data derived from observation and/or experimentation. For example, consider the following list of empirical beliefs:

1. The window is open.
2. Water and oil do not mix.
3. Value clarification is a methodology that causes children to develop positive self-concepts.
4. Population tends to increase beyond the means of production.
5. Children learn to talk through a process of differential reinforcement.

How can you confirm that the window is open? One way is by looking at it, that is, by observing it. A similar form of confirmation—by what is called simple observation—is also an appropriate way to confirm that water and oil do not mix. You need only add some oil to a container of water, shake the liquid, and observe. Confirmation by simple observation, then, is the confirmation of the truth or falsity of a belief by reference directly and exclusively to the data derived from what one can see, touch, hear, taste, or smell.

Confirmation by simple observation is not possible for all empirical beliefs, however. The third belief on the list, "Value clarification is a methodology that causes children to develop positive self-concepts," cannot be confirmed merely by direct observation. There are two reasons for this. In the first place, it is a causal belief. That is, it asserts that value clarification *causes* the development of a positive self-concept. And it is not possible to directly observe a causal relationship. The most that one can see is that a certain event precedes another in time. This is not the same as seeing one thing "causing" the other. In addition to observation, the confirmation of a causal belief must involve experimentation. For instance, sophisticated experiments must be conducted in order to establish that value clarification and not some other factor—for example, the teacher's personality—is the significant variable here.

The second reason for the inadequacy of simple observation in confirming the belief about value clarification is that the supposed effect, a positive self-concept, is itself not directly observable. That is, it is not possible to actually *see* a positive self-concept. Rather, it must be inferred from that which is directly observable, namely, what the person says and does.

The fourth belief on the list, "Population tends to increase beyond the means of production," suggests yet another factor in the matter of confirmation: the limits to experimentation. It is not possible to construct experiments in which the variables of this belief can be controlled. Whereas the belief about value clarification is more or less amenable to what we think of as "laboratory" procedures, the belief about population clearly is not.

If a formal experiment cannot be constructed, how then do we confirm the truth (or falsity) of this belief? The answer is implicit in the belief itself. Since the claim concerns population in general, and not for instance the present population of the United States, data concerning the growth of all populations past and present are relevant here. Historical and statistical procedures, then, will have to be employed in gathering evidence. And consequently the presuppositions of these procedures will be relevant to the confirmation of the belief.

Confirming the last empirical belief on the list, "Children learn to talk through a process of differential reinforcement," involves only some of the methods applicable in confirming the four previous beliefs. Observa-

In recent years, many educators and others concerned with improving the education of poor, inner-city children have called for the production of new kinds of reading materials. In particular, they have argued that the textbooks used by poor minority children living in urban areas should not have as their main characters white, middle-class individuals who live in the suburbs. They have claimed that textbooks for these children should deal with "relevant" and familiar situations to which they can easily relate. In an attempt to confirm or disconfirm the empirical belief that inner-city children prefer such reading materials, Jerry Johns, a college professor and reading specialist, undertook a research study to gather pertinent data. He begins the report on his research by noting that

> . . . it is commonly assumed that multi-ethnic basal readers have provided a new incentive for inner-city children to learn to read and/or to improve their reading efficiency. . . . A crucial assumption, either stated or implied, is that inner-city children prefer to read stories which depict urban settings, characters, and/or group interactions.
>
> The central focus of this investigation was to explore this assumption as it related to the reading preferences of inner-city children in grades four through six. . . .
>
> Study participants were 597 fourth, fifth and sixth grade children who were selected in a non-random fashion from school districts in four large midwestern cities. . . . [The] sample [was] evenly distributed between and within grades and sexes.
>
> The racial composition of the sample was divided into blacks (515) and others (82). . . .
>
> A questionnaire was prepared with 15 forced choices, all taken from modern realistic fiction books for children. Five choices were between illustrations and descriptions depicting either the stark, crowded conditions of inner-city living or uncrowded, pleasant conditions in urban and suburban areas. Another five choices were between descriptions of characters with positive and negative self-concepts. The last five choices were between descriptions of characters in positive and negative group interactions. . . .
>
> The results of the statistical tests . . . indicate that inner-city children in the intermediate grades expressed a statistically significant reading preference for stories or books which depicted middle-class settings, characters with positive self-concepts, and characters in positive group interactions. (Jerry L. Johns, "Reading Preferences of Urban Students in Grades Four Through Six," *Journal of Educational Research* 68, no. 8 [April 1975], pp. 306–08.)

Is the belief that Johns is trying to disconfirm here one concerning the manner, the matter, or the outcomes of education? Why is this belief an empirical one? Does Johns supply strong evidence to disconfirm the belief in question?

In what sense did Johns try out materials under controlled conditions? Do you think that many people are making too many recommendations about matter and manner without any evidence? What evidence do *you* have to back up your position?

tion is relevant because one must study children learning to talk and the environment in which they exist. But, strictly speaking, it is not possible to directly observe learning taking place. One can only observe certain signs from which it is usually inferred that learning has taken place. Statistical procedures, which appeared to apply in some of the preceding cases, do not seem especially relevant here; the same is true of historical investigation. Experimentation is a different matter. The construction of an experiment in confirming this belief is not only possible but crucial.

On the basis of these considerations, we can now define "empirical belief" more precisely. An *empirical belief* is a belief that describes or explains a state of affairs, with the presupposition that the description or explanation can in principle be confirmed by exclusive reference to the data derived from observation and/or experimentation.

When people make decisions concerning the manner, matter, or outcomes of education, their empirical beliefs often play a significant role. For example, the current controversy concerning whether schools should "return to the basics" revolves in part around different beliefs regarding what the consequences of such a "return" would be. Some advocates of the "back to basics" position hold the empirical belief that such a change in curriculum would more effectively prepare children for various adult roles. Many opponents believe that a return to the "basics" would retard the development of creativity and sensitivity in children, who would then

---

In explaining why the "back-to-basics movement" is gaining momentum in American education, one observer makes the following points:

1. Parents, often at the behest of educators, have taken a larger part in school affairs. As they delve deeply into the task, they don't like, or don't understand, what they see. They try to reshape policies and programs in accordance with their views.

2. Blacks and Hispanics claim, rightly or wrongly, that their children are ignored or shortchanged with respect to instruction in basic skills. The ghetto has been a hot bed for the basics.

3. Over the years, teachers have been urged to focus on creativity, on humanistic objectives, on development of independent thinkers. It has not always been clear to the classroom practitioner whether these were to be in addition to, or instead of, mastery of the skills. . . . (Ben Bodinsky, "Back to Basics: The Movement and Its Meaning," *Phi Delta Kappan,* March 1977, p. 523.)

Identify the empirical beliefs in the preceding excerpt. Explain why they are empirical. Which do you think are true and which do you think are false? What evidence do you have for your beliefs?

be less prepared for adult roles. Of course, there are many other areas of disagreement among the parties to this dispute. However, the point of this example is that disagreements over what the manner, matter, or outcomes of education ought to be often involve disagreements about the truth of certain empirical beliefs—especially those having to do with the effectiveness of producing certain consequences.

There are, however, many cases in which the empirical beliefs that enter into a person's educational decisions are not concerned principally with effectiveness; their main concern is theory—psychological, sociological, or the like. For example, some people hold the theoretical belief that all learning results from experience. On the basis of this belief, many teachers attempt to structure their teaching so that children are actively involved in and directly experience what they are supposed to learn.

Clearly, most people have very many empirical beliefs concerning education. And just as clearly, these empirical beliefs range over many different areas: psychology, sociology, biology, political science, anthropology, economics, history, the effectiveness of various teaching methodologies, and so on. The point that needs to be recognized here is that if someone uses any empirical beliefs as reasons for educational decisions, then those beliefs are part of that person's philosophy of education.

PHILOSOPHICAL BELIEFS

The philosophical beliefs that accompany empirical beliefs in a person's philosophy of education can be characterized as metaphysical, epistemological, logical, or normative.

Generally speaking, metaphysical beliefs deal with questions concerning reality as a whole. For the most part, metaphysics is an attempt to provide a theory or group of rational principles that accounts for, and hence explains, everything that exists. It is the study of Being as a whole. Consequently, metaphysical beliefs are about or have implications for *all* of Being and are not just about specific parts thereof. For instance, biology is the study of a particular part of Being, namely, living matter. Since there is matter that is not living, a biological theory cannot be considered a theory that explains (or attempts to explain) everything that is. The other areas of study that man has identified—for example, physics, psychology, sociology, politics, ethics, and so on—are likewise delimited by the domain of their respective subject matters. In each case, some particular aspect of Being—some categorial division of everything that exists—is differentiated and examined. The result of the examination is the acquisition of various beliefs concerning this or that part of Being. However, metaphysical theories and beliefs are not particularized in this sense. And that is to say once again that metaphysical beliefs are about *all* that exists, not just a particular part of what exists.

This distinction between theories concerning all that exists and theories concerning part of what exists may be further clarified as follows. Many people believe that everything that exists is comprised of matter and hence that only material things are real. Anything else is illusory and unreal. Many other people disagree. They believe, for example, that the human being is not merely a material body but a unique combination of body and nonmaterial soul. Such a belief is a direct contradiction of the assertion that everything is material. Implicit in this belief is the position that Being in itself cannot be correctly characterized as being exclusively material, since there are some aspects of Being, namely souls, that are non-material.

This implication suggests a familiar metaphysical theory. We know that many people subscribe to the metaphysical belief that there is a God and that, if anything exists, it does so only through God's will. God is the creator and sustainer of everything that exists. Every grain of sand, every gnat, every person, the earth, the stars, the universe—these all exist only because God wills that they exist. In other words, if you ask the question "Why?" long enough, the final answer according to this theory must necessarily be, "Because God wills it to be so."

At this point, a caution is necessary. The theory that God is the creator of all that exists is only one example of a metaphysical theory. Metaphysical theories do not have to refer to God or have any theological overtones. That is, you should not generalize from this example and think that all metaphysical theories involve theological beliefs. The significant factor in this example is that a metaphysical theory attempts to provide an explanation of everything that exists. The particular theory in this example relies on God's will to provide such an ultimate explanation. However, there are many other metaphysical theories that make no such reference in their attempts at explaining the nature and origin of all that exists.

In addition to the fundamental issue of the nature of reality, there are other, related metaphysical questions. Among these are those concerning the reality of the self and the body. Is a person a body only? Or is the real person something other than a body? Perhaps a soul or a mind (but not a physical brain)? Another metaphysical topic is the problem of free will versus determinism. Are human beings ever free to choose, or are all choices (and hence actions) causally determined? Moreover, what exactly is the nature of the cause-effect relationship, and of matter, space, and time? If you have any particular beliefs concerning these issues, they are metaphysical beliefs.

Philosophical beliefs also include epistemological beliefs, that is, beliefs concerning the nature, limits, or conditions of knowledge. What is it to "know" something? How does knowing differ from believing and having an opinion? How is knowledge acquired? Must something be directly perceived through one of the five senses in order to be known? Or are some things knowable without sense experience? These and similar questions concerning the nature of knowledge and the status of knowledge claims are epistemological questions. The various answers to them are epistemo-

Differing metaphysical views are often classified according to various "schools" of thought. With the caution that this way of considering metaphysics can be misleading, a few of these "schools" and their fundamental beliefs are identified below for your consideration.

IDEALISM   Ultimate reality is ideational or spiritual (that is, not material). Physical, material things *appear* to be real, but they are not. That is, even though there are "physical things," they are not what they appear to be. The physical appearance is merely the appearance of a more fundamental, underlying reality which is ideational. For example, one version of this position claims that everything that exists does so because God thinks it. It exists as an idea (a nonmaterial thing) in the mind of God. Many idealists believe that the human being is essentially a mind or soul. For this reason, some argue that a person's choice is not subject to any supposed "laws" of the physical realm, but that all choices are free and undetermined. Other idealists have a problem with the free-will issue, because they subscribe to the view that everything is a thought in the mind of God. If you do something because God thinks it, how can your doing it have been an act of free will?

REALISM   Reality is material. All that is real (everything that exists) is material, and, moreover, it exists independently of being thought. In addition, this material, real, world is law-like, and any change takes place according to the "laws of nature." Many realists deny that the human being is a "mind" or "soul." Rather, they claim that a person is a biological, material organism only. And since as a material object one is totally subject to the laws of nature, some claim that people have no free will. On the other hand, other realists hold the view that, while some actions are determined, others are chosen freely. It is, however, difficult to show that all of reality is material and law-like and that people can make free decisions.

PRAGMATISM   Reality is exactly what we experience. That is, reality is not ideational only or material only. Reality is law-like in certain respects and unpredictable and non-law-like in other respects. For most pragmatists, the dualisms of real and apparent, mind and body, free and determined are untenable and incorrect ways of viewing reality. Reality is interactive; it is the human being's interacting with (experiencing) his environment. Characteristic of reality is the fact of change, because a person's relationship to the environment is one of change. We can as thinking beings impose a certain order and regularity on our environment—and thus see reality as being somewhat law-like. But at the same time, our environment requires us to alter that imposed order from time to time. Consequently, reality is always changing.

logical beliefs. For example, those who say, "You can know something only if you experience it yourself" are expressing an epistemological belief. They are identifying personal experience as a necessary condition for knowing anything.

Traditionally, there has been agreement that in order to know something a person must also believe that thing. However, the opposite does not appear to be the case. That is, in order to believe something a person does not have to know it. Can you think of any things that you know and also believe? Can you think of any things that you believe but would not claim to know? Finally, can you think of any things that you know but do not believe? Most philosophers have claimed that the answer to this last question must be "No."

Now, if knowing something requires that you believe it, how does knowing differ from believing? Many epistemologists have maintained that one major point of difference is that a person can have a false belief but not false knowledge. In other words, if a person knows something, that thing must be true. But if a person only believes it (and does not know it), then it may be true or it may be false.

Think of some things that you claim to know. If someone could convince you that what you claimed to know was actually false, would you continue to claim to know it? Or would you perhaps say something like, "I felt so sure that I was right, but I guess I *didn't* know what I was talking about"?

Historically, many philosophers have agreed on the two preceding points, but have disagreed widely on a third issue. If being false differentiates false beliefs from knowledge, what differentiates a true belief from knowledge? Other related, controversial epistemological issues concern the role and reliability of sense perception, whether we can know anything by the use of reason alone, and whether anything can ever be known with certainty. Your answers to these questions are epistemological beliefs.

A third kind of philosophical belief typically found in a person's philosophy of education are logical beliefs, beliefs about the criteria for strong reasons. If you think that you have strong reasons for a decision, you must have some beliefs about what makes those reasons strong ones. If you have no idea what the criteria for strong reasons are, you cannot rationally claim that a particular reason is a strong one.

It is fairly obvious how logical beliefs are included in a teacher's philosophy of education. In the first place, most teachers attempt to teach their students how to think logically. Consequently, they must have some beliefs concerning what logical thinking is. Secondly, teachers sometimes make a critical examination of their own beliefs and decisions. They ask whether they themselves are thinking well or poorly, or whether they have strong reasons for what they believe. And when they do this, they must use some logical beliefs.

Moreover, logical beliefs are obviously intimately involved in any attempt at making a rational educational decision. As we saw in Chapter 2, a necessary condition for making a rational decision is that you have some reasons that you believe support your decision. And the belief that your reasons support your decision is a logical belief.

Like metaphysical views, differing epistemological positions are sometimes classified according to various "schools" of thought. Remembering that such classifications can be misleading, consider the following "schools" and some of their basic epistemological claims:

IDEALISM   Many idealists maintain that we cannot have knowledge of anything that we perceive through our senses. One reason often given for this is that we can never be certain of the information provided by sense perception. Our senses, it is argued, sometimes deceive us. For instance, when we look at an oar that is partially immersed in water, the oar appears to be bent. Our sense of sight is providing us with false information. If our senses can deceive us in some instances, how can we be certain that they do not deceive us in others? And if our senses are not reliable sources of information, we can never be certain of the accuracy of our perceptions. Thus, we cannot have knowledge of anything that we perceive through our senses. Knowledge is given to us only through our minds, independent of our senses. Through our minds, and our minds alone, we are able to understand the truth of things. And the only "things" that we can know (and know about) are the things of the mind, that is, ideas, concepts, and so on.

REALISM   To know something is to have a true belief that corresponds to reality, that is, to the material world. If you believe that the chair is brown, your belief is true if the material chair is actually brown. And you know whether it is or not by observing it with your senses. Knowledge comes through and from sense perception. Sometimes our senses provide us with knowledge directly, but in other instances (such as in many scientific experiments) our senses are aided by various instruments.

PRAGMATISM   Beliefs are "instruments" that we use in solving life's problems. As an instrument (a tool of sorts), a belief is raised to the status of knowledge insofar as it is useful in solving problems. But it is not so much that our senses provide us with knowledge (as realists claim). Rather, when presented with a problem, a person acts upon certain beliefs in attempting to solve it. If the action is successful (that is, if the problem is solved), then the beliefs were "warranted." Even though it is through observation that such a person determines whether or not an action is successful, the observation itself does not show that the belief is true. Insofar as a belief regularly leads to the successful solution of problems, a person can be said to know it. Nevertheless, in the future the belief may not prove successful and hence the person would have to give it up.

Finally, perhaps the most apparent, distinctively philosophical beliefs included in a person's philosophy of education are normative beliefs, beliefs that something is good or bad, right or wrong, or ought or ought not to be done or occur. It should be clear that practically anyone connected with education will have some normative beliefs concerning its manner, matter, and outcomes. For instance, the belief that a certain teaching method ought to be used is a normative one. Because logical and normative beliefs are so important for making educational decisions intelligently, we will examine them much more thoroughly in subsequent chapters.

PHILOSOPHY OF EDUCATION AS JUSTIFICATION

Although "philosophy of education" ordinarily means a person's set of beliefs about education, there is another sense of the phrase that is also important. This is the notion of philosophy of education as an *activity of justification*, that is, the activity of trying to prove or confirm the truth of philosophical beliefs that are relevant to education.

When you engage in the activity of philosophy of education, you are "philosophizing about education" or simply "thinking philosophically about education." In general, thinking philosophically about education involves doing one or both of the following: (1) trying to show (by giving reasons) that a philosophical belief relevant to education is true; (2) critically examining reasons that are offered in support of philosophical beliefs relevant to education.

Many—possibly most—people think philosophically about education by giving reasons for certain of their philosophical beliefs concerning education. But it is equally important to critically examine the reasons that are given. Do those reasons support that philosophical belief? How well do they support the belief? Are there stronger reasons for thinking that the belief is true? Are there perhaps any reasons for thinking that it is false? Merely offering reasons for your philosophical beliefs is not enough. You must also critically examine them to determine how well they support your beliefs.

Similarly, when you make an educational decision rationally, you must—as we have seen—have reasons for that decision. In particular, you must have reasons for thinking that pursuing the alternative you decide upon is better than pursuing some other. You must also critically examine those reasons. And doing this will involve you in the activity of philosophy of education. In other words, you cannot avoid thinking philosophically about education if you are to make rational educational decisions.

Like other activities, however, thinking philosophically about education can be done well or poorly. One person may be able to support certain philosophical beliefs much better than someone else can. That is, one person may hold those beliefs more rationally than the other.

Thinking philosophically about education is also like other activities in that you can improve your skills through practice. However, unguided practice in this context is more often than not unproductive and results in little real improvement. Thus the remainder of this text will attempt to guide you in developing your abilities to make better, and more rational, educational decisions and to develop stronger reasons for your philosophical beliefs.

R. S. Peters, a British philosopher, identifies the following as some of the reasons for including the study of philosophy of education in teacher preparation programs:

There was a time, I suppose, when the view was defensible that teachers could pick up their art entirely on an apprenticeship system from experienced practitioners on the job. Education had relatively agreed upon aims; procedures were more or less standardized; few fundamental questions were raised about principles underlying school organization, class management and the curriculum; the general standards of the community, which they were meant to pass on in training the character of children, were relatively stable; and little was known about the psychology of children and the social conditions under which they lived which transcended common-sense. . . .

I do not want to minimize the importance of this learning on the job under skilled direction. Indeed I think we would all agree that it must be the lynchpin of any system of training. I need hardly comment much either on its limitations as a sufficient type of training under modern conditions. The point is that nowadays just about none of the conditions obtain which provided the milieu in which the old apprenticeship system was viable. Education no longer has agreed aims; procedures are constantly under discussion and vary according to what different people conceive themselves as doing in teaching the various subjects; fundamental questions concerned with principles underlying school organization, class management and the curriculum are constantly being raised; and in the area of moral education the task is made more perplexing by the variations of standards which characterize a differentiated society. The question therefore is not whether a modern teacher indulges in philosophical reflection about what he is doing; it is rather whether he does it in a sloppy or a rigorous manner. . . . (R. S. Peters, "The Place of Philosophy in the Training of Teachers," *Paedagogica Europa* 3 [1967], pp. 152–53.)

Do you agree or disagree with the position taken by Peters? How well does he support his position? What reasons do you have for agreeing, or disagreeing?

Review

1. Define each of the following terms used in this chapter:

Empirical belief	Logical belief
Metaphysical belief	Normative belief
Epistemological belief	

2. Explain what a philosophy of education is and describe the different kinds of beliefs ordinarily found in a person's philosophy of education.
3. Show how a philosophy of education is related to a person's attempts at making educational decisions rationally.
4. Give some examples of metaphysical, epistemological, logical, and normative beliefs and suggest how each might function as a reason for a practical educational decision.
5. Explain why a person must necessarily engage in the activity of philosophy of education in order to make a rational educational decision.
6. Identify some of the elements of your philosophy of education.

Beliefs, Propositions, and Truth

This book is ultimately concerned with identifying guidelines for making educational decisions more intelligently. Yet before we can directly consider these guidelines, there are some important things that must be understood about beliefs. For as we have seen, beliefs are central to making educational decisions intelligently.

BELIEFS AND PROPOSITIONS

To begin, let us reconsider some of what has been said concerning a philosophy of education as a set of beliefs. Given that ordinary meaning of "a philosophy of education," if we ask someone, "What's your philosophy of education?," he will answer by articulating some of his beliefs about education. That is, his response will have the form

I believe that p

where p represents whatever his particular belief is. For instance, p might represent any one of the following:

> The schools should be more sensitive to the needs and interests of children.
>
> Learning can occur only in an atmosphere of mutual trust and respect.
>
> Phonics is the most effective way to teach reading.

Now if each of these is a possible replacement for p in the sentence, "I believe that p," each must in turn be a belief. More specifically, if someone (let's call that person McX) truly says, "I believe that phonics is the most effective way to teach reading," then "Phonics is the most effective way to teach reading" is one of McX's beliefs.

In general, to say that McX believes that p is simply to say that p is a belief of McX. Conversely, if p is one of McX's beliefs, then McX believes that p. But what is this "p" that McX believes and what does believing it mean?

In the first place, what McX believes is a *proposition;* and a proposition is the kind of thing that is either true or false.* That is, in sentences of the form

> McX believes that p

p must be a proposition. Unless p is a proposition, McX cannot legitimately be said to believe it. Saying,

> McX believes that children

makes no sense. The reason that it makes no sense is that "children" is not a proposition. "Children" is neither true nor false. It does, however, make sense to say

> McX believes that children are by law compelled to go to school.

For "Children are by law compelled to go to school" is a proposition. It is either true or false. If we are not prepared to say that what p represents is either true or false, we cannot properly say that McX believes that p—whatever else p may be.

Secondly, believing is the affording of a degree of psychological assent to the truth of a particular proposition. When McX believes that phonics

---

* Along with our earlier claims, this implies that metaphysical and normative beliefs are either true or false—which is not an uncontroversial view. For a discussion of alternative views, consult any of the books listed at the end of Part Three.

is the most effective way to teach reading, McX assents to the truth of the proposition

Phonics is the most effective way to teach reading.

The actual degree of assent McX affords the proposition may vary from quite weak to very strong. Yet unless McX gives some degree of assent, it would not be proper to claim that McX has this belief.

Now, even though we have defined *belief* in terms of psychological assent, our study of the nature of a philosophy of education need not be overly concerned with the psychological processes involved in believing. Of more immediate importance is an understanding of that which one believes, namely propositions. The primary reasons for this are as follows.

Suppose that you were to examine your philosophy of education. To begin you would have to identify specifically what your philosophy of education is. And this can and will consist in nothing other than the specification of your beliefs about education. But such a specification will be essentially a listing of only those propositions about education that you believe, that is, those to which you give assent.

Consequently, in examining your philosophy of education, what you (or anyone else) have to deal with is basically a set of propositions. The fact that you believe that these propositions are true is significant only

---

In *Crisis in the Classroom,* Charles Silberman expresses some of his philosophy of education concerning the preparation of teachers.

> What is wrong with the way teachers and administrators . . . are educated has less to do with the fact that they are given inadequate mastery of the techniques of teaching . . . than with the fact that they are not trained to think about either the purposes or the processes, the ends or the means of education. . . . They all need an education that equips them to ask why, to think seriously and deeply about what they are doing. . . . (Charles E. Silberman, *Crisis in the Classroom* [New York: Random House, Vintage Books, 1971], p. 380.)

Do you agree or disagree with Silberman's beliefs here? How *strongly* do you agree or disagree? Make a list of your beliefs relative to Silberman's position and indicate how strongly (very strongly, strongly, moderately, weakly) you believe each of them.

Do you have any reasons for the beliefs that you listed? Is there a correlation between how good your evidence for a belief is and how strongly you assent to it?

for identifying them as members of the set that is *your* philosophy of education. Once identified as members of that set, the fact that you believe them is irrelevant to any further consideration of their truth or falsity.

PROPOSITIONS AND TRUTH

Having a belief, then, is tantamount to affording some degree of psychological assent to a proposition. And the proposition, with which this assent is associated, is either true or false; it cannot be both.

Many people find this difficult to "accept," for they have been persuaded to believe, in some strange way, that a proposition can be true for one person but false for another. Still others believe that the truth or falsity of a proposition can change from time to time or place to place. For instance, it is often said that what was true yesterday is no longer true today or what is true today may be false tomorrow. When one or another of these views is expressed, the propositions involved usually concern such controversial areas as religion, politics, ethics, or education.

Few, however, are disposed to maintain the position that truth is relative where "scientific" matters are concerned. For example, consider the following situation. Two people are examining a .45 caliber pistol. One of them believes that it is loaded, the other believes that it is not. The truth of the proposition "This pistol is loaded" is in dispute. Now clearly, this proposition is either true or it is false. Furthermore, whether anyone believes that it is true (or that it is false) is irrelevant to its actual truth (or falsity). Suppose now that the individual who believes that the pistol is not loaded points it at the other person and pulls the trigger. The gun fires, wounding the other person. What can the first person say? "I did not believe that it was loaded." Well, perhaps he did believe that it was not loaded. But the *truth* is that it was!

The truth or falsity of a proposition is not dependent on anyone's believing it. For example, whether or not anyone believes that the earth is not flat is irrelevant to the truth of the proposition

The earth is not flat.

A comparatively short time ago, most (perhaps all) people believed that "The earth is not flat" was false. Nevertheless, it was and is true.

This all goes to show that

I believe that the earth is flat

does not imply that

The earth is flat.

More generally, we can show that for any proposition, p,

McX believes that p

does not imply that

p is true.

The argument is fairly straightforward. If "McX believes that p" implies that "p is true," then the proposition "The earth is flat" would have to be true if McX believed that the earth is flat. Now we know that there have been some people (McX) who have actually believed that the earth is flat. Yet we know that "The earth is flat" is false. Therefore, it is false that "McX believes that p" implies that "p is true." Believing that a proposition is true has no bearing on the actual truth or falsity of that proposition.

We can now consider the mistake inherent in popular misconceptions concerning the relativity of the truth of beliefs. As suggested above, the most common misconceptions are:

(1) Any proposition is both true and false at the same time.
(2) The truth of any proposition may change over a period of time.

There are many reasons why (1) above is false, but perhaps the most telling is the following. Let q = "Any proposition is both true and false." Now if q is true, then clearly *any* proposition is both true and false. However, q is itself a proposition. Hence, if q is true, it follows that q is false. And if q is false, then it is *not* the case that *any* proposition is both true and false. In other words, q implies its own negation. It is inherently contradictory.

There are other rather obvious reasons for the falsity of (1), and each in its own way is grounded in essentially the same thing. The example of the loaded .45 pistol is a case in point. The proposition "This pistol is loaded" is either true or it is false. Certainly, it is not *both* true and false at the same time. It is not, and cannot be, the case that the pistol is loaded and at the same time is not loaded. And insofar as it is true that "This pistol is loaded" is either true or false but not both true and false, then it follows that (1) above is false. For if we can find just one case where a given proposition is not, and cannot be, both true and false, this is sufficient for showing that (1) is false. We have identified such a case. Moreover, any number of similar cases can be cited as evidence for the falsity of (1).

Finally, we should note the rather common confusion that lies at the root of such comments as "What is true for you may not be true for me." This confusion arises out of the failure to distinguish between a person's believing something and what that person believes. Obviously, it is pos-

It is not uncommon for teachers and researchers to argue that some educational proposition is true because many people *believe* that it is. In other words, concensus is often used as the criterion for truth. A favorite way of gathering such "data," and hence showing concensus, is the poll. For instance, consider the following poll of school board members and administrators regarding criticisms of standardized testing:

	Agree or tend to agree (percent)	Disagree or tend to disagree (percent)
Many current standardized tests discriminate against minorities.	57	43
Grade-level equivalent scores (allowing statements like "The Jones School kids average 1.2 years below grade level") are meaningless.	39	61
Standardized testing programs are not worth their required investment of time and money.	21	79
Most citizens do not understand test results and misinterpret them.	88	12
Most school board members do not understand standardized test results and misinterpret them.	51	49
Most school administrators do not understand standardized test results and misinterpret them.	15	85
Most teachers do not understand standardized test results and misinterpret them.	26	74
Most news reporters do not understand standardized test results and misinterpret them.	82	28
Schools rely heavily on standardized tests out of ignorance about the tests' limitations.	38	62

—Herbert C. Rudman, "The Standardized Test Flap,"
Phi Delta Kappan, Nov. 1977, p. 184.

What conclusions can be properly made on the basis of the statistics reported in this poll? In particular, what can you properly conclude about the truth or falsity of the propositions on which the educators were polled? Discuss the mistake that a person would be making if he or she claimed that this data shows that most school board members understand standardized test results and do not misinterpret them.

sible that you could believe that p is true while someone else believes that p is false. And if you carefully analyze what people mean when they say, "p is true for you but not for me," you will find that this frequently means simply, "You believe that p, but I do not." So far there is no problem. The propositions

>You believe that p is true
>I believe that p is false

are not inconsistent. That is, they may both be true at the same time. But remember: the fact that someone believes that p is true does not imply that p *is* true. Likewise, the fact that someone believes that p is false does not imply that p *is* false. The mistake that many make is to forget this.

They recognize that different people believe different things, but then they proceed to make the following incorrect inference:

>You believe that p is true and I believe that p is false
>p is true for you, but p is false for me
>p is both true and false

The incorrect move here centers on the second step. Reasoning from the first to the second step is correct if "p is true for you" means "You believe p is true," and "p is false for me" means "I believe p is false." However, if one remembers these meanings, it becomes clear that the third step does not follow from the second for the reasons already mentioned: "You believe that p is true" does not imply "p is true."

Likewise, the other aspect of the relativity of truth expressed in

>(2) The truth of any proposition may change over a period of time

is also false. This misconception is significantly different from the first. For (1) states that a proposition is both true and false at the *same* time. However, (2) implicitly maintains that, at any given time, a proposition is either true or false but not both. And insofar as this is the case, it is free of the particular deficiencies adduced above against (1).

Yet even though it is different from (1), (2) is nevertheless false. For the truth of a proposition does not change. If a proposition is true today, it must be true tomorrow. Indeed, if it is true today, it must be true *forever*. Similarly, if it is true today, the proposition *was always* true. The truth of a proposition, in other words, is atemporal. And, of course, the same holds for falsity. If a proposition is false, it always was and always will be false.

Consider the proposition "It snowed in Boston, Massachusetts, on December 6, 1966." If this proposition is true on December 6, 1966, clearly it will always be true. After a period of time the perception of this truth may change—records may be lost, people may forget, perhaps many may disbelieve—but such a change will be irrelevant to the truth of the proposition.

Time *per se* is not relevant to the truth of propositions, unless the proposition explicitly or implicitly makes reference to a period of time. For instance, the proposition

Elizabeth is queen of England

contains an implicit time reference. It says, in effect, that Elizabeth is *now* (that is, at the time the proposition is being articulated) queen of England. Without the implication of that time reference, the locution is ambiguous; one does not know precisely and specifically what is being claimed. Moreover, an ambiguous locution is not, properly speaking, a proposition.

Once the proposition is stated clearly and precisely, it is obvious that the truth (or falsity) of the proposition is atemporal. Time, then, is not relevant to the truth (or falsity) of a proposition unless the proposition explicitly or implicitly makes reference to a period of time. Even if there is such a time reference, time can in no way affect the truth of the proposition.

Misconception (2) above is generated in most instances by a confusion similar to the one at the root of misconception (1). When people maintain that the truth of a proposition changes (or may change) with time, they are usually thinking of situations like the following. Suppose that you have an ice cube in a glass. The proposition

(i) The water in this glass is frozen

is true. Then, five hours later you look at the glass and find that the ice has melted. Now the proposition

(ii) The water in this glass is frozen

is false. The question is whether the truth of the proposition has changed. Clearly, proposition (i) was true five hours ago; and just as clearly, proposition (ii) is false now. And it *appears* that (i) and (ii) are the same proposition. Hence, one wants to conclude that the proposition was true and then became false. The mistake, of course, is in thinking that (i) and (ii) are the same proposition. They are not. A more precise statement of proposition (i) would be

(i) The water in this glass is (now, at time T) frozen

whereas, a more precise statement of proposition (ii) would be

(ii) The water in this glass is (now, at time T + 5 hours) frozen.

When both are stated precisely, it becomes obvious that proposition (i) is *not* at all the same as proposition (ii). Since they are different propositions, the truth of (i) is compatible with the falsity of (ii); there is no need to conclude that the truth of (i) has changed. As long as you allow for the time reference implicit in a proposition and realize that a different time reference means a different proposition, you will avoid the mistake of thinking that the truth of a proposition changes with time.

Some people confuse methods of teaching with propositions. They correctly believe that a certain teaching method may work for one teacher and not for another. But then they make the incorrect inference that the *proposition* "This method works" is true for the one person and false for the other.

Identify a teaching method that you believe works for some people but not for others, and explain how or why this happens. Then, identify the propositions in your discussion.

Can you explain why some people confronted with the proposition "This method works for some people but not for others" incorrectly infer "The proposition 'This method works' is true for some people but false for others?"

Another confusion of methods of teaching and propositions leads some people to conclude that certain propositions concerning methods are true at certain times and false at others. In other words, they make such claims as " 'This method works' used to be true, but it no longer is."

Can you show precisely what their mistake is and explain how it is made?

TRUTH AND PROOF

You might easily agree with much of the preceding argument and still have difficulty "accepting" the position that *any* proposition is either true or false but not both. It is easy to understand that there is or is not a bullet in a gun, or that the earth is or is not flat. But when it comes to what should be done in our schools, the situation seems not nearly as clear cut.

Now, we may well grant that knowing what should go on in schools is much more complex than knowing that there is a bullet in a gun or that the earth is not flat. Nevertheless, even propositions related to educational issues follow the rules we have discussed: no proposition relevant to education can be true and false at the same time, nor can its truth change over time.

We have already considered some of the sources of many people's unwillingness to "accept" this fact, but there is another that needs to be mentioned here. Many of these reluctant people confuse the truth of a proposition with the proof of a proposition.* They believe that if a proposition cannot be proven true, then it is not true; or that then it is neither true nor false. This rather common view warrants our examination.

To begin, consider the Pythagorean theorem in geometry. Practically all schoolchildren, at one time or another, learn something about this theorem. The theorem, you will remember, states that "The sum of the squares of the two legs of a right triangle equals the square of the hypotenuse." Now although they have studied this theorem, most people cannot actually prove that it is true. Nevertheless, few, if any, of these individuals would claim that this inability of *theirs* is a reason for saying that the theorem is false. Indeed, most would maintain that the theorem is true. Moreover, recognizing that several different proofs of the Pythagorean theorem are possible, none would argue that the theorem becomes *more true* with each new proof adduced. To do so would suggest a complete ignorance of the nature of mathematical proof.

Some people confuse truth and proof mainly because they do not understand exactly what a proof is. They do not realize that proving a proposition is only showing that the proposition is true. A proof does not make a proposition true; it merely exhibits or demonstrates the truth of a proposition. It discloses what is already there.

By way of analogy, imagine someone searching for a lost coin. The coin is under a chair, but he does not see it. If he were to move the chair, he would see the coin. Yet moving the chair is not the only way to disclose the whereabouts of the coin. He might simply look under the chair without moving it and thereby see the coin, and there are other, less conventional ways of disclosing the presence of the coin under the chair. But regardless of how it is found, indeed regardless of whether it is found, the coin *is* under the chair. The truth of a proposition is like the coin under the chair. How (and whether) disclosure is made has no effect on the proposition's truth. Truth does not come through proof, nor is it necessarily absent in the absence of proof. If a proposition is proven to be true, it was true prior to the provision of the proof and would have remained so had no proof been given. Again, a proof only demonstrates or discloses the truth of a proposition.

Now as we have seen, if you believe something, what you believe is always a proposition. And since this is the case, your *belief* will be either true or false—the fact that you believe it to be true having no bearing on its actual truth or falsity. Consequently, your philosophy of education may be made up exclusively of true beliefs, exclusively of false beliefs,

---

* In order to streamline the present discussion, "proof" is used here to indicate either "deductive proof" or "inductive confirmation." These latter notions are developed in Part Two.

or—what is most likely—of some true beliefs and some false ones. Of course, which of these alternatives holds depends upon the specific propositions that are included in your philosophy of education.

BELIEFS AND RATIONAL EDUCATIONAL DECISION-MAKING

We are now in a position to understand more clearly what is involved in making rational educational decisions. As we have seen, whenever you make an educational decision rationally, you must decide upon one alternative from among many alternatives open to you, and you must have some reasons for your choice. In addition, you must have some *normative belief* about your decision, such as:

This decision is one that I ought to have made.
This decision is a good one.
This decision is better than another decision I could have made.

Now consider the proposition "This is a good decision" as representative of the kind of belief you must have in order to make an educational decision rationally. Since any proposition is either true or false, "This is a good decision" is either true or false. Moreover, whether or not you believe that this proposition is true is fundamentally irrelevant to the matter. For, as we have seen, your believing a proposition to be true has no bearing on its actual truth. Consequently, your believing that your decision is a good one has no bearing on whether it actually is a good one. Yet, at the same time, your decision is a good one or it is not a good one.

You can try to increase the probability of making good educational decisions by basing your decisions on some reasons. However, it is important to recall that rational decision-making by itself does not "guarantee" that the decision will be a good one or that it will be better than some other decision you could have made. In Part Two we will consider some ways of determining how rationally educational decisions have been made and some guidelines for improving your philosophical reasoning abilities.

Review _____

1. Define each of the following terms used in this chapter:

Belief
Degrees of belief
Proposition

2. Explain why any belief is either true or false; include an explanation of why the truth (or falsity) of a proposition is not relative to a person's beliefs or time.
3. Identify some common problems and confusions inherent in saying, "p is true for you, but it is false for me."
4. Explain why it is false that the truth of a proposition may change over a period of time.
5. Differentiate between the truth of a proposition and its proof.

Broudy, H. S., et al. *Philosophy of Education.* Urbana, Ill.: University of Illinois Press, 1967.
> A good, comprehensive annotated bibliography of books, articles, and dissertations concerned with topics in philosophy of education.

Frankena, William. *Three Historical Philosophies of Education.* Glenview, Ill.: Scott, Foresman, 1965.
> A critical study of the philosophies of education associated with Aristotle, Immanuel Kant, and John Dewey, showing not only how these philosophies of education have influenced teaching practice but also how they stand up to the test of reason.

Green, T. F. *The Activities of Teaching.* New York: McGraw-Hill, 1971.
> Chapters 3, 4, 5, and 8 of this work provide an analysis of the epistemological issues surrounding the concepts of belief and knowledge, including how they are related to truth and falsity and to decisions by teachers.

Lucas, Christopher, ed. *What Is Philosophy of Education?* New York: Macmillan, 1969.
> A collection of essays that considers the nature and role of philosophy of education from many different viewpoints.

McClellan, J. E. *Toward an Effective Critique of American Education.* New York: Lippincott, 1968.
> A critical study of the philosophies of education associated with Conant, Brameld, Barzun, Skinner, and Goodman.

Nagel, Ernest, and Brandt, Richard, eds. *Meaning and Knowledge.* New York: Harcourt Brace Jovanovich, 1965.
> An excellent collection of essays that examine philosophical issues surrounding the nature of beliefs, propositions, and truth.

Peters, R. S., ed. *The Philosophy of Education.* New York: Oxford University Press, 1973.
> A series of essays presenting different philosophical views on the matter, manner, and outcomes of education.

Scheffler, Israel. *Conditions of Knowledge.* Glenview, Ill.: Scott, Foresman, 1965.
> A systematic analysis of major philosophical issues surrounding the nature of belief, knowledge, and truth.

Strain, J. P., ed. *Modern Philosophies of Education.* New York: Random House, 1971.
> A collection of essays that provides an introduction to contemporary philosophies of education, including several about which little has been printed.

Ulich, Robert, ed. *Three Thousand Years of Educational Wisdom.* Cambridge, Mass.: Harvard University Press, 1971.
> A collection of well-known presentations of various philosophies of education, including those associated primarily with Islam, Judaism, and Christianity.

PART TWO

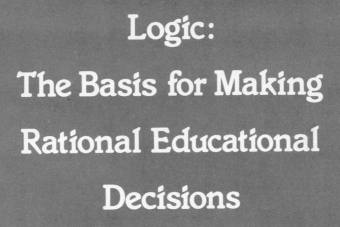

Logic:
The Basis for Making
Rational Educational
Decisions

Logic is not the science of belief, but the
science of proof or evidence. Insofar as belief
professes to be founded on proof, the office of
logic is to supply a test for ascertaining
whether or not the belief is well grounded. . . .

By far the greatest portion of our knowledge,
whether of general truths or of particular
facts, being avowedly a matter of inference,
nearly the whole, not only of science but of
human conduct, is amenable to the authority
of logic.

—John Stuart Mill

CHAPTER

5

Deductive Arguments

As we have seen, making educational decisions intelligently requires having reasons for your decisions. However, having just any reasons is not sufficient—even if all of those reasons are true. In addition to being true, the reasons must provide some actual evidence for the belief that your decision is a good one. The branch of philosophy that is concerned with identifying how well certain reasons function as evidence for particular beliefs is known as logic. You will need to know some logic in order to determine how intelligently you are making your educational decisions.

ARGUMENTS

Our study of logic will begin with an examination of the nature of logical arguments, which, you should recognize at the outset, are not quarrels or disagreements. The word "argument" here has a more limited meaning. In logic, an *argument* is a set of propositions, in which some of the propositions, the premises, are offered in evidential support of another of the propositions, the conclusion.

Whenever you offer some reasons for a belief, you are offering an argument. Suppose, for instance, you believe that as a teacher you should meet the needs of your students. And suppose your reasons are that all teachers should meet the needs of their students and that you are a teacher. The full structure of your argument is as follows:

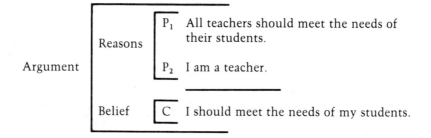

Argument — Reasons:
P_1 All teachers should meet the needs of their students.
P_2 I am a teacher.

Belief:
C I should meet the needs of my students.

In this argument, the propositions labeled P_1 and P_2 are called the premises and the proposition labeled C is called the conclusion. The *conclusion* of an argument is that proposition whose truth the argument is intended to prove or confirm. And the *premises* of an argument are the reasons that are offered in evidential support of the conclusion.

In general, an argument may be represented by the following schema:

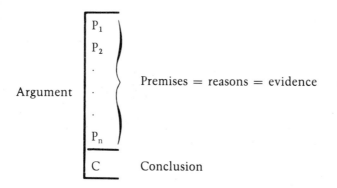

Argument:
P_1
P_2
.
.
.
P_n
} Premises = reasons = evidence

C   Conclusion

In this schema, P_1 represents the first premise, P_2 the second premise, and so on through P_n, the last premise in the argument. Consequently, if an argument had four premises, the last premise would be represented by P_4. In any argument, the number of premises is finite; that is, n must always be some specific whole number. However, while an argument may have any number of premises, it can have only one conclusion.

This schema—that is, this way of *arranging* premises and conclusion— is helpful in analyzing arguments, and we will continue to use it throughout this section of the book. You should be aware, however, that arguments are seldom presented in so orderly a fashion. Many times, the conclusion is stated at the beginning of the discussion and then the premises are presented. Frequently, some premises are given first, then the conclusion, and then additional premises. The point here is that there are many different ways in which arguments may be presented. And you should not expect to find the premises and conclusion of actual arguments arranged as in the schema. On the other hand, arguments may be reconstructed in accordance with this schema, and such an arrangement makes the analysis of an argument easier.

It is also important to recognize that by itself a specific proposition is neither a premise nor a conclusion. Whether a proposition can or cannot be properly called a premise is dependent upon its function in a particular argument. If it is offered as a reason for some other proposition, then it is a premise in the argument. Otherwise, it is not a premise in that argument; a proposition is a premise only if it is offered as a reason. Similarly, whether a proposition can or cannot be properly called a conclusion is dependent upon its function in a particular argument. If reasons are offered in support of a particular proposition, that proposition functions as the conclusion in that argument. Thus a given proposition may be a premise in one argument and the conclusion in another—and, of course, if no argument is offered, the proposition is neither a premise nor a conclusion.

Whenever any argument is offered, the understood claim is that the premises provide evidence that the conclusion is true. Offering an argument, then, is an attempt at proving or confirming its conclusion. Until this point, we have used the terms *prove* and *confirm* without saying precisely what they mean. Now, we must make a clear distinction between them.

In the following paragraph an educational psychologist discusses his belief that, if schools are going to be more adaptive to individuals, they must take seriously the fact of individual differences. He is especially concerned that the aptitude tests used by so many schools do not, and cannot, help teachers adapt to the needs of individuals:

> Current aptitude tests used, having been designed primarily for purposes of selection in a relatively fixed system, do not necessarily provide a basis for deciding how instruction might be designed to increase the probability of successful performance. They are not designed to identify particular capabilities and talents that can become the bases for learning. The general scholastic intelligence tests predict success under "typical" instructional conditions. They do not assess the influence of more specific acquired abilities that might be related to success if alternate means of instruction were available. (Robert Glazer, "Adapting to Individual Differences," *Social Policy,* Sept.–Oct. 1977, p. 30.)

Identify the premises and the conclusion in this argument, then rearrange them in accordance with the schema presented in the text. Why do you agree (or disagree) with Glazer's beliefs?

DEDUCTIVE VERSUS INDUCTIVE ARGUMENTS

There are basically two kinds of arguments: deductive arguments and inductive arguments. In a deductive argument the truth of the premises absolutely guarantees that the conclusion is true. That is, *if* the premises in a deductive argument are true, its conclusion must necessarily be true. It is in this sense that we shall henceforth use the word *prove*. A deductive argument with all true premises *proves* its conclusion to be true.

An inductive argument, on the other hand, does not prove its conclusion—even if all of its premises are true. However, strong inductive arguments do provide some very good evidence for thinking that their conclusions are true. This is the sense in which we shall hereafter use the word *confirm*. An inductive argument with true premises *confirms* its conclusion to some degree; the stronger the inductive argument, the greater the degree of confirmation it affords its conclusion. No inductive argument can ever prove, that is, absolutely guarantee, the truth of its conclusion. At the very best, inductive arguments confirm their conclusions to a high degree.

Given this distinction between *proof* and *confirmation*, we should perhaps elaborate a point made in the previous chapter by asserting now that neither the proof *nor the confirmation* of a proposition makes a proposition true. The proof of a proposition merely discloses its truth, and the confirmation of a proposition partially (but never fully) discloses its truth. Any argument is an attempt at disclosing the truth of its conclusion. The attempt may, or may not, be fully successful.

In order for an argument to be fully successful at disclosing (that is, proving) the truth of its conclusion, at least two conditions must exist: (1) the conclusion of the argument must actually be true; (2) the premises of the argument must be related to the conclusion in such a way as to fully disclose the truth of that conclusion. With regard to the first condition, if the conclusion of the argument is false, then there is *no* argument that could ever prove it true. In terms of our earlier analogy, no amount of moving the chair can disclose the presence of the dime under it if the dime is not there.

With regard to the second condition, if the premises are not related to the conclusion in such a way as to disclose its truth, then even if the conclusion is true, the argument will not be fully successful. For the whole point of offering an argument is to disclose the truth of the conclusion *through* the evidence supplied by the premises.

For instance, suppose that the dime is actually under the chair and that you want to disclose its presence there. Now if your effort is limited to moving the sofa, you will not achieve your goal. Your attempt at disclosure will be unsuccessful because what you are doing (that is, moving the sofa) is not related to disclosing the dime's presence under the chair. A similar situation prevails when you offer an argument. If the premises of

In discussing the difference between deductive and inductive arguments, one contemporary logician identifies

> two fundamental misconceptions about the difference . . . that ought to be chased away at once, just in case anybody is likely to be a victim of them.
>
> *Misconception 1:* "A deductive argument involves reasoning from the premises to the conclusion, and an inductive argument involves reasoning from the conclusion to the premises."
>
> The first thing to notice is that the misconception is blatantly wrong in characterizing arguments. Both inductive and deductive arguments involve premises and a conclusion. That's what an argument is, after all. But what's more, both inductive and deductive arguments rely upon the premises to *establish* the conclusion, to provide grounds or reasons for it. It is just plain nonsense to talk about the conclusion of an argument being used to establish the premises. . . .
>
> *Misconception 2:* "A deductive argument involves reasoning from the general to the specific, and an inductive argument involves reasoning from the specific to the general."
>
> . . . All we have to do is to present an inductive argument in which we reason from the "specific" to the "specific." Here's one:
>
> The chocolate cake I bought at Tom's Bakery was stale.
> The coconut cake I bought at Tom's Bakery was stale.
> _____
> The next cake I buy from Tom's Bakery will be stale.
>
> . . . Take a look at this deductive argument. It's one in which it's not possible even to make the distinction between "general" and "specific" which the misconception relies upon.
>
> If public school teachers do not receive a wage increase,
> then they will be forced to strike.
> They will not receive a wage increase.
> _____
> They will be forced to strike.
>
> With tongue in cheek we can summarize in this way: the misconception is a misconception, not because it's not true in some specific cases, but because it is not true in general, that is, in *all* cases. (Ronald Munson, *The Way of Words: An Informal Logic* [Boston: Houghton Mifflin, 1976], pp. 216–18.)

In what other ways can you show the falsity of the two "misconceptions" described above? Identify some other common misconceptions regarding deductive and inductive arguments.

your argument are not related to disclosing the truth of the specific conclusion of the argument, then the argument cannot be fully successful in proving the truth of its conclusion. In the remainder of this chapter, we will be examining deductive arguments, those arguments whose premises, if true, do serve to disclose the truth of their conclusions. Inductive arguments will be considered at greater length in Chapter 6.

FORM

In an argument, the premises are related to the conclusion through the argument's "form." Any argument has both form and content. And in attempting to determine how the premises of an argument are related to its conclusion, we must focus our attention on the argument's form rather than its content.

The difference between the form and the content of an argument can be likened to the difference between the form and the content of a statue. For instance, it is possible for there to be several statues of Socrates that have the very same shape or form. Yet they could be very different in content, each being made of a different material. One could be made of bronze, another of marble, the third of clay, and so forth. In an argument, the content is the particular propositions that are the premises and the conclusion. The *form* of an argument is the logical relationship between the premises and the conclusion. For example, consider the following argument:

Argument 1

If Deb wants to become a physicist,
then she must learn calculus.

Deb wants to become a physicist.

_____

She must learn calculus.

If we let p* represent the proposition "Deb wants to become a physicist," and q represent the proposition "She must learn calculus," we can represent the form of Argument 1 as

If p, then q

p

_____

q

Notice that in the argument, the first premise is an "if . . . then" proposition. Also, in the argument, the second premise is the same proposition

---

* Letters used to signify propositions are called propositional variables. The forms of certain arguments may be represented by assigning each proposition a different propositional variable and by substituting that propositional variable for the proposition wherever it appears in the argument.

as the if-clause of the first premise. Hence, in representing the form of Argument 1, we replace both the second premise and the if-clause of the first premise with the same propositional variable: p. For similar reasons, we replace the then-clause of the first premise and the conclusion with the variable q.

It is important to recognize here that an argument and an argument form are two different things. An argument, you will recall, is a set of propositions. But an argument form is not a set of propositions. For instance, in the following argument form

> if p, then q
>
> p
> _____
>
> q

"p" is not a proposition, but rather stands for a proposition. Similarly, "q" and "if p, then q" represent propositions but are not themselves propositions. Consequently,

> if p, then q
>
> p
> _____
>
> q

is not a set of propositions and hence not an argument. It is instead an argument form representing a logical relationship that may exist between any propositions labeled "p" and "q." An infinite number of arguments can have this particular form—for example, Argument 2 below:

Argument 2

If Dave has studied logic, then he can reason well.

Dave has studied logic.
_____

He can reason well.

Argument 2 must be considered a different argument because the propositions that comprise it are not those that comprise Argument 1. Nevertheless, while they obviously differ in content, the two arguments have the same form.

VALIDITY VERSUS INVALIDITY

As we have seen, in deductive arguments the premises are related to the conclusion in such a way that *if* the premises are true, the conclusion *must necessarily* be true. In other words, the forms of these arguments

Much of the theoretical foundation for the current emphasis on providing equal educational and social opportunities for all children was developed many years ago by the American philosopher and educator John Dewey. Consider, for instance, Dewey's position concerning the nationalization of American education:

> Since the idea of the nation is equal opportunity for all, to nationalize education means to use the schools as a means for making this idea effective. There was a time when this could be done more or less well simply by providing schoolhouses, desks, blackboards and perhaps books. But that day has past. Opportunities can be equalized only as the schools make it their active serious business to enable all alike to become masters of their own industrial fate. . . . If [education] is so constructed in practice as to produce merely more competent hands for subordinate clerical and shop positions, if its purpose is shaped to drill boys and girls into certain forms of automatic skill which will make them useful in carrying out the plans of others, it means that, instead of nationalizing education in the spirit of our nation, we have given up the battle, and decided to refeudalize education. (John Dewey, "Nationalizing Education," *Journal of Proceedings of the 54th Annual Meeting of the National Education Association of the United States,* 1916, p. 189.)

This quotation contains the following argument:

> If opportunities ought to be equalized, then schools ought to make it their active serious business to enable all alike to become masters of their own industrial fate.
>
> Opportunities ought to be equalized (since this is the idea of the nation).
>
> ———————
>
> Schools ought to make it their business to enable all alike to become masters of their industrial fate.

Using the propositional variables p and q, represent the form of this argument. Do you think the logical relationship between the premises and conclusion is a strong one? Do you share Dewey's belief that the conclusion of the argument is true?

absolutely guarantee that their conclusions are true, *if* their premises are true. For this reason, deductive arguments are often called valid arguments. A *valid argument* is any argument that has a valid form.

An argument has a *valid form* if and only if it is impossible, given that form, to have all true premises and a false conclusion. In other words, if it has all true premises and a valid form, an argument proves with absolute conclusiveness the truth of its conclusion—it fully discloses the truth of that conclusion. Any argument that does not have a valid form is, regardless of the truth of its premises, an *invalid* argument.

The argument form discussed in the preceding section,

> if p, then q
>
> p
> _____
>
> q

is a deductive argument form called "affirming the antecedent." (In an "if . . . then" proposition, the if-clause is called the *antecedent* and the then-clause is called the *consequent.*) In any argument having this form, the second premise, p, is the affirmation of the antecedent contained in the first premise.

"Affirming the antecedent" is a valid argument form, for any argument with this relationship among its propositions and all true premises cannot possibly have a false conclusion. And since any argument that has a valid form is a valid argument, the argument

> If Tim is a good teacher, then
> he can motivate students.
>
> Tim is a good teacher.
> _____
>
> Tim can motivate students.

for example, is valid: it has the valid form of "affirming the antecedent."

Now consider an argument that looks somewhat like the preceding one.

> If Tim is a good teacher, then
> he can motivate students.
>
> Tim can motivate students.
> _____
>
> Tim is a good teacher.

This argument has the form

> if p, then q
>
> q
> _____
>
> p

which is called "affirming the consequent." In arguments having this form, the second premise, q, is the affirmation of the consequent contained in the first premise.

Although the argument form "affirming the consequent" looks much like the argument form "affirming the antecedent," "affirming the consequent" is an invalid form. That is, it *is possible* for an argument having this form to have all true premises and a false conclusion. For instance, consider the argument

> If Douglas MacArthur was President of the United States,
> then he was a United States citizen.
>
> Douglas MacArthur was a United States citizen.
> _____
> Douglas MacArthur was President of the United States.

Clearly the premises of this argument are true and, just as clearly, its conclusion is false. Hence, since it allows even one example of an argument having a false conclusion and all true premises, the argument form "affirming the consequent" cannot be valid.

This example illustrates an important point. One way to show that an argument is invalid is to first identify the form of the argument and then identify another argument having the same form and also having obviously true premises and an obviously false conclusion. Such an argument is called a "counter-argument." If you can identify one counter-argument for a given argument form, you will have shown that form to be invalid. And hence, you will have shown that any argument having that form is invalid—including the original argument.

Next, consider another common argument form, called "denying the consequent":

> if p, then q
>
> not-q
> _____
> not-p

In arguments having this form, the second premise, not-q, is the denial of the consequent contained in the first premise. "Denying the consequent" is a valid form, for any argument that has this form and true premises must necessarily have a true conclusion.

An invalid argument form that looks somewhat like "denying the consequent" is the form known as "denying the antecedent":

> if p, then q
>
> not-p
> _____
> not-q

The invalidity of this argument form can be shown by means of the following counter-argument:

> If Einstein was a biologist, then
> he was a scientist.

Einstein was not a biologist.

He was not a scientist.

Clearly, the counter–argument has true premises and a false conclusion. And this is sufficient for showing that the argument form "denying the antecedent" is invalid.

Any argument, then, is either valid or invalid. And whether it is valid or not depends exclusively upon its form. If the form of an argument is such that it is impossible for *any* argument having that form to have all

---

The following passage contains two arguments:

> The schools have ... never been places for the stimulation of young minds. If all through school the young were provoked to question the Ten Commandments, the sanctity of revealed religion, the foundations of patriotism, the profit motive, the two-party system, monogamy, the laws of incest, and so on, we would have more creativity than we could handle. In teaching our children to accept fundamentals of social relationships and religious beliefs without question we follow the ancient highways of the human race, which extend backward into the dawn of the species, and indefinitely into the future. There must therefore be more of the caveman than of the spaceman about our teachers. (Jules Henry, *Culture Against Man* [New York: Random House, 1963], p. 288.)

We may reconstruct one argument as follows:

If all through school the young were provoked to
question the Ten Commandments, the sanctity of
revealed religion, the foundations of patriotism, the profit
motive, the two-party system, monogamy, the laws of
incest, and so on, we would have more creativity than
we could handle.

It is not the case that all through school the young are
provoked to question such matters (that is, schools have
never been places for the stimulation of young minds).

We do not have more creativity than we can handle.

Notice that the conclusion is not explicitly stated in the passage. Nevertheless, the *context* makes it clear that this is the proposition the writer of the passage wished to establish. It is important to realize that often the conclusion of an argument is left unstated and the reader or listener must supply it.

Identify the form of the argument as reconstructed. Why is this argument valid (or invalid)?

true premises and a false conclusion, then the argument is a valid argument. On the other hand, if the form of an argument is such that it is possible for *even one* argument having that form to have all true premises and a false conclusion, then the argument is an invalid argument.

TRUTH VERSUS VALIDITY

Even if we establish that an argument form is valid, we cannot thereby conclude than any argument having that form has a true conclusion. It is possible for a valid argument to have a false conclusion. Truth and validity are not the same. For example, consider the argument

> If Douglas MacArthur was an admiral, then
> he was not in the army.
>
> Douglas MacArthur was an admiral.
> _____
> He was not in the army.

This argument is valid, because it has the valid form "affirming the antecedent." But clearly it has a false conclusion.

If an argument is valid and has a false conclusion, at least one of the premises of the argument must be false. If an argument is valid and has one or more false premises, it does not prove its conclusion true—even if the conclusion is indeed true. Notice that in the preceding argument the second premise, "Douglas MacArthur was an admiral," is false. Nevertheless the argument is valid, its validity depending only upon its form, not the actual truth or falsity of its premises or conclusion.

The following chart shows all of the true-false combinations that are possible for the premises and conclusion in a valid argument:

Premises	Conclusion
All true	True only
Some true and Some false	True or false
All false	True or false

The only combination that is *not* possible in a valid argument is

Premises	Conclusion
All true	False

It is important to realize that this combination, all premises true and conclusion false, is *not* excluded by an invalid form. That is, it is possible for an argument having an invalid form to have all true premises and a false conclusion. (Of course, it is also possible for an invalid argument to have a true conclusion.) The evidence supplied by the premises of an invalid argument—even if all of those premises are true—is never sufficient to fully disclose the truth of the conclusion. In terms of our earlier analogy, offering an invalid argument is somewhat like moving the sofa with the intention of disclosing the presence of the dime under the chair. The action simply fails to provide full disclosure. Remember, however, that this failure

---

In opposition to the welfare state and in defense of capitalism as a necessary condition for the improvement of education and the social order, the American sociologist and educator William Graham Sumner once offered the following argument:

> It is impossible that the man with capital and the man without should be equal. To affirm that they are equal would be to say that a man who has no tool can get as much food out of the ground as the man who has a spade or a plough; or that the man who has no weapon can defend himself as well against hostile beasts or hostile men as the man who has a weapon. If that were so, none of us would work any more. We work and deny ourselves to get capital just because, other things being equal, the man who has it is superior, for attaining all the ends of life, to the man who has it not. . . .
>
> It follows from what we have observed that it is the utmost folly to denounce capital. To do so is to undermine civilization, for capital is the first requisite of every social gain, educational, ecclesiastical, political, or other. (William Graham Sumner, *The Challenge of Facts and Other Essays,* ed. Albert Galloway Keller [New Haven: Yale University Press, 1914], p. 97).

We may reconstruct this argument as follows:

> If the person with capital is equal to the person without capital, then people do not work and deny themselves in order to get capital.
>
> People do work and deny themselves in order to get capital.
>
> ———————
>
> The person with capital is not equal to the person without capital.

Identify the form of this argument. If the premises of the argument are true, why is this fact sufficient (or insufficient) to prove that the conclusion is true?

of an invalid argument has nothing to do *per se* with the actual truth or falsity of its premises. It is due exclusively to the argument's form—to the relationship that exists between its premises and its conclusion.

VALIDITY AND FORM

So far, we have merely *said* that the validity of its form guarantees that an argument must have a true conclusion if all of its premises are true. In this section, we will examine a particular argument in order to illustrate just how the validity of an argument's form provides this guarantee.

Consider the argument

> All teachers are intelligent people.
>
> All intelligent people are logical.
> _____
> All teachers are logical.

The first premise of this argument asserts a relationship between teachers and intelligent people, a relationship that can be represented by means of the following diagram:

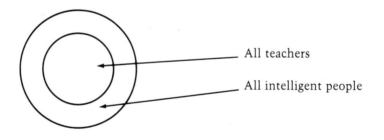

Similarly, we can represent the relationship asserted by the second premise as

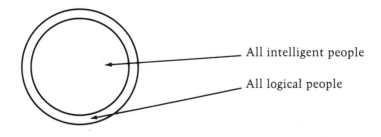

Now, if we consider all of the premises together, we see that they assert a certain relationship among teachers, intelligent people, and logical people:

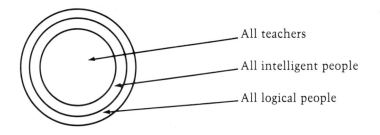

In addition to this, the conclusion of the argument, "All teachers are logical," identifies a relationship between teachers and logical people:

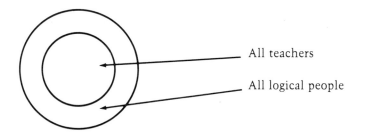

The relationships expressed by the premises and the conclusion of this argument can be summarized as follows:

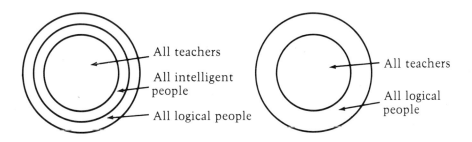

It is obvious that *if* the premises are true, the conclusion must necessarily be true. That is, the argument is valid. The validity of this argument does not depend upon whether all teachers are actually intelligent or upon whether all intelligent people are logical. The truth of the premises is inconsequential. Rather, the validity of the argument, as we have explained, depends only on the logical relationship between its premises and conclusion, that is, on its form.

When the variables X, Y, and Z* are substituted for the groups or classes mentioned in the propositions, the argument's form may be represented as

All X is Y

All Y is Z

All X is Z

The class variables X, Y, and Z have replaced "teachers," "intelligent people," and "logical people," respectively. If these variables were in turn replaced with other class terms, we would have a different argument. However, this new argument would have the same form as the original one.

As we have said, it is because of this form that the original argument is valid. Notice the relationship among X, Y, and Z in this form.

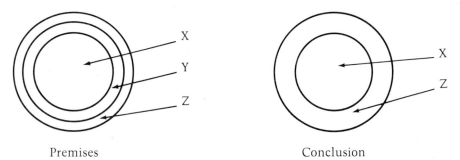

Premises   Conclusion

If X is totally contained in Y and Y is totally contained in Z (as asserted by the premises), then X *must necessarily* be totally contained in Z. In other words, if an argument has this form *and* if it has all true premises, it *must necessarily* have a true conclusion. Thus, if *any* argument has this form, it is a valid argument.

The preceding analysis has illustrated how the validity of an argument depends upon its form and not its content. Clearly, the argument and the form in the example are very simple ones. You should not be misled by this; that is, you should not think that all valid arguments are as simple or that the validity of their forms is as obvious.

FORMAL VERSUS INFORMAL ASSESSMENTS

In this chapter, we have considered only a few valid arguments and valid argument forms. There are, however, an infinite number of valid argu-

---

* The letters used to signify classes are called class variables. Notice that class variables are different from propositional variables. Class variables do not represent propositions. The forms of certain arguments may be more adequately represented using class variables than using propositional variables.

ment forms; and for each valid form, there are an infinite number of different arguments. So, we have examined not only very simple arguments, but also a very small percentage of the possible valid forms and arguments.

As suggested, the major reason for considering these arguments has been to show how the validity and invalidity of arguments depends upon their forms. Circular diagrams, such as those in the preceding section, are useful for illustrating this dependence in a concrete and visual way. They provide a "formal" assessment of an argument's validity, that is, an assessment of the argument's form.

It is important to recognize that the circular diagram technique is only one way of formally assessing the validity of deductive arguments. There are other (and, in many cases, more functional) techniques for formally assessing validity. A discussion of the other techniques lies beyond the scope of an introductory text, however. (Several of the texts listed at the end of Part Two include a systematic treatment of these formal techniques and should be consulted for other ways to establish the validity of deductive arguments.)

There are also certain "informal" techniques that in many instances can be successfully employed in assessing an argument's strength. These informal techniques involve considering arguments not only in terms of their form but also their content. What is said, how it is said, the relevance of evidence—these are all significant in the informal assessment of an argument's strength. In Chapter 8, we will consider how you can informally assess the strength of educational arguments. But before we do that, you will need to have a clearer understanding of inductive arguments.

Review

1. Define each of the following terms used in this chapter:

Reasons	Deductive argument	Valid argument
Argument	Inductive argument	Invalid argument
Conclusion	Argument form	
Premise	Argument content	

2. Explain why you must offer an argument in order to make an educational decision rationally.
3. Explain why an understanding of logic is important in determining how rationally an educational decision was made.
4. Explain why only a valid argument can prove the truth of a conclusion.
5. Explain why validity alone does not guarantee the truth of an argument's conclusion.

Inductive Arguments
and Fallacies

Sometimes you may not be able to produce a valid deductive argument for a certain belief or decision. You may have reasons for your belief and these reasons may seem to you to provide fairly good evidence for thinking that your belief is true. But, nevertheless, when you examine the resulting argument, you find that it is invalid. Such a finding does not necessarily mean that your argument is worthless or that you did not have good reasons for your decision. For some invalid arguments do provide good (although never conclusive) reasons for thinking that their conclusions are true. These arguments are called strong inductive arguments.

In this chapter, we will explore further the differences between inductive and deductive arguments. Then, we will consider some types of inductive arguments commonly employed in attempts at rationally holding educational beliefs and making educational decisions. In addition, since inductive arguments—unlike deductive ones—have varying degrees of strength, we will consider ways of increasing the strength of various kinds of inductive arguments. We will also examine some of the fallacies common to educational argumentation.

INDUCTIVE VERSUS DEDUCTIVE ARGUMENTS

As we saw in Chapter 5, an inductive argument is any argument that is not deductive. All inductive arguments are invalid. That is, in any inductive argument, the truth of the premises does *not* guarantee the truth of the conclusion; the most that the truth of the premises can do is to supply *probable* (but never conclusive) evidence that the conclusion is true. It is in this sense that inductive arguments *confirm* their conclusions to greater or lesser degrees, but do not fully prove them. For since all inductive arguments are invalid, it is always possible—although it may not be probable—that an inductive argument has all true premises and a false conclusion.

In terms of our previous analogy, offering a deductive argument with all true premises is like moving the chair and thereby fully disclosing the presence of the dime. But offering an inductive argument with all true premises is like doing something that in itself cannot fully disclose the presence of the dime under the chair—something that will, at best, be highly suggestive of the dime's presence there. Rather than being like the actual moving of the chair, a strong inductive argument is more like looking under the chair in a dim light and seeing *something* shining there. You may be able to distinguish some features of what you see but not enough to be certain that it is in fact the dime. The more suggestive the features are of a dime, the better your reasons for thinking that the dime is under the chair. It is in this sense that some inductive arguments are stronger than other inductive arguments. The premises of a stronger inductive argument provide better reasons for believing that its conclusion is true than do the premises of another, weaker argument.

Consider, for instance, the following inductive arguments:

Argument 1

John was successfully taught how to read by using the phonics method.

The phonics method is the most effective way to teach anyone how to read.

Argument 2

A group of randomly selected children were taught under controlled conditions how to read by using the phonics method.

Another group of randomly selected children were taught under controlled conditions how to read by using the sight method.

> As measured by objective tests, the group
> taught by using the phonics method
> learned how to read with greater speed
> and comprehension than did the group
> taught by the sight method.
>
> _____
>
> The phonics method is the most effective
> way to teach anyone how to read.

Both of these arguments are clearly not valid. In neither argument does the truth of the premises necessitate or guarantee that the conclusion is true. Nevertheless, Argument 2 is much stronger than Argument 1. Even if the premise in Argument 1 is true, it does not provide very good evidence for the conclusion. On the other hand, if all of the premises in Argument 2 are true, they provide stronger—but still not conclusive—evidence for the argument's conclusion.

Some inductive arguments, then, are stronger than others. If in an inductive argument the premises supply substantial evidence indicating that the conclusion is true, then the argument is a strong one. If the premises provide only little evidence that the conclusion is true, the argument is weak. Indeed the degree of strength of an inductive argument can be so small that the argument is completely worthless. This is the case when the truth of the premises bears no relation at all to the conclusion. For instance, consider the argument

> Birds fly.
>
> _____
>
> The phonics method is the most
> effective way to teach anyone
> how to read.

In this argument, the premise is completely irrelevant to the conclusion. That is, even if the premise is true, its truth has no bearing at all on the truth or falsity of the conclusion. Such arguments are worthless.

You can view the strengths of arguments as ranging over a continuum, from those that have no strength at all (and hence are worthless) to those that are the very strongest—deductive arguments. In these strongest arguments the premises, if true, supply conclusive evidence that the conclusion is true. In arguments that have no strength at all, the premises supply no evidential support for the conclusion. Between the strongest and the weakest arguments are those whose premises supply some evidence for the truth of their conclusions, but not evidence strong enough to fully disclose the truth of the conclusion. Whereas deductive arguments all have the same high degree of strength, inductive arguments vary in strength from worthless to quite strong.

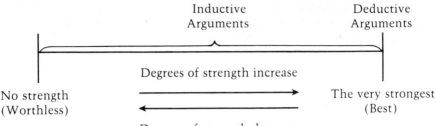

CONTINUUM OF ARGUMENT STRENGTHS

In the following sections of this chapter, we will examine several types of inductive arguments and consider how the strengths of arguments of each type increase and decrease. For each type, we will be concerned with identifying (1) the basic form of the type of argument, (2) the conditions by which you can assess the degree of strength possessed by arguments of that type, and (3) some counter-arguments that may successfully be offered to arguments of that type.

ENUMERATION

A common type of inductive argument is the *argument by enumeration,* an argument whose premises refer to some members of a class and whose conclusion refers to all members of that class. The basic form of an argument by enumeration is:

Some members of S are P
_____

All of the members of S are P

     (where the number of members of S referred to in
     the premises does not equal all of the members of S)

This is considered the "basic" form of the argument because an argument by enumeration may (and indeed for strength must) possess additional premises. Moreover, an argument by enumeration need not have a premise of the specific form "Some members of S are P," as long as it has some premises that are equivalent to a premise of that form. For example, both of the following are arguments by enumeration because they meet the conditions specified in the basic form:

This bird flies.   Crows are birds and fly.
That bird flies.   Eagles are birds and fly.
The other bird flies.   Sparrows are birds and fly.
_____   _____

All birds fly.   All birds fly.

Now consider the following argument by enumeration.

Argument 3

None of my ninth-grade math students
can read well.

No ninth-grade math students in my school
can read well.

It is obvious that the premise of this argument could be true and the conclusion false. Yet it is equally clear that the premise is not irrelevant to the conclusion. That is, *some* logical relationship exists between the premise and the conclusion. The degree of strength of Argument 3 depends upon just how strong this relationship is. And, in fact, it is not very strong at all.

We could, however, produce a stronger argument having the same conclusion, but with additional premises.

Argument 4

None of my ninth-grade math students
can read well.

Of the ninth-grade math students in my
school, 95 percent are mine.

No ninth-grade math students in my
school can read well.

Argument 4 is a different argument because the propositions that comprise it are not the same as those that comprise the preceding argument. Argument 4 is stronger than Argument 3; that is, it more adequately meets the conditions for assessing the strength of an argument by enumeration:

1. The number of members of the class S referred to in the premises is large relative to the number of members of the whole class S.

2. The members of the class S referred to in the premises are representative of all the members of the whole class S.

Since Argument 3 contains no premise relating one teacher's ninth-grade math students to the number of ninth-grade math students in the school, neither the first condition nor the second has been adequately met. Hence, that argument is a very weak one. Argument 4, on the other hand, meets both conditions to a very high degree and thus is a very strong inductive argument.

In general, the more adequately any argument by enumeration meets the two conditions, the stronger it is. Moreover, it should be noted that these two conditions are interrelated: often the larger the number of members referred to in the premises, the greater the degree to which those members will be representative of all the members of the class. And if the members referred to in the premises are highly representative of the members of the whole class, the argument may be strong even if Condition 1 has not been adequately met. For since the conclusion of an argument by enumeration refers to all the members of a class, if the group referred to in the premises is highly representative of all the members of the class, this increases the probability that what is true of all the members of the representative group is also true of all the members of the class of which it is representative. In other words, as the degree of representation increases, the significance of Condition 1 in assessing the strength of the argument decreases.

This last fact is of particular importance in assessing the strength of many educational arguments. In attempting to provide a rational foundation for their educational decisions and beliefs, many people often offer arguments by enumeration. Yet in many instances, it is difficult or impossible to observe enough cases to adequately meet Condition 1. Nevertheless, we can still produce a strong inductive argument, if we can meet Condition 2 to a high degree.

Some of the most effective attempts at meeting Condition 2 employ a special procedure for selecting the members of the group that will ultimately be referred to in the premises. This procedure is known as *random selection.* The selection of members for such a group is random if *each* member of the *whole* class, excluding those previously selected, has an equal chance (probability) of being selected as the n-th member of the group.

In order, then, for an argument by enumeration to be strong, the premises must include propositions referring to

(a) the number of individuals referred to in the premises in relation to the number of members of the whole class referred to in the conclusion

and/or

(b) the degree to which the individuals referred to in the premises are representative of all the members of the class referred to in the conclusion.

If an argument by enumeration contains no such premises (see Argument 3), then it is considered a very weak argument. However, having premises that make the requisite reference does not guarantee strength. Those premises must adequately meet Conditions 1 and 2.

This fact suggests a way in which you can argue against an argument by enumeration. As we have seen, whenever you argue against an argument, you are offering what is called a counter-argument. One type of counter-argument against an argument by enumeration attempts to show that the enumeration fails to adequately meet one or both of the conditions for assessing the strength of an argument by enumeration. Such a challenge represents an attack on the strength of the argument, rather than an attack on the truth of the conclusion.

If, for example, someone offered the argument

> I was a substitute teacher in a suburban school, and all of my students were stupid.
> _____
> All suburban children are stupid.

you might produce the following successful counter-argument:

> If your argument is an argument by enumeration, and if Conditions 1 and 2 are not met, your argument is a very weak one.
>
> Your argument is an argument by enumeration.
>
> The number of suburban children referred to in the premises is very small relative to the number of members in the whole group, suburban children—that is, Condition 1 is not met by your argument.
>
> Your argument contains no premise concerning how representative the children in your classes were of all suburban children—that is, Condition 2 is not met by your argument.
> _____
> Your argument is a very weak one.

Notice that the counter-argument does not directly challenge the truth of the conclusion of the other argument. Instead, it shows that the original argument is weak because it fails to adequately meet the requisite conditions and hence fails to provide any good reasons for believing that "All suburban children are stupid" is true.

Another way of arguing against an argument by enumeration is to directly challenge the conclusion by showing that it is false. You can do this successfully by finding one instance of S that is not a P. That is, since the conclusion of an argument by enumeration must be of the form "All members of S are P," showing just one member of S to be not P is sufficient to prove that the statement "All members of S are P" is false. In other words, you offer a counter-argument having the form

> One member of S is not P
> _____
> It is not the case that all members of S are P

This is a valid argument form, and it can be used to prove *conclusively* that the conclusion of an argument by enumeration is false.

In attempting to confirm certain beliefs concerning the relationship between patterns of high-school preparation and college success, two psychologists employed random selection in their gathering of data:

> The subjects were students attending the University of California, Riverside, during the winter quarter of 1973. The registrar's office maintains class standing broken down by enrollment in the five colleges of the campus. . . . A fixed percentage (25%) [which equaled 429 students] was sampled randomly from the junior and freshman classes in each college. Most of the college GPA's [grade point averages] were based on at least two quarters of college work. (Dennis W. Sexton and Roy D. Goldman, "High School Transcripts as a Set of 'Nonreactive' Measures for Predicting College Success and Major Field," *Journal of Educational Psychology,* 67, No. 1 [Feb. 1975], p. 32.)

Using their findings concerning the students in the sample, the psychologists attempted to confirm conclusions concerning college students in general. One of their arguments is essentially the following:

> Among the students in the sample, college success (rank) was virtually unrelated to the number of classes in English, mathematics, science, history, and foreign language taken in high school.
>
> The students in the sample were selected randomly.
>
> ———————
>
> The college success (rank) of all college students is virtually unrelated to the number of classes in English, mathematics, science, history, and foreign language taken in high school.

Evaluate this argument with regard to the conditions for a strong argument by enumeration.

STATISTICAL INDUCTION

Similar to arguments by enumeration are arguments called *statistical inductions,* which have the following basic form:

> Y percent of some of the members of S are P
>
> ———————
>
> Y percent of all the members of S are P
>
> (where Y does not equal 100 or 0)

As in the preceding section, the phrase *basic form* is used to indicate that there are variations permissible. Specifically, such an argument may have more than one premise, but at least one of the premises must be equivalent to the form

Y percent of some of the members of S are P

The conclusion of a statistical induction must be of the form

Y percent of all of the members of S are P

The conditions for assessing the strength of a statistical induction are the same as those for assessing the strength of an argument by enumeration:

1. The number of members of the class S referred to in the premises is large relative to the number of members of the whole class, S.

2. The members of the class S referred to in the premises are representative of all the members of the whole class S.

A statistical induction, like an argument by enumeration, can be argued against in two basic ways: by challenging the strength of the argument and by challenging the truth of the conclusion. A successful challenge of the first type must show that the statistical induction fails to adequately meet the conditions regarding strength in a statistical induction. Such a counter-argument is essentially of the same sort used to show weakness in an argument by enumeration.

The second type of argument against a statistical induction, one that questions the truth of the original argument's conclusion, is significantly different from that kind of challenge to an argument by enumeration. For instance, consider the following arguments:

Argument by Enumeration	*Statistical Induction*
All of the students I have observed dislike school.	Nearly 73 percent of the students questioned do not like school.
All students dislike school.	Nearly 73 percent of all students do not like school.

As we have seen, the conclusion of the enumerative argument can be shown to be false by identifying just one student who likes school. Yet it is clear that finding one student who likes school would not be sufficient to show that the conclusion of the statistical induction is false.

The only way to *prove* that the conclusion of a statistical induction is false is to provide a valid argument with all true premises and a conclusion that denies the conclusion of the statistical induction. If such a de-

Many parents and educators believe that early entrance into nursery schools or kindergartens is beneficial to children. Nevertheless, consider the following argument against sending children to school before they reach age six:

> Advocates of early schooling usually start from two well-proved points: the fact of incredibly rapid growth in the child's intelligence between birth and age five, and the need for the child's social development to keep pace with his intellectual maturity. But then they go on to make unfortunate twin assumptions: that a child's intelligence can be nurtured by organizing it, and that brightness means readiness for the world of schooling. In short, their happy vision is that early schooling offers the best garden for a child's budding intelligence and developing social awareness.
>
> These assumptions, however comforting or promising, are contradicted by clear-cut experimental evidence. . . . Early schooling, far from being the garden of delights its advocates claim, may actually be a damaging experience. . . .
>
> . . . It is hard to escape the conclusion that early schooling is little short of crippling. A few indicative studies by well-regarded researchers give a sense of the situation. . . .
>
> In Grosse Point, Michigan, Paul Mawhinney describes a study of children who were selected by psychologists because they were considered mature enough or bright enough to be admitted to kindergarten before age five. An evaluation of all those children remaining in the school system after fourteen years showed that more than one-fourth of the select group were below average or had repeated a grade. (Raymond S. Moore and Dennis R. Moore, "The Dangers of Early Schooling," *Harper's Magazine,* July 1972, pp. 58–59).

The preceding argument may be restated as follows:

> A group of children who were considered mature enough or bright enough to be admitted to kindergarten before age five were studied.
>
> More than 25 percent of those children who began school early were—after fourteen years—below average or had repeated a grade.
> _____
> More than 25 percent of all children who begin school early will be below average after fourteen years or will have repeated a grade.

Explain why this reconstructed argument is a statistical induction. Why is it a strong (or weak) argument? Do you believe that sending children to school before they are six years old helps or harms them with regard to later schooling? Assess the strength of your argument.

ductive argument cannot be produced, the best that you can do is offer a strong inductive argument having as its conclusion a proposition to the effect that the conclusion of the statistical induction is false. Ironically, often the strongest counter-argument of this type is itself a statistical induction. Such inductive counter-arguments can never be conclusive, of course. But if it can be shown that your inductive counter-argument is stronger than the original argument, you have provided a successful challenge to that argument. You have shown that there are better reasons for believing that the conclusion of the original argument is false than for believing that it is true. You have not, however, proved that the conclusion is actually false.

ANALOGY

Another type of inductive argument commonly used in making educational decisions is the *argument by analogy*, which has the following basic form:

$x_1, x_2, \ldots, x_m$ have the properties $Q_1, Q_2, \ldots, Q_n$

$x_1, x_2, \ldots, x_{m-1}$ have the property R

---

x_m has the property R

In an argument by analogy, two or more things ($x_1, x_2, \ldots, x_m$) are compared and claimed to share certain properties ($Q_1, Q_2, \ldots, Q_n$). Next, all but one of the things are claimed to share some other property, R. The conclusion is that the remaining thing (x_m) has the property R as well. Typical of the many analogical arguments teachers employ is the following:

My students this year, like my students last year, are second graders, numbering as many boys as girls, and all from middle-class homes.

My students last year were very receptive to the teaching method I used.

My students this year will be very receptive to the same teaching method.

The strength of an argument by analogy can be determined by reference to the following conditions:

1. The number of things ($x_1, x_2, \ldots, x_m$) compared.

2. The number of different properties ($Q_1, Q_2, \ldots, Q_n$) all of the things share.

3. The relevance of the properties $Q_1, Q_2, \ldots, Q_n$ to the possession of property R.

The significance of Condition 1 is readily apparent. For instance, suppose that the science book you read last week is the only science book you have read and that you found it difficult to understand. If you conclude on the basis of this experience alone that the science book just given to you will also be difficult to understand, you will have a very weak argument. However, had you read seven science books and found them all difficult to understand, then you would have a much stronger argument for your belief that the new science book will be difficult to understand. The greater the number of things compared, the stronger the analogical argument.

Condition 2 indicates that the smaller the number of properties shared by all of the things compared, the weaker the argument. The following argument, for example, does not measure up very well in regard to this condition:

> Pat and Mary are both girls.
>
> Pat is very intelligent.
>
> ———————————
>
> Mary is very intelligent.

As the number of properties shared by the things compared increases, the strength of the argument will not increase substantially unless Condition 3 is also satisfied. That is, merely identifying additional common properties does not *in itself* result in a stronger argument. Those properties must also be relevant to the possession of the property identified in the conclusion. For example, consider this elaboration of the preceding argument:

> Pat and Mary are both girls, have brown hair
> and brown eyes, and weigh 115 pounds.
>
> Pat is very intelligent.
>
> ———————————
>
> Mary is very intelligent.

This argument identifies several more properties shared by Pat and Mary than does the preceding one. Yet, since none of the additional properties is relevant to being intelligent, this argument is no stronger than the original. But what about the following argument?

> Pat and Mary are both girls who wear glasses.
>
> Pat is very intelligent.
>
> ———————————
>
> Mary is very intelligent.

Is poor eyesight relevant to intelligence? The importance of Condition 3 in assessing the strength of an analogical argument cannot be overstated. You cannot merely *assume* that the possession of the properties mentioned in the premises of a given analogical argument is relevant to the possession of the property mentioned in the conclusion. You must be able to produce an *additional* argument for this implied relevance.

As with the two preceding types of inductive arguments we have discussed, you can argue against an argument by analogy by challenging either the strength of the argument or the truth of the conclusion. Challenging the argument's strength involves showing that the argument fails to adequately meet one or more of the conditions for assessing the strength of an argument by analogy. The most successful challenge to the truth of an analogical argument's conclusion is, of course, a valid deduc-

---

Among the more engaging analogies common in education are those that relate the developing child to a developing plant. The natural unfolding of the (good?) potentials of a child is likened to the natural unfolding of the potentials contained in the seed of a plant. If the proper conditions for growth are present, the seedling grows strong and hardy, producing stem, leaf, flower, and more seeds as the natural fulfillment of itself. And so it is suggested of the child. If nurtured properly (by the teacher), the child will develop and fulfill his or her potential.

One of the classic statements of this sort of analogical argument is presented by the eighteenth-century philosopher Jean Jacques Rousseau in his novel *Emile:*

> Everything is good as it comes from the hands of the Maker of the world but degenerates once it gets into the hands of man. . . . Not content to leave anything as nature has made it, he must needs shape man himself to his notions, as he does the trees in his garden.
>
> But under present conditions, human beings would be even worse than they are without this fashioning. A man left entirely to himself from birth would be the most misshaped of creatures. . . . He would fare like a shrub that has grown up by chance in the middle of a road, and get trampled under foot by the passers-by.
>
> Plants are fashioned by cultivation, men by education. We are born feeble and need strength; possessing nothing, we need assistance; beginning without intelligence, we need judgment. All that we lack at birth and need when grown up is given us by education. . . . (William Boyd, ed., *The "Emile" of Jean Jacques Rousseau* [New York: Teachers College Press, 1956], p. 11.)

Reconstruct this argument, identifying its premises and conclusion. Then, assess its strength according to the conditions appropriate to arguments by analogy. How strong is this argument?

tive argument having all true premises and a conclusion to the effect that the conclusion of the analogical argument is false. If such a deductive argument cannot be produced, the best that you can do is offer a *stronger* inductive argument to the effect that the conclusion of the analogical argument is false.

HYPOTHETICAL ARGUMENTS

One of the more important types of inductive arguments is the *hypothetical argument.* A cornerstone of modern science, it is also indispensable for making certain educational decisions rationally.

Suppose, for instance, that you want to confirm the following:

> Children who have mastered the "basics" will be more
> financially successful as adults than their peers who have
> not mastered the basics.

As the proposition to be confirmed, this statement would be called your *hypothesis.* Notice that this hypothesis has certain logical implications or consequences. For example, if the hypothesis is true, each of the following is true:

> If ten-year-old Janine has mastered the "basics," she will
> be more financially successful as an adult than will ten-
> year-old Charles, who has not mastered the "basics."

> If seven-year-old Pietro has mastered the "basics," he will
> be more financially successful as an adult than will nine-
> year-old Christopher, who has not mastered the "basics."

And there are countless other implications of the hypothesis.

A hypothesis may be confirmed or disconfirmed by means of its implications. For example, if you were to observe that the above implications were true, your observation would count as evidence *for* the original hypothesis. Whereas, should you observe that one or another of the implications is false, this fact would be evidence toward disconfirming the original hypothesis.

In general, the basic form of a hypothetical argument has two parts. With certain important qualifications to be made later, we can say that the first part of the hypothetical argument involves a *deductive* argument to the effect that if the hypothesis is true, certain implications must be true. That is, a valid argument must be offered to the effect that

> H is true
> ———————————
> I is true

where H represents the hypothesis and I represents the implications of the hypothesis. Then, the second part of the argument is offered to the effect that since the hypothesis has these implications (that is, since if H is true, I is true), and since the implications themselves are true, the hypothesis is confirmed. In other words, the second part of a hypothetical argument has the form

> If H is true, I is true
>
> I is true
> _____
>
> H is true

This part of a hypothetical argument is clearly an inductive argument. (Notice that it has the invalid form "affirming the consequent.")

In the schema above, I represents any number of different implications of H. As more and more of these implications are shown to be true, the hypothesis is confirmed to higher and higher degrees. For example, as we find more instances of people who have mastered the "basics" and who are more financially successful than those who have not mastered the "basics," the degree of confirmation of the hypothesis increases.

In many cases, however, it is not possible to deduce the relevant test implications from the hypothesis alone. Certain auxiliary hypotheses must be employed. In other words, there are cases in which the argument

> H is true
> _____
>
> I is true

is not valid but the argument

> H is true *and* A is true
> _____
>
> I is true

is valid, A representing certain auxiliary hypotheses. For example, consider this hypothesis:

> Only intelligent students can master calculus.

In trying to confirm this hypothesis by means of the implication

> If someone scores 85 percent or more on certain calculus tests, then he or she will score 120 or above on IQ tests

certain auxiliary hypotheses must be employed, for in this case the argument

> H is true
> _____
> I is true

is not valid. In addition to H, some auxiliary hypotheses are necessary; for instance:

> If someone scores 85 percent or more on certain calculus tests, he or she has mastered calculus.
>
> If someone is intelligent, he or she will score 120 or above on IQ tests.

If these auxiliary hypotheses are used in conjunction with the original hypothesis, they do imply the test implication mentioned above.

In order to strengthen a hypothetical argument, you should identify many different implications of your hypothesis (or of your hypothesis and auxiliary hypotheses). The more implications you show to be true, the more highly you confirm your hypothesis. Moreover, you should try to identify different kinds of implications, thus employing diverse conditions for confirming the hypothesis. The greater the number of conditions and the more diverse they are, the more highly will the truth of the implications confirm the hypothesis.

You can successfully challenge the strength of a hypothetical argument by showing that only a small number of implications have been employed in trying to confirm the hypothesis and/or that the implications have not been sufficiently diverse. However, it is important to remember that a challenge to the strength of an argument is not necessarily a challenge to the truth of its conclusion.

One way to challenge the *truth* of the conclusion of a hypothetical argument depends upon the first (that is, the deductive) part of the argument. If some implication I is validly deducible from H directly (that is, without the use of any auxiliary hypotheses), you can show H to be false by showing I to be false. In other words, the form of the counter-argument is:

> If H is true, I must be true
>
> I is false
> _____
> H is false

This counter-argument has the valid argument form "denying the consequent" and can be used to conclusively prove that H is false.

But this sort of counter-argument is successful only if I is deducible directly from H. It cannot be employed when I is deduced from H plus some auxiliary premises A. The reason for this is that the argument

If H and A are both true, then I must be true

I is false

_____

H is false

is *not* valid. It is not an instance of "denying the consequent," for its conclusion is not the denial of the *whole* antecedent of its "if . . . then" premise.

When I is deduced from H plus some auxiliary premises A, determining that I is false is sufficient for showing that *either* H *or* one or more of the auxiliary premises A is false. But it is not sufficient for showing that H is false. Another way of saying this is that the argument

If H and A are both true, then I must be true

I is false

_____

It is not the case that both H and A are true

is valid. Notice that this argument *does* have the form "denying the consequent."

For example, finding someone who scored 85 percent or more on certain calculus tests *and* who did not score 120 or above on any IQ tests would be sufficient for concluding that *at least one* of the following was false:

Only intelligent students can master calculus.

If someone scores 85 percent or more on certain calculus tests, he or she has mastered calculus.

If someone is intelligent, he or she will score 120 or above on IQ tests.

In other words, even though the falsity of the test implication is established, the original hypothesis may still be true. The choice of auxiliaries may be the problem. One or more of the auxiliary hypotheses may be false. Standard IQ tests may be inadequate for measuring intelligence, or the calculus tests may be inadequate for determining mastery of calculus. This example also illustrates the important fact that many major educational hypotheses are never tested alone, but are always tested along with some auxiliary hypotheses.

Thus, if someone has offered a hypothetical argument in which I is deduced from H *and* A, a successful counter-argument must show two things: (1) that I is false, and (2) that there is good, independent evidence for believing that each of the auxiliary hypotheses is true. If you can establish both of these points, your counter-argument will be a strong one.

FALLACIES

In each of the types of inductive arguments we have considered, the premises stand in some relationship to the conclusion. Consequently, arguments of each type have some degree of strength. In the remaining sections of this chapter, we will examine a group of arguments that have no strength at all, that is, arguments in which there is no logical relationship between their premises and conclusion.

As we have seen, some arguments are obviously worthless. But there are other worthless arguments whose lack of strength is not nearly so obvious. Such an argument is called a *fallacy*. Fallacies "masquerade" as very strong arguments, and too often people find them quite persuasive. However, when a fallacy is stripped of its adornment and stated in its briefest form, its worthlessness as an argument is usually quite evident. It is when the propositions comprising the fallacy are spread out over several pages or throughout a lengthy, convoluted dialogue that it gains in its power to deceive. The following types of fallacies will each be illustrated by a brief form that allows you to see its essential weakness.

POST HOC ERGO PROPTER HOC

One of the most common mistakes that teachers make in their thinking is captured in the formula, "Try it and see if it works." Usually, some strategy of teaching is being considered and the question is whether the teacher ought to employ it. The teacher reasons that if this year's students do better than last year's, then the decision to employ this new strategy will have been a correct one. The fallacy involved in such reasoning is pernicious, because of its subtlety.

The general form of the argument is

X (temporally) followed Y

X was caused by Y

The fallacy represented by such an argument is called the *post hoc ergo propter hoc* (after this, therefore because of this) fallacy. It is a worthless argument to the effect that because one thing preceded another in time, the first is a cause of the second. The mere fact that Y occurred prior to X is not a good reason for concluding that Y caused X.

Yet many teachers are continually misled into thinking, for example, that since a particular teaching strategy was employed prior to their students' achievement of certain learning objectives, it was the strategy that caused the learning. The major weakness of such reasoning is that it disregards the possibility that other factors in the environment may have had a causal effect with regard to the students' learning; it was perhaps mere *coincidence* that the realization of the learning objectives followed

In an article in the magazine *Learning,* Kim Marshall describes some of his experiences as a white, sixth-grade teacher at Boston's previously all-black Martin Luther King, Jr., Middle School during its first year of court-ordered desegregation:

> The improvement in teacher attitude was indeed dramatic. The integration plan seemed to offer a chance for a fresh start, and the entire King staff was willing to make every effort to make it work. In the euphoria of the opening weeks of school, one teacher's warning that we might not be able to maintain the enthusiasm went almost unheeded. . . .
>
> I started the kids off at integrated tables and allowed them to talk and interact. . . . I was delighted to see one close interracial friendship after another forming. The kids seemed almost unaware of race in choosing their friends, relying instead on the inexplicable chemistry that naturally draws people to one another. . . .
>
> A conflict early in the school year reaffirmed our commitment to integration. An administrative order ruled that the school elect a biracial student council by a balloting process that allowed the students to vote only for representatives of their own race. Kids throughout the school reacted strongly; several white kids in my class were furious that they couldn't vote for their black friends. Everyone resisted when told to line up for two separate assemblies, one for black students, one for white students. . . .
>
> While the black kids were down at their assembly, rumors circulated that they were plotting ways to beat up the white kids. When they returned to the classroom, several white students actually hugged their black friends when they learned it wasn't true. . . .
>
> The school didn't sustain its strong beginning; by March it showed most of the symptoms of being a standard ghetto school again, complete with several ugly interracial incidents in the corridors. As the teacher had warned at the beginning of the year, the greatest danger was in not sustaining our effort and enthusiasm. . . ." (Kim Marshall, "The Desegregation of a Boston Classroom," *Learning,* Aug.-Sept. 1975, pp. 33–40.)

Identify and discuss the *post hoc ergo propter hoc* fallacy committed in the excerpt above.

the employment of the teaching strategy. Moreover, this fallacy fails to take into account the possibility that the students may have learned *in spite of* the use of the teaching strategy.

ARGUMENT *AD HOMINEM*

Less subtle than the *post hoc ergo propter hoc* fallacy is the argument *ad hominem* (argument directed toward the man). This fallacy, a staple of political campaigns, is usually offered in one of three variations.

In the first, the argument that is presented is supposed to show that a particular proposition is true. But the proposition goes all but unexamined; the only reasons offered for believing it are praises for someone identified with the proposition. Consider the following:

Case 1

Schools should give students more freedom. John Hart
says so, and he is a well-known author who has written
many books.

Some individuals presented with this argument may possess great respect for Hart or may be somewhat in awe of all famous authors. It may be possible to misdirect their approval and positive inclination for the *person* who supports the proposition to the proposition itself.

The second version of the *ad hominem* fallacy plays on disapproval instead of approval. The arguer tries to get others to believe that a certain proposition is false by associating it with something of which they disapprove:

Case 2

Mitchell's statement that contemporary American schools
are inhumane institutions is obviously false. As everyone
knows, Mitchell is a dedicated communist.

The argument above attempts to use many people's disapproval of communism to undermine Mitchell and a particular educational belief. While supposedly challenging that belief, it directs its attack against the person rather than against what the person affirms.

The third version of the *ad hominem* fallacy attempts to get people to assent to a proposition because of some special condition in which they find themselves:

Case 3

How can you, who profess to be a humanist, be against
these psychological and pedagogical theories? Since they
are among the most popular humanist theories, you must
agree with them.

In Cases 1 and 2 the person toward whom attention is misdirected is someone who is not a party to the argument. In Case 3, the person being persuaded is also the focus of the misdirected attention. The argument attempts to get the person to believe that a certain proposition is true (or false) because to do so would be in harmony with some personal facts or self-image. No relevant reasons for the truth of the proposition are provided.

To summarize, the argument *ad hominem* concludes either (1) that a proposition is true because it was asserted by a certain person, (2) that a

Analyze the *ad hominem* fallacy in the following passage:

> We usually think of a curriculum as having high standards if "it" covers ground, requires much and difficult reading, demands many papers, and if the students for whom it is intended do not easily get "good" grades. Advocates of "high standards" characteristically and unwittingly invoke other revealing metaphors. One of the most frequently used of these is "basic fundamentals." The most strident advocates of "high, and even yet higher standards" insist that these be "applied" particularly to "basic fundamentals." Indulging our propensity to inquire into the language of education, we find that the essential portion of the word "fundamental" is the word "fundament." It strikes us as poetically appropriate that "fundament" also means the buttocks. . . . We will resist the temptation to explore the unconscious motives of "fundamentalists." But we cannot resist saying that *their* "high standards" represent the *lowest possible standards imaginable* in any conception of a new education. (Neil Postman and Charles Weingartner, *Teaching as a Subversive Activity* [New York: Delacourt Press, 1969], pp. 66–67.)

proposition is false because it was asserted by a certain person, or (3) that a person ought to assent to a proposition because of some personal circumstance or attitude.

ARGUMENT FROM IGNORANCE

Another common mistake in reasoning, especially where philosophical issues are involved, is known as the *argument from ignorance.* In such an argument, the arguer attempts to prove that a proposition is true because it has not been proven false (or that a proposition is false because it has not been proven true). A recurring illustration of this fallacy is the contention that there must be flying saucers and visitors to earth from outer space because no one has ever proved these phenomena do not exist. In academic matters, this fallacy is often committed through the use of a rhetorical question like "Who's to say?" The following situation is typical; in it, one person attempts to persuade another that her belief is false simply because no one else has proved that it is true:

> Danielle and John are discussing what the aims of education ought to be. Danielle says that the aim of education ought to be to produce knowledgeable people. John responds, "Who's to say that that should be the aim of education? People have been arguing this issue for centuries. Thus, you are no doubt wrong."

Consider the following argument:

> If it be protested that education needs more time to take effect, let's try a wide-angle glance back toward the Middle Ages. H. G. Wells suggests that in the medieval church's attempt to strengthen its grip on Europe by theological thought-control via education, what happened was the precise opposite of what was intended. . . . In trying to mold the minds of tomorrow's leaders, it [the church] succeeded only in setting those minds free and forfeiting its supremacy in Europe. . . .
>
> There were, to be sure, other forces at work; but not least important, as a side effect of education, was the appearance of "common man, the unofficial outside independent man." . . .
>
> Education sowed the seeds of Renaissance, Reformation, and Revolution—unintentionally. With its spread came criticism, dissent, protest, rebellion—inadvertently. Maybe these phenomena constituted social progress and reform, but they were not exactly in the curricular game plan.
>
> Whether one accepts this reading of history or not, the negative fact seems indisputable: In the long run, the church's behavioral objectives were not attained. The conclusion can scarcely be avoided that, whatever else instruction accomplishes, its ultimate outcomes are indeterminable and unpredictable. (T. Robert Bassett, "It's the Side Effects of Education That Count," *Phi Delta Kappan,* September 1972, p. 16.)

Identify the "argument from ignorance" contained in the passage above. Next, simplify the passage to show the argument by enumeration it also contains. Why is this argument a weak one?

THE FALLACY OF EQUIVOCATION

Somewhat different from the preceding fallacies is the *fallacy of equivocation.* It primarily involves mistakes concerning the meanings of words. Many words or phrases have more than one meaning. For instance, the word *blue* may mean a color or a mood. The fallacy of equivocation occurs when the different meanings of a word or phrase are confused in an argument:

> The study of biology has shown that all biological organisms have certain needs. In fact, no organism can survive for very long if these needs are not satisfied. Among the needs that human beings have is the need to be allowed to make decisions for oneself. Therefore, children must be allowed to make decisions for themselves; otherwise, they will not be able to survive for very long.

This is a fallacious argument because it confuses two different senses of the word *need.* In the first two premises, *need* refers to biological need; but in the third premise it refers to psychological need. Indeed, the third premise is credible only when "psychological need" is taken as the meaning of *need.* For if that premise is understood to maintain that being allowed to make decisions for oneself is a biological need, it is clearly false. When these different meanings of *need* are kept separate, it becomes obvious that the premises of the argument do not support its conclusion.

Another version of the fallacy of equivocation occurs when a word with a well-established meaning is given a new meaning but allowed to retain some elements of the old one. In educational discussions, examples of this fallacy often involve such fundamental words as *growth, teaching, learning,* and even *education.* For instance, some psychologists have recently redefined *learning* in terms of "measurable, observable behavior." Employing the word *learning* in its new meaning, they conduct experiments and offer arguments concerning ways to maximize "learning," factors that inhibit or prevent "learning," and so forth. As long as only the new meaning of the word is meant and understood no fallacies are committed by such arguments. However, there is the persistent chance that the psychologists or, more likely, interpreters of their works will present them as though they dealt with learning in the older, more ordinary sense. Thus, because of the fallacy of equivocation, studies that established relatively little may come to influence educational practice in ways far beyond what their evidence warrants.

Review

1. Define each of the following terms used in this chapter:

Inductive argument	Fallacy
Argument by enumeration	*Post hoc ergo propter hoc* fallacy
Statistical induction	*Ad hominem* fallacy
Argument by analogy	Argument from ignorance
Hypothetical argument	Fallacy of equivocation

2. Explain the difference between inductive arguments and deductive arguments.
3. Explain how it is that inductive arguments have varying degrees of strength.
4. Explain the difference between proving a conclusion and confirming a conclusion.
5. Devise and assess the strength of:
   a. an argument by enumeration
   b. a statistical induction

      c. an argument by analogy

      d. a hypothetical argument

6. Develop an original example of:

      a. a *post hoc ergo propter hoc* fallacy

      b. an *ad hominem* fallacy

      c. an argument from ignorance

      d. a fallacy of equivocation

Language and Educational Arguments

Arguments are expressed in language. The reasons for decisions or beliefs are communicated mainly by means of language. Consequently, when you attempt to determine how rationally a decision has been made or why a belief is held, you must deal with arguments that are presented in language. Thus, in this chapter we will examine aspects of language that you need to understand in order to properly assess the strength of educational arguments.

EMOTIVE FORCE

One of the more apparent—albeit often confusing—aspects of language is the fact that it has many different functions. Language is used to state propositions, ask questions, give commands, express emotions, persuade others, engender emotions in others, make promises, and so forth. It does not function only to state propositions. Moreover, many of the functions of language are not mutually exclusive. That is, it is possible to use language to do several things simultaneously. For instance, in saying "Children need to learn the basics," a teacher might be trying to (1) state a proposition, (2) express a positive emotion concerning children's learning the basics, (3) persuade others to implement a program of basic education in a school, (4) arouse positive emotions in others with regard to children's learning the basics.

When in books, articles, and everyday conversation different language functions are employed without careful attempts to distinguish them, the undifferentiated juxtaposition causes little or no difficulty. However, the effect is usually very different where formal arguments are concerned. If you want to properly formulate or assess such an argument, you must be careful to separate out all language which does not state propositions. And this is not always as easy as it may appear. Nevertheless, the separation must be made. For, as we have seen, arguments legitimately contain *only* propositions.

One of the primary sources of confusion in the language used to express educational arguments is the fact that many words and phrases have, in addition to cognitive meaning, considerable emotive force. A word or phrase has an *emotive force* if it tends to arouse one or more emotions in those who hear or read it. For example, the word *fascist* has a negative emotive force for many people, because it tends to arouse in them such emotions as hatred, anger, fear, and contempt.

Whether or not a particular word has an emotive force depends upon the person who hears or reads it. That is, a word may have a particular emotive effect on you, but not on someone else—especially if your experiences have been vastly different. But since the backgrounds of most speakers of the same language are very similar in some respects, many words tend to have a standard or conventional emotive force.

It is not uncommon for people to come to believe that the proposition expressed by a given sentence is true (or false) simply because of the emotions aroused in them by some of the words that occur in it. For instance, consider the following sentence:

> The little children suffer horribly when wrenched from the comfortable environment of their own neighborhood school and bussed all the way across the city.

The sentence above states a proposition, but some of its phrases arouse emotions in many people. The phrases that tend to arouse positive emotions are *little children, comfortable environment,* and *neighborhood.* Those that tend to arouse negative emotions are *suffer, horribly,* and *wrenched.* If the sentence caused you to associate the negative emotions you have for these words with bussing, you might thereby be persuaded to believe that schoolchildren should not be bussed to a school beyond their neighborhood. Of course, if you came to believe this only as a consequence of your emotional responses to the words and had no sound reasons for believing the sentence, you would be reacting irrationally. The danger posed by words having an emotive force is that they can be used to persuade a person to hold a belief or make a decision without having good reasons for it.

With specific regard to educational arguments, the propositions that comprise the arguments will be expressed by means of sentences. And those sentences may (and frequently do) contain words that have emotive force. In order to properly offer or criticize such an argument, you must separate the emotive force of the sentences from their propositional function. And then you should consider *only* the propositions that the sentences express.

The writer of the following paragraphs appears to be attempting to show that the student who is motivated will learn:

> He learns who *wants* to learn. This is the first law of education. You can, perhaps, teach a person against his will; but to do so is like pushing a car uphill with the brakes locked. This desire to learn, educators and psychologists call *motivation*. . . .
>
> To appreciate the value of motivation, reflect upon your own experience. Perhaps you accompanied a friend to a lecture on a subject in which you had utterly no interest and in which, furthermore, you saw no possibility of any value accruing to yourself or to your work. You sat, however, listening deferentially, but without enthusiasm or interest, to all that was said. As you reflect upon that experience, how much was your behavior changed as a result of it? Probably not at all.
>
> Now, contrast this experience with another one. You have an opportunity for advancement. It means increased status, a raise in pay, better hours, and improved working conditions. The supervisor calls together a group of potential candidates for the position. You are one of them. The lecture begins. This time you are far from apathetic. You listen intently. To get every word, to act upon it judiciously, means your future. In this situation there is no doubt of your interest—nor of your motivation. . . . That you are motivated, there is not the slightest doubt. For in this instance you really *want* to learn. (Thomas F. Staton, *How to Instruct Successfully* [New York: McGraw-Hill, 1960], p. 10.)

Identify the emotive language used in the preceding statement; then reconstruct its argument, using only the propositional elements of the sentences. Devoid of the emotive language, is the argument a very strong one? Explain.

AMBIGUITY

In addition to the difficulties caused by the emotive force of many words and phrases, there are difficulties that arise from ambiguity. Linguistic ambiguity has two major sources: (1) the multiple meanings of some words and phrases and (2) faulty sentence structure. If a word is used in such a way that it is not clear which of its several meanings is intended, that use of the word is *semantically ambiguous.* The following sentence is ambiguous in this way:

He has learned the multiplication tables.

It is not clear whether the sentence means (a) "He is able to recite the multiplication tables," or (b) "He understands the multiplication tables." In some instances, comprehending the wrong proposition would lead to the rejection of a whole argument.

The second type of ambiguity arises when the position of words or the punctuation in a sentence makes unclear exactly what proposition the sentence is meant to express. The faulty sentence is said to be *syntactically ambiguous.* Consider the following faulty construction:

When Mr. Chernak punished his class on the advice of a more experienced teacher he spoke quietly.

It is syntactically ambiguous, because it could mean either (a) "On the advice of a more experienced teacher, Mr. Chernak spoke quietly when he punished his class," or (b) "When Mr. Chernak, on the advice of a more experienced teacher, punished his class, he spoke quietly."

Both types of ambiguity must be avoided in your attempts to offer proper reasons for your beliefs and decisions. Happily, it is not especially difficult to do so. In order to avoid semantic ambiguity, you should first determine whether any of the words or phrases you use to express your beliefs and reasons has more than one common meaning. Then, you should determine whether the context in which you are using such a word or phrase makes clear which of its meanings is intended. If the context does not make the meaning clear, an explicit statement that does so should be provided. Syntactic ambiguity can be avoided if you are careful in constructing and punctuating your sentences and if you always proofread your material.

It is important to avoid ambiguity in attempting to make educational decisions rationally or in assessing how rationally such decisions have been made. Educational decisions can be made rationally only if reasons have been given and reasons must be propositions. But if a linguistic formulation is ambiguous in either of the senses identified here, it will be impossible to determine *precisely* what proposition is expressed by the linguistic formulation. And if this is not possible, there will be no way of identifying *precisely* what reasons have been offered for the decision. Hence, if the linguistic formulations that are put forward as expressing reasons are ambiguous, there can be no way (short of removing the ambiguity) of determining how rationally the decision was made.

VAGUENESS

Somewhat similar to the problems generated by ambiguity are those resulting from the vagueness of many expressions. A word or phrase is *vague* if in certain situations it is, in principle, impossible to determine whether it properly applies; such a word or phrase lacks clarity and precision of meaning. The word *old*, for instance, is vague, because it is not clear what age someone or something must be in order to be properly called old. There are no criteria that precisely distinguish old people from people who are not old. Although there are clearly some people who definitely are old and some who are not, there is no clear line of demarcation between old people and people who are not old. Consequently, there are many cases where it is *in principle* impossible to determine whether "old" does or does not properly apply. That is, there is in principle no way of determining in certain situations whether a person is old or not.

For any vague expression, there is a set of cases in which the expression clearly applies, a set of cases in which it just as clearly does not apply, and a set of cases in which it is in principle impossible to determine whether the expression applies. These groupings may be represented as follows:

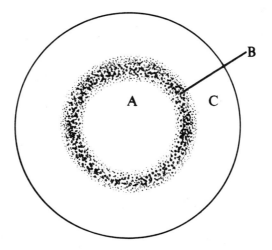

Area A represents that set of cases in which the expression clearly applies. Area C represents that set of cases in which the expression clearly does not apply. And area B represents that set of cases in which it is in principle impossible to determine whether it applies. Although B separates A from C, there is no hard and fast line of division between A and B, or between B and C, or between A and C.

Vague terms in an argument may or may not cause problems. If the vague term is used in a context concerning *only* those cases in which it clearly does or does not apply, there will be no special difficulties. In such an event, the term functions *as if* it had a precise, that is, non-vague, meaning. To the degree that the term is used with the precise part of its meaning, the sentence in which it occurs may properly function to state a proposition.

On the other hand, if the term is used concerning cases where it is in principle impossible to determine whether it applies, then it is *in principle* impossible to determine whether the sentence in which the term occurs properly functions as either a premise or conclusion in an argument. For if we cannot determine precisely what proposition a sentence states, we cannot be certain that it actually functions to state a proposition. And since an argument is comprised only of propositions, if it is impossible to determine whether a given sentence states a proposition or precisely what proposition it does state, then it is also impossible to determine whether the sentence functions to express a premise or conclusion in the argument.

These latter points require some elaboration. Suppose that McX says, "John is old." If we know John and know that he is 103 years of age, we can readily agree with McX. Indeed, we could have good reason for believing that "John is old" expresses a true proposition. For we know that in such a context *old* means at least "over 100 years of age." More specifically, on the basis of our understanding of part (a *precise* part) of the meaning of "old," we know that the proposition "If John is over 100 years of age, then John is old" is true. Consequently, we are able to argue that since this is true and since John is 103 years of age, then "John is old" must be true. So long as we employ only this precise, albeit partial, meaning of *old*, each of these sentences expresses a specific proposition. And insofar as this is the case, we may properly say that here we have an argument with premises and conclusion.

Such certainty is not possible, however, when the term is used in a context in which it is in principle impossible to determine whether it applies. Suppose that McX says, "David is old." We may know David and know that McX knows that David is about 30 years of age. So what understanding of the term *old* do we employ? We are now dealing with the term's inherent vagueness; no precise partial meaning presents itself as it did in the preceding case. In this context, we have no partial (or complete) meaning to employ in determining *precisely* what proposition is expressed by the sentence "David is old." Certainly, we would know that "If David is over 100 years of age, then David is old" is true. And we would know that "If David is not over 2 years of age, then David is old" is false. Yet because being 30 years of age falls within that set of cases in which it is in principle impossible to determine whether *old* applies, it is

The writers of the following paragraphs on classroom management employ the term *cohesiveness* with less than maximum precision:

> Some degree of cohesiveness must develop in order for group organizations to function efficiently and thus to provide satisfactory conditions for members. This means that it is characteristic of groups to seek to develop and maintain structural stability, cooperativeness, and functional operativeness. It might be said that groups are concerned with unity and loyalty, and with achieving some common values. Although a class group is fairly large, and many of its operations are routine, it appears that many behavior patterns exhibited by members of classroom groups indicate that unity and integration are valued, and classroom work is set aside when the group must devote its efforts to developing a stable system of relationships..... .
>
> Terms such as solidarity, loyalty, morale, attractiveness, and atmosphere have been used to describe the group property of cohesiveness. Cohesiveness has also been called mutual attraction or group attractiveness. This condition, which usually exists to some degree in most groups at some time, has been likened to glue, and has been called the quality, substance, or force which binds the group members together, for members of cohesive groups do stick together. They think of themselves as being bound together in some way. (Lois V. Johnson and Mary A. Bany, *Classroom Management: Theory and Skill Training* [New York: Macmillan, 1970], p. 138.)

In what ways is *cohesiveness* a vague term in the paragraphs above? How does the vagueness of the term affect the authors' argument?

in principle impossible to determine whether "David is old" is true or false. In this context, it is not clear precisely what proposition is stated by the sentence "David is old." Indeed, without clarification, we have no warrant for thinking that it states *any particular* proposition.

Difficulties generated by vagueness are especially acute when you attempt to be rational about educational beliefs or decisions, because at present so many expressions central to educational discourse are vague. For instance, consider the expression "teach." Is a person teaching, if his students are not learning? If a person has told his students to form groups and discuss a particular issue, is he teaching if he is now only observing the discussions? What exactly are the criteria in terms of which we can determine whether the word *teach* has been properly used? These questions begin to point up the inherent vagueness of "teach" as it is ordinarily used in educational discourse and attempts at argumentation. Asking similar questions about other expressions central to educational discourse will likewise disclose their inherent vagueness. But disclosure of the source of a problem is one thing; remediation is another.

Consider another definition of *cohesiveness* among human beings:

> Man has been aware of one of the major features of groups at least since he began to record his history. Military commanders and athletic coaches long ago discovered the importance of teamwork, group loyalty, and morale. The troop or team that coordinated its activity and acted quickly as a unit was effective, and sometimes its members would be stimulated to extraordinary effort. They would catch fire and sustain one another in a maximum attempt at victory. Members of a group develop loyalty, a feeling of belonging, and a willingness to work for the good of everyone. Students of group methods refer to this feeling of loyalty and *esprit de corps* as *cohesiveness*. (Ernest G. Bormann, *Discussion and Group Methods: Theory and Practice* [New York: Harper & Row, 1969], p. 139.)

Explain how this definition of *cohesiveness* differs from the Johnson-Bany definition in the preceding box. In what respects are they similar? Is the second definition vague? Explain.

DEFINITION

The problems associated with semantic ambiguity and vagueness can be overcome, or at least minimized, if you state clearly and precisely just what you mean by potentially troublesome words or phrases—that is, if you provide definitions. There are many highly complex philosophical issues surrounding the matter of definition; however, they lie beyond the scope of this text. For our purposes here, we shall take a definition to be a proposition that sets forth or specifies a meaning of a word or phrase.

In many cases it is obvious that someone giving you a definition is telling you only what he or she means by the particular word or phrase. For instance, suppose that someone says that *bifortang* means "a triangle with two forty-degree angles." She is telling you what she means by *bifortang*; she is not necessarily claiming that this is what you or anyone else means by it. Such a definition is called a stipulative one.

A *stipulative definition* is essentially an announcement by someone that by the word W he or she means M. As long as it does not contradict itself—that is, as long as it does not imply that some proposition is both true and false—a stipulative definition cannot be false. Anyone may use a particular word or phrase to mean whatever he or she wants it to mean. For example, it would be quite proper for a friend to say to you, "By the word *dog*, I mean what is ordinarily meant by the word *chalk*." Clearly, this cannot be false, if he is only announcing what *he means* by the word.

Suppose he goes on to say such things as "Please bring me a piece of dog," "This piece of dog is yellow and I wanted a white one," "That dog is too brittle," and so on. You might appropriately point out that other people mean something else by the word *dog*, that it is really weird to use *dog* to mean what he means, or that his unusual use of the word is likely to be confusing to other people. But you could not properly claim that his definition is false. And so it is with any stipulative definition. Of course, once someone offers a stipulative definition for a given word or phrase, he or she may not properly change the meaning without an additional announcement.

As we have said, a definition is at bottom a proposition that sets forth or specifies a meaning of a word or phrase. Yet frequently when a person claims to be giving a "definition," he or she is—and intends to be—doing more than just specifying a meaning. In most cases, the person is also claiming to report a conventional or common meaning of the word. Such a definition is termed a *reportive definition.* Whereas a stipulative defi-

---

The following paragraphs on modern education are taken from a paper titled "Accountability Defined":

> The public has lost faith in educational institutions. Traditional acceptance of educational programs on the basis of their past performance and apparent but unsubstantiated worth is no longer the rule. The public has demanded that schools demonstrate that resources are being utilized "properly." But this has meant far more than mere financial accounting, to ensure that funds have not been illegally spent or embezzled. What is demanded instead is that schools demonstrate that the outcomes they are producing are worth the dollar investment provided by communities. In short, what has been called for is a system of "educational accountability." . . .
>
> In this paper we will tentatively settle on a definition of accountability as:
>> *Accountability is a negotiated relationship in which the participants agree in advance to accept specified rewards and costs on the basis of evaluation findings as to the attainment of specified ends. . . .*
>
> At the heart of all of the above noted elements is the concept of "negotiation." Negotiation, for example, is suggested in the kind of dialogue which leads to mutual acceptance of a position, or in the acceptance of a negotiated, specified end. Negotiation frequently involves the allowable constraints, such as the students to be worked with and the instructional materials to be utilized. (Marvin C. Alkin, "Accountability Defined" in *Accountability for Educational Results,* ed. R. W. Hostrop, J. A. Mecklenburger, and J. A. Wilson [Hamden, Conn.: Linnet Books, 1973], p. 51.)

Explain why this definition of *accountability* is a stipulative definition.

nition is essentially an announcement of a meaning, a reportive definition is an empirical claim about the conventional meaning of a word or phrase. Such an empirical claim is either true or false.

People frequently search for and debate the "real" definitions of words; they expect timelessness and uniformity. However, there are no "real" definitions. Words are dynamic human creations. In the initial stage of a language, sounds and sets of marks are more or less arbitrarily selected to express meanings. As a language grows, it usually gains in sophistication; some more or less practical grounds are found for standardization, and rules for expressing new meanings preempt most of the arbitrary selection of sound patterns and sets of marks. Nevertheless, in the final analysis, there is no *necessary* relationship between a given word and a particular meaning.

People who seek "real" definitions do not fully understand this fact. In most instances, they are actually wanting only the conventional meaning of some term. The tendency is to think that the conventional meaning is the "real" meaning.

Although it is proper to criticize a reportive definition on the grounds that it does not adequately capture the common meaning of the term, it is not appropriate to criticize a definition on the grounds that it is not the real definition of the word or phrase. It is quite different to claim "That's not the *ordinary* meaning of the word" and "That's not the *real* meaning of the word." To talk of "ordinary" meanings, rather than "real" meanings, takes a great deal of the mystery (and perhaps mysticism) out of the situation. It also helps to avoid a possible source of confusion when you deal with definitions.

Another problem with thinking that there are such things as "real" definitions is that it often prevents a person from being open to and accepting a stipulative definition which someone might offer. This is an unfortunate consequence, for introducing *new* meanings through stipulation is important in the development of knowledge.

There is also a particular danger here. Sometimes when people talk about the "real" definition of a word, they are offering a *persuasive definition*—a definition that appears to be (but is not) a reportive definition and that has (or is intended to have) the effect of persuading the listener to adopt a certain belief or attitude. For example, suppose that McX wants to convince you that a particular educational proposal ought to be implemented. He might argue as follows:

> McY wants you to allow children to set their own goals because, he says, education is a process of development from within, an unfolding. Students develop from their own reserves much as flowers develop from seeds.
>
> But that is not what education *really* is. Education is really the process of leading the ignorant toward knowledge. And obviously since this is what *education* really means, students cannot be expected to set proper

goals for themselves. The setting of goals must be done by a teacher who already knows the way and hence can lead students in the right direction.

Notice that McX's *purpose* here is to convince you that McY's proposed educational policy should not be adopted—and perhaps that McX's policy should be. If McX can convince you to adopt his definition of *education* by calling it the "real" definition, then he will have significantly increased the chances that you will accept his recommendations regarding educational policy. For it is likely that you already hold beliefs involving the term *education.* Presumably, many of these beliefs have policy implications. For instance, you might believe that schools should be structured so as to provide children with the best education possible. If McX can convince you to adopt his definition of *education*, the natural tendency will be for you to retain the previous wording of your beliefs about education but to substitute his meaning of the term for the one you had pre-

---

In attempting to achieve some clarity concerning the meaning of the phrase *equal opportunity,* one writer on education has offered the following distinctions:

> What exactly the phrase "equality of opportunity" means is not clear. Roughly it implies a fair start in life, an opportunity for all children to develop their faculties and to proceed into adult life and employment without being adversely affected by poor homes and families. But, to use the metaphor of a running race, "equality of opportunity" can mean variously the opportunity to start together, the opportunity to benefit from staggered starts, the opportunity to finish together—and sometimes no more than the opportunity to run on the same track. Arguments have shifted ground, involving at different times different ideas of educational ability and social justice and different concepts of the ways in which ability can be measured and exploited. The two main strands of the theme—educational and social—are interwoven so that at various times and in various arguments one or the other takes precedence: in terms of education it can mean the provision of equal facilities and attention and in social terms it can mean the use of education to achieve a more equal society. Disillusion with the ability of education by itself to make for a more equal society has led to a concentration upon ways in which society can be made more equal in order to encourage more equality of opportunity in education. (Michael Locke, *Power and Politics in the School System: A Guidebook* [London: Routledge & Kegan Paul, 1974], pp. 77–78.

Using the distinctions set forth above, construct two or three persuasive definitions of *equal educational opportunity.*

viously employed. The result will be at least the altering of your beliefs and possibly some changes in educational policy.

Of course, one need not talk of "real" definitions in order to offer a persuasive definition. The point here is that a persuasive definition has (or is intended to have) the effect of persuading a person to adopt some belief or attitude. In educational contexts, the intention is often to persuade a person to be for or against an educational policy.

Being able to detect a persuasive definition offers two major benefits. The first of these is that you are less likely to be misled in your acquiring of new beliefs. Persuasive definitions do not constitute good reasons for affirming propositions or making decisions. The second advantage in being able to detect persuasive definitions is that it can help you avoid being drawn into irrelevant or rationally unresolvable discussions. The introduction of a persuasive definition often turns an argument away from its central issue, and the focus becomes what is or is not the "real" definition of a particular term. There is in such diversion the mistake of criticizing a definition on the grounds that it is not the "real" definition. More importantly, the search for the "real" meaning of a term can cause a significant policy matter to go unresolved or to be decided on the basis of irrelevant evidence.

THE IMPORTANCE OF DEFINITION

In attempting to make educational decisions rationally, it is important that you be able to offer reasonably clear definitions. Unfortunately, the language used in discussions of education today is for the most part "ordinary" language. It does not include a specialized or technical vocabulary such as that found in the fields of mathematics, physics, and biology. The words in these fields tend to have much more precise meanings than do those in ordinary language. For instance, compare the word *life* as it is ordinarily used and the term *half-life* as it occurs in physics.

The varying degrees of precision in ordinary language cause remarkably few difficulties in conducting our everyday, nonprofessional affairs. In private matters, people tend to overlook imprecision, and adjust. Indeed, in many cases the lack of precision is beneficial. However, the opposite tends to be the case when it comes to public matters, such as education. In particular, the problems created by imprecision become especially acute in attempting to make educational decisions rationally.

If you are to offer good reasons for your educational decisions, you must understand what your reasons are. And if you use the words and phrases of ordinary language, you must have a fairly clear understanding of what you mean by them. We are so used to hearing and using certain words that we often mistakenly think that we have a clear understanding of their meanings when we do not. If in fact you do not have a reasonably clear understanding of the meanings of certain terms and nevertheless em-

A book on modern secondary education offers this definition of *discipline:*

> Basic to all questions of discipline is the need to agree on what the term means and what kind of discipline we want in our schools. One complication in defining discipline is the fact that most people have widely divergent views on the subject. To some, discipline means the ability to control the behavior of individuals. Others see it as conformity to regulations. Memories of the birch rod and physical punishment persist in the minds of some adults as representing school discipline. . . .
>
> For years discipline in schools meant punishment for the violation of rules and the enforcement of regulations imposed upon students by the authorities. Webster recognizes these concepts but points out that discipline is also a process of education designed to improve and perfect behavior; furthermore, discipline may have as its goal obedience to rules based on self-control or self-discipline. Present-day educators are in general agreement that, although discipline still involves the establishment of rules and regulations, the major emphasis should be on securing a high degree of self-discipline. . . .
>
> As society has become increasingly complex, and as fates of nations depend more and more upon reasoned judgment in human relations and international affairs, the need to help future citizens develop behavior controlled from *within* rather than imposed from without has become critical. . . .
>
> School discipline in harmony with the above viewpoint has the following characteristics: (1) Student behavior is largely self-controlled, (2) authority is vested primarily in humanitarian principles rather than in a person, (3) obedience to rules and regulations is based on an understanding of the reasons for such requirements rather than on accepting someone's word for them, (4) school activities and classroom experiences are designed to provide opportunities to develop socially acceptable behavior, and (5) emphasis is on treating behavior problems according to the background of individual students. (Lester W. Anderson and Lauren A. Van Dyke, *Secondary School Administration* [Boston: Houghton Mifflin, 1972], pp. 409–10.)

In what respect is this a persuasive definition? Does it suggest that there is a "real" meaning of the term *discipline?* Or does it suggest that *discipline* is a word with multiple reportive definitions? What, if any, ambiguous or vague terms are included in this definition of *discipline?* Is there an argument *ad hominem* here?

ploy them in formulating reasons for your beliefs and decisions, a great deal of confusion can result.

Consequently, whenever you offer reasons for your beliefs, you should also be able to provide reasonably clear definitions of the words used to express those reasons. If you cannot do this, people will have good reason for believing that you are not at all clear on just what your reasons are.

Indeed, if in such a case you were unable to provide any clear definitions, we would have to seriously question whether your sentences were anything more than empty verbal formulations.

SOME GUIDELINES FOR OFFERING DEFINITIONS

The formulating of definitions does not lend itself to hard and fast rules, but the following guidelines should be helpful.

A definition should be as precise as possible. One of the most effective ways to define a word precisely is to specify the necessary and sufficient conditions that must be satisfied in order for the word to be employed properly. To say that N is a *necessary condition* for the proper use of W is to say that W may be properly used only if N has been satisfied. For example, given ordinary meanings, something is properly called "a bachelor" only if that thing is a man. Being a man, then, is a necessary condition for being a bachelor. However, being a man is not sufficient for being a bachelor. To say that S is a *sufficient condition* for the proper use of W is to say that if S has been satisfied, then W may properly be used. That something is a triangle is a sufficient condition for calling it a "polygon," but it is not a necessary condition.

While specifying necessary and sufficient conditions is an effective way of defining precisely, it may not always be possible to identify such conditions. This is often the case with regard to words whose ordinary meanings we try to capture in reportive definitions. As we have discussed, the ordinary meanings of many words are very imprecise. For instance, are there necessary and sufficient conditions for the proper use of the word *chair?* If the ordinary meaning of a word does not contain both necessary and sufficient conditions, then we cannot properly impose the impossible requirement that they be specified in the reportive definition. If the necessary precision cannot be achieved with a reportive definition, then it would be appropriate to use a stipulative definition.

A definition should be consistent with definitions already given in the same context. Two definitions are consistent if, and only if, they do not imply a contradiction. The following definitions, for example, are inconsistent:

> *Education* is the process whereby an individual teaches himself or herself what is valuable.
>
> *Teaching* is the act of promoting learning in another person but not in oneself.

Given these definitions, it would be impossible to educate anyone.

A definition should incorporate conventional meanings whenever possible. This is a practical requirement, for it would be foolish to regularly

An article in a professional journal for elementary school principals prefaces its recommendations for changing schools with the following definition:

> I use the term "school" to mean people—the people connected with each individual school: the principal, the teachers, the children, the parents, and anyone else the school wishes to bring in. (John I. Goodlad, "The Child and His School in Transition," *The National Elementary School Principal*, January 1973, p. 30.)

Evaluate how well the statement above follows the guideline regarding precision in definitions. Does the explanation of the stipulative definition of *school* fall back on that word's ordinary meaning? Rewrite this part of the statement substituting the stipulative definition for the term defined.

create new languages. However, since many conventional terms—especially those central to educational discourse—are quite vague, this guideline should be followed only insofar as doing so does not necessitate the violation of other guidelines.

A definition should not contain terms that are unclear or ambiguous. Since the point of defining a term is to make its meaning clear and explicit, using words that are themselves unclear will not contribute to a definition's success. For example, under most circumstances, it would not be helpful to define *education* as

> the process through which humans grow intellectually and emotionally.

The word *grow* is not an especially clear term. On the other hand, if you could go on to give a reasonably clear definition of *grow* as it is used in this definition, the initial problem of lack of clarity would be diminished.

Ambiguous terms are also undesirable in definitions. If for some reason you have to use an ambiguous term, you should immediately make clear which of its several meanings is employed in the definition. For example, suppose that you define *basic education* as

> education that provides the student with an ability to read, write, and do arithmetical calculations.

The word *write* is ambiguous. It could mean either "to form words or letters on a surface (such as paper) using some instrument (such as a pencil)"—which could mean only good penmanship—or "to express one's ideas clearly and logically by forming words"—which does not necessarily mean good penmanship.

Many teachers, administrators, and parents seem to be in favor of educational policies that will enhance a child's "creativity." But what does the term *creativity* mean? The reportive definition is not especially clear or precise. And neither is the following:

> Creativity, best defined, is a form of intelligence based on divergent thinking. It is partly innate and partly learned or developed. The main characteristics of divergent thinking are fluency, flexibility, originality and elaboration. It exists, therefore, as a potential for creativity. The person in whom divergent thinking is highly developed tends to think in unconventional patterns; he searches for different solutions rather than converging on the single correct, or logical answer. He is likely to be innovative and original. (Stephanie Z. Dudek, "Teachers Stifle Children's Creativity: A Charge Too Easily Made," *Learning,* August-September 1976, p. 102.)

Evaluate the statement above with regard to the guidelines for definitions, especially the suggestions on clarity and ambiguity. Devise your own definition of *creativity*.

SOME WAYS OF DEFINING

The preceding section identified some guidelines you can use in offering definitions. In this section, we will consider some specific ways in which you can construct your definitions.

One obvious way to define a word is to use a single word that has the same meaning—that is, a *definition by synonym.* For example, you might say that *motherland* means the same as *fatherland* or that *car* means the same as *automobile.*

Although the definition by synonym is common, it may not be very helpful in serious educational discussions. There are simply no easy synonyms for many educational terms. Sometimes there are words close in meaning but not close enough. In such a case, offering a definition by synonym may be more misleading than helpful. It will also be inaccurate. Even a slight difference in meaning can be important. For instance, in many cases it would be misleading to define *teaching* as "instruction" because there are subtle, but significant, differences in their meanings.

One way to make clear the subtle differences between meanings is to offer a *definition by necessary and/or sufficient conditions,* that is, a definition specifying conditions for the proper use of the word. We have already discussed this sort of definition, but it seems appropriate to reemphasize here that it is often impossible to offer a correct reportive definition of this kind for words in our "ordinary" language.

In defining some words or phrases as they are used in "ordinary" language, it is often useful (and sometimes most accurate) to offer a *definition by listing*—a definition that lists some or all of the things to which the term refers. For example, you might define the phrase *great works of literature* by listing such works as Shakespeare's *Hamlet,* Dostoyevsky's *Crime and Punishment,* and Plato's *Republic.* Usually, the clarity of a definition by listing increases as the number of items increases. A complete list is often impractical, however. An exhaustive listing of great works of literature, for example, would be a major chore. In most situations, listing several examples is usually sufficient. So as not to be misleading, the sample list should be a varied one.

The final method of definition we will consider is the *ostensive definition,* which involves physically pointing out something the word refers to. So, for instance, you might offer an ostensive definition of *teaching* by taking a person around a school and pointing out actual instances of what you consider to be teaching.

In defining a word ostensively, it is usually necessary to point out a fairly large number of cases. Sometimes it is also helpful to point out cases that do not illustrate the word. For instance, imagine teaching a child the meaning of the color word *blue.* You might say the word while pointing out many things that are blue in color. You might also point out things that are not blue, identifying them negatively as "not blue" or positively by their color.

Review

1. Define each of the following terms used in this chapter:

Emotive force	Sufficient condition
Ambiguity	Definition by synonym
Vagueness	Definition by necessary and/or
Stipulative definition	sufficient condition
Reportive definition	Definition by listing
Necessary condition	Ostensive definition

2. Identify and discuss some of the different uses of language.
3. Discuss the problems created by the emotive force of various words and phrases.
4. Explain the two major sources of ambiguity.
5. Discuss the ways to avoid vagueness in educational arguments.
6. Explain why a stipulative definition cannot be false so long as it is not contradictory.
7. Explain why a reportive definition can be either true or false.
8. Explain why it is inappropriate to criticize a definition on the grounds that it is not the "real" definition of a particular word.
9. Identify and discuss some guidelines for offering definitions.
10. Identify and discuss some different ways of defining.

How to Assess

Educational Arguments

We can now show how the preceding discussion of logic and language applies to actual cases. In doing so, we will outline a procedure that you can employ in assessing how rationally you or others hold educational beliefs and make educational decisions.

IDENTIFYING PREMISES AND CONCLUSION

We have seen that in order to make an educational decision rationally, you must have some reasons for your decision; that is, you must be able to offer an argument. Yet before you can assess such an argument, you must be able to identify its premises and conclusion. This is usually not too difficult when the argument is your own. But when you are considering someone else's argument, it may not always be clear what the premises and conclusion are. For in the "real world," the propositions of an argument are usually presented in a maze. They are not often stated in the clear, schematic ways we have considered thus far. As we have noted, the conclusion may be given toward the beginning or in the middle of the argument rather than at the end. The premises may come after the conclusion or may be offered both before and after the conclusion.

In addition—and this further complicates things—there may be several sentences interspersed throughout the presentation of an argument that express neither a premise nor the conclusion. Such sentences are not actually a part of the argument, and they may obscure and confuse matters considerably.

Consider, for example, the following paragraph:

[1]A teacher cannot conceal his real views and values from his students. [2]To think that he can is a mistake. [3]There is nothing that he can do or say that will long disguise his personal beliefs. [4]I cannot imagine that anyone would seriously think otherwise. [5]A teacher teaches by what he says and does. [6]If a teacher really likes children, this attitude will come through in his teaching. [7]If he dislikes them, his negative feeling will be known. [8]Similarly, if a teacher is not especially interested in his subject matter, his students will sense his indifference and be uninterested themselves.

The paragraph contains an argument, but not all of its sentences are part of that argument. The conclusion is stated in the first sentence, and the second and third sentences are merely reaffirmations of that conclusion. The fourth sentence is neither a premise nor a conclusion; hence, it is not a part of the argument. The premises of the argument are presented in sentences five through eight.

Now, if we were to reconstruct this argument in terms of our schema, having omitted any sentence that is not part of the argument, we would have the following:

[5]A teacher teaches by what he says and does.

[6]If a teacher really likes children, this attitude will come through in his teaching.

[7]If he dislikes them, his negative feeling will be known.

[8]If a teacher is not especially interested in his subject matter, his students will sense his indifference and be uninterested themselves.

———————————

[1]A teacher cannot conceal his real views and values from his students.

This, of course, is not a good argument, but that is not the point at the moment. It serves to illustrate how nonessential sentences are often interwoven with the premises and conclusion of many of the arguments you are likely to encounter. It is important that you begin to develop the skill of separating premises and conclusion from sentences that are not actually part of the argument.

The following paragraph contains an argument. Number each sentence; then reconstruct the argument identifying its premises and conclusion. Omit those sentences that are not part of the argument.

The growing child learns to talk unconsciously by imitating his parents and others. Most children learn to speak and a few develop excellent patterns of speech but the majority of them need specific instruction to speak effectively. Effective speaking is not accidental: it is learned. Most experiences the child has are reflected in his competency in oral communication. Few activities can be isolated as being unrelated to social discourse. Therefore, the entire curriculum in the elementary school contributes to the speech growth of each child. Physical education, music, and art provide training and creative outlets for the child which help him to become a better speaker. Regular classroom activities provide experiences for the development of necessary oral communication skills. The home provides opportunities for the continuation of group interaction. The responsibility for the speech education program is shared by administrators, parents, classroom teachers, special teachers, and consultants. Every person who has contact with a child from the day he enters kindergarten until he completes the twelfth year influences, either directly or indirectly, his speaking patterns. (Lois Shefte Potter, "A Plan for Individualized Speech Activities in the Elementary School," *The Speech Teacher* 15 [Summer 1966], p. 200.)

Explain why the sentences you omitted were irrelevant to the argument.

In trying to identify premises and conclusions of real arguments, key words can often be helpful. Such words as *therefore, thus, hence, so,* and *consequently* usually signal that what follows them is the argument's conclusion. Reasons are sometimes preceded by the words *because, since, for,* and the like. You should never depend solely on key words, however. They tend to have several grammatical functions and are often misused.

CLARITY OF KEY TERMS

Once you are sure that you have identified all of the premises and the conclusion of an argument, you can begin to assess it. Your first consideration should be the key or central terms used in its presentation. Are they sufficiently clear? Does the author of the argument appear to be using them to convey their standard meanings? Do the words have sufficiently clear standard meanings so that the author need not provide definitions? If not, are the necessary definitions included? If the key terms in an argument are vague or unclear to any degree, the argument

A textbook for health science teachers offers the following argument for employing a "conceptual approach" to health instruction:

> A *concept* can be thought of as a relatively complete and meaningful idea in the mind of a person. Essentially it amounts to the understanding of something. . . .
>
> This derived understanding results from one's sensory perception and cognitive interpretation of a particular learning experience. . . . Such understanding is tempered by a multitude of external and biological forces. Needless to say, it is the subjective product of *our* (each of us) way of working meaning from things we have perceived or experienced. . . .
>
> Concepts are helpful in imposing an order of sorts within the idea system that we all possess. Concepts can be helpful in placing the knowledge within a given field in perspective. By identifying basic concepts to be stressed in the instructional process, we isolate the focal points around which lesser ideas are grouped. Once this task has been completed, the body of knowledge is so ordered that appropriate instructional objectives, learning experiences, and evaluation techniques can be evolved.
>
> Careful concept formation therefore provides the foundation around which organized health education experiences transpire. The resultant outcome of such an approach will hopefully be understanding on the part of the student. There is no question but that the student's health behavior is influenced by what he understands or perceives as being a positive and healthy life-style.
>
> There is no substitute for understanding. Cognitive mastery enables the student to better understand himself and the world around him. Conceptual learning assists in the educational process by providing the basis for meaningful understanding. Once health information becomes meaningful and relevant, it is more likely to be utilized by students to guide everyday life experiences. (Walter D. Sorochan and Stephen J. Bender, *Teaching Secondary Health Science* [New York: Wiley, 1978], pp. 181–82.)

Identify the premises and conclusion of the argument—it may be helpful to number the sentences—then identify its key terms. Are they sufficiently clear? Does each key term seem to have its standard meaning? Are the standard meanings sufficiently clear? Assess the definition of *concept* in terms of the criteria discussed in Chapter 7.

will be deficient; the more vague or unclear the key terms, the poorer the argument. For instance, consider the following statement:

> Many of the advocates of early schooling argue that young children need social interaction outside the home. They maintain that contact with other young children is needed. However, these claims are just not true. Young children need close and fairly continual contact with their parents more than they need contact with other children. Indeed, the greatest

need of young children is loving maternal care, which few—if any—
schools can provide.

There are several unclear claims in the statement. What exactly is
meant by "early schooling," for example? Does the phrase mean kindergarten at age three, first grade at age four, or day-care centers for infants?
Clearly, the author of the argument is against "early schooling," but this
verbal formulation does not tell us much. We have to know more precisely what he means by "early schooling." The lack of clarity in the use of
this key phrase seriously weakens the argument. Until the author clarifies
what he means by "early schooling," we cannot even be sure what proposition he is trying to establish. Similar problems surround the use of the
phrase "young children."

Difficulties also arise through the use of the word "need," for it is quite
ambiguous. The context offers no clue as to whether it means "physical
need," "emotional need," or "intellectual need." In addition, given this
ambiguity, the argument may also contain a fallacy of equivocation:
"need" may be used with one meaning in the premises and another in the
conclusion. With flaws such as these, the argument will require additional definitions if it is to be made clear.

In general, you can criticize an argument on the grounds that some (or
all) of its key terms are unclear. The more unclear and the more central
the terms, the more deficient the argument. In the face of such a criticism, it is up to the author of the argument to clarify as precisely as possible what he means by these terms.

The criterion of clarity should always be applied judiciously, however.
In most cases, it would be impractical for the author of an argument to
define every term that is used. Most terms have sufficiently clear and
standard meanings (reportive definitions). Thus, unless there are good
reasons for thinking that the author does not intend the standard meanings, it is not reasonable to expect that each key term will be defined.

TRUTH OF PREMISES

After you have identified the premises and conclusion of an argument
and have assured yourself that they are sufficiently clear, you should focus your assessment on the truth of its premises. Remember that the function of premises is to supply evidence for the conclusion. If some or all
of the premises are false, the argument is defective.

For example, consider the following argument:

> If every child enjoys school, every child will learn much
> more.
>
> Every child enjoys school.
> _____
>
> Every child is learning much more.

This obviously is a valid argument, because it has the valid form of "affirming the antecedent." Yet it is not a good argument, since the second premise is patently false. If a premise is false, it does not supply any evidence for the truth of the conclusion. In general, it is a serious and damaging criticism of an argument to show that its premises are false.

You may not always be certain that a particular premise is false. Your reasons for suspecting that it is false may be good but inconclusive. For instance, consider the premises in the following argument:

> Some critics claim that [1]many educational programs—especially compensatory programs—are doomed to failure. [2]This is almost certainly true. [3]To be successful, any educational program must focus on students with IQs over 85. But [4]many of these compensatory programs are for children whose IQs are below 85. Thus, [5]the critics are correct.

Relevance in education is a continuing concern of parents, students, and teachers. The author of the following passage argues for injecting a certain kind of relevance into the curriculum:

> The curriculum should be made more relevant to the lives of the children and youth for whom the curriculum exists. Through their reading materials, for example, city children must often meet people like themselves, rather than always encounter the legendary Dick and Jane and Spot of suburban life. The world of the city must itself become part of the subject matter if young city dwellers are to improve human relations, develop citizenship, widen horizons, and meet the problems of urban living. . . .
>
> Nor are the suburbs exempt from the blight of irrelevance. Though some suburban young people have an economic head start in life, they, too, are sometimes cheated. When communities are bland and homogenized and indifferent to reality, the young are sometimes cheated of the opportunity to know people of varied races, religions, nationality backgrounds and social classes. (William Van Til, "The Key Word is Relevance," *Today's Education: NEA Journal* 58, no. 1 [January 1969], p. 17.)

After numbering each sentence in the passage, reconstruct the author's argument. Identify the premises and conclusion and omit any sentences that are not distinct propositions of the argument. Next, identify the key terms of the argument and evaluate their clarity.

Are there any emotive terms in the statement? If so, what effect, if any, do they have on your assessment of the argument? What is your assessment of the argument? Do you think that any of the premises is false? If so, which one(s)? How strong is your argument for thinking so?

The argument offered in the preceding statement is

[3]To be successful, any educational program must focus on students with IQs over 85.

[4]Many compensatory (educational) programs are for children whose IQs are below 85.

---

[1]Many educational programs—especially compensatory programs—are doomed to failure.

You may not be certain that the first premise is false, but you may have some good reasons for doubting that it is true. Unless the author of the argument shows you that your reasons for questioning this premise are not really good ones or provides better reasons for accepting the premise than you have for rejecting it, you would be justified in considering the argument a weak one.

RELEVANCE OF PREMISES

Sometimes the premises of an argument are all true and the argument is still not a good one, for some of them are irrelevant to the conclusion. When a reason is relevant to a conclusion, the truth or falsity of that reason has bearing on the truth or falsity of the conclusion. For example, the truth of the proposition "It is 10:12 p.m. in Boston, Massachusetts" is relevant to the truth of the proposition "The sun is not shining in Boston, Massachusetts" but irrelevant to the truth of the proposition "The sum of the squares of the legs of a right triangle is equal to the square of the hypotenuse."

If an argument contains irrelevant premises, it is generally not a very good one. And, of course, if all of the premises are irrelevant to its conclusion, the argument is worthless.

If, on considering the relevance of premises in someone's argument, you have good reasons for thinking that one or more of them are irrelevant to the conclusion, it is incumbent upon the author of the argument to show that they are relevant. Unless he or she shows you that your reasons for questioning the relevance of the premises are not really good reasons or provides better reasons for thinking that they are relevant, you will have to conclude that the original argument is not a very good one because it has irrelevant premises.

The issue of the relevance of reasons is a very important one with regard to making educational decisions intelligently. As we will see in subsequent chapters, it is not always readily apparent as to whether certain reasons are relevant to the different kinds of decisions which must be made. In order to assess how intelligently you (or others) make educational decisions, you will have to be able to assess the relevance of the reasons offered in support of the decision.

The following statement contends that the junior high school is an inappropriate part of the American school system.

Perhaps the most publicized and valid indictment of the program of the junior high school is that it mimics that of the senior high school. The name itself implies that if there is a "junior" version of an institution there must also be a "senior" counterpart. Almost from the time of the establishment of the junior high school protesting voices have been raised against its name. For the past fifty-odd years the protest has continued. What is there about the junior high school that approximates the senior high? There are many such characteristics—not all are found in every junior high, but these practices are sufficiently spread throughout the country to indicate that they are typical. Varsity teams in football, basketball, baseball, and track are to be found in most junior high schools. The accouterments—marching bands, cheerleaders, pep rallies—also approximate those of the high school. In most instances high school athletic coaches and band directors look upon the junior high school as a training ground for their future teams and bands. . . . Athletes in junior high schools may even receive varsity letters, an indication of prestige. The student body is expected to look upon these youngsters who are physically gifted as individuals who are a cut or so above the average student.

Another marked similarity between the program of the junior and senior high schools is the offering of organizations and clubs. Very few are designed specifically for children in this age group; most are junior versions of those offered in the high school—language clubs, dramatics clubs, choral societies, cotillions, science clubs, and the various service clubs found in high schools. (William M. Alexander, et al., *The Emergent Middle School,* 2nd ed. [New York: Holt, Rinehart and Winston, 1969], pp. 52–53.)

Reconstruct the argument above. Are any of its premises obviously false or questionable? Are any of its premises irrelevant to the conclusion that junior high schools are inappropriate? Evaluate the strength of this argument.

STRENGTH OF THE ARGUMENT

An argument with premises that are true and relevant to its conclusion may still not be a strong argument. After you have determined the truth and relevance of the premises, you must assess how strongly they support the conclusion.

Of course, the strongest possible support is provided if the argument has a valid form as well as true and relevant premises. To assess an argument's validity you can use formal tests (such as those described in Chapter 5) or the informal test of asking whether the conclusion must necessarily be true if the premises are true. Are there any conceivable circumstances (regardless of how outrageous they might be) under which it would be possible for the premises to all be true and for the conclusion to be false? If you can imagine just *one* situation in which the premises could be true and the conclusion false, this is sufficient for determining that the argument is not valid. On the other hand, if you are not able to think of such a situation, the argument is not necessarily valid; such a situation may exist even though it eludes you. Nevertheless, if after serious consideration you are unable to imagine any situation where the premises could be true and the conclusion false, you then have good reason for thinking that the argument is valid.

But what if you determine that the argument is *not* valid? Does this mean that it is not a good one? Obviously not, for it may be a strong in-

---

Are there good reasons for teaching social studies in the secondary school? Are there good reasons for *requiring* all secondary school students to take courses in social studies? The following passage answers these questions affirmatively.

The claim that the foremost objective of the American system of precollegiate public education is the development of good citizens for a democratic society is probably one of the most frequently stated goals in the professional literature. This educational "fact" has most significant implications for the secondary school social studies curriculum. Obviously, citizenship values are claimed for all areas of the secondary curriculum. However, of all the subject areas comprising the secondary curriculum, the social studies program is the field most directly responsible for the transmission of those values, ideals, and elements of the cultural heritage to the nation's youth with the ultimate objective of producing "democratic citizens." Thus, the social studies program is more directly responsible for the development and perpetuation of strong feelings of loyalty and patriotism among the nation's inhabitants and, hence, a high degree of national viability and cohesion than any other subject matter area. The inculcation of citizenship education based upon a high degree of nationalism among the populace will continue to be the ultimate rationale for social education in the secondary school. (Randall C. Anderson, *Current Trends in Secondary School Social Studies* [Lincoln, Nebraska: Professional Educators Publications, 1972], p. 14.)

Identify the premises and conclusion of the argument. Why is the argument a strong (or weak) one?

ductive argument and hence provide very good (albeit not conclusive) evidence for the conclusion.

As we discussed in Chapter 6, there are ways to identify and assess the strength of different types of inductive arguments. Once you have determined what kind of inductive argument you are dealing with, you can assess its strength in terms of the appropriate conditions. If you determine that the argument is an inductive one, but not of a familiar type, you can assess its inductive strength by asking yourself the question "How well do the premises confirm the conclusion?" and then providing the strongest reasons you can in support of your answer.

You can always criticize an inductive argument by showing that there is another, stronger argument having all true and relevant premises and having a conclusion to the effect that the conclusion of the original argument is false. Consequently, when you are assessing the strength of an inductive argument, you should take into consideration everything that you know that could count as evidence against the original conclusion. In weighing this evidence, you will be considering whether a stronger counter-argument exists. If you identify such a counter-argument, then you will have shown that—in the absence of any further evidence—the original argument does not contain good enough reasons for rationally accepting the conclusion.

A CASE STUDY

We can now apply this procedure in assessing a complex educational argument. The following argument has been offered in opposition to the application of affirmative action principles to school admissions:

[1]American society is fast becoming a meritocracy—[2]social rewards are given to people on the basis of their abilities and skills. But [3]colleges are resisting this trend by having affirmative action admissions policies. Indeed, [4]in most cases, they are completely out of line with the times. [5]Instead of rewarding students for their abilities and achievements, some colleges have affirmative action admissions policies. [6]A medical school will accept a student who is a black or a woman, simply because the student is a black or a woman. But [7]we live in a democratic society. And [8]in a democratic country, everyone should have an equal opportunity to succeed. [9]Hard work and ability should be rewarded—not a person's skin color or sex. [10]Schools should reflect the dominant values of the broader society in which they exist. [11]Affirmative action admissions policies do not afford everyone an equal opportunity to succeed, because [12]they give some students unfair advantages based on factors other than ability and achievement. [13]Colleges should take immediate steps to change their resistance to the social mainstream and eliminate affirmative action admissions policies.

Attempting to identify the premises and conclusion of the argument, we find that there are actually two major arguments here. The first is

[1]American society is fast becoming a meritocracy.

[3]Colleges are resisting this trend by having affirmative action admissions policies.

[10]Schools should reflect the dominant values of the broader society in which they exist.

---

[13]Colleges should take immediate steps to change their resistance to the social mainstream and eliminate affirmative action admissions policies.

The second argument is

[7]We live in a democratic society.

[8]In a democratic society, everyone should have an equal opportunity to succeed.

[11]Affirmative action admissions policies do not afford everyone an equal opportunity to succeed.

---

[13]Colleges should take immediate steps to change their resistance to the social mainstream and eliminate affirmative action admissions policies.

Beginning with the first of these arguments, we examine each of the sentences to see if the key terms are sufficiently clear. We find, for example, that the use of the word *reflect* is not at all clear. What exactly does it mean to say that schools "reflect" the dominant values of society? Do they "have exactly the same," "have most of," or "have some of" the dominant values? The sentence in which *reflect* appears could be stating any one of three very different propositions. This lack of clarity represents a serious defect in the argument, and it is a good reason for considering the argument a poor one.

"Dominant values" presents another problem. What exactly is a "dominant value"? Since the context does not explain such terms, we will have to assign them the clearest meanings we can—as long as this is done reasonably and fairly—in order to pursue the questions of the truth and relevancy of the premises.

When we do consider the truth of the premises, we find that the first premise,

American society is fast becoming a meritocracy,

is not obviously true; indeed, it seems to be false. Experience and mere observation contradict it: most of us can think of recent cases in which jobs and money (that is, rewards) were obtained less because of ability than because of "credentials" and connections. And perhaps more reliable are the findings of recent scholarly research, which indicate that ethnic background, sex, early economic status, and so on are more significant in determining a person's "social rewards"—particularly, income—than are natural abilities or acquired skills. In other words, the first premise of this argument is not obviously true and there are some good reasons for thinking that it is false. Unless the author of the argument can counter this evidence with stronger evidence for the premise, we have no warrant for thinking that it is true and good evidence for thinking that it is false.

The second premise,

> Colleges are resisting this trend by having affirmative
> action admissions policies,

is questionable. Clearly, many—and probably most—American colleges have affirmative action policies; but that this fact is an instance of "resisting the trend to a meritocracy" is another matter. For in questioning the truth of the first premise, we became reasonably confident that there is no "trend" toward a meritocracy. And if there is no such trend, colleges cannot be in any legitimate sense "resisting" it. So as it is stated, the second premise is false if the first premise is false.

The first two premises are empirical propositions. The third premise,

> Schools should reflect the dominant values of the broader
> society in which they exist,

is a normative proposition. Consequently, in considering whether this is true, we are not so much concerned with whether *in fact* schools reflect the values of society, but rather with whether they *should*, that is, ought to, reflect those values.

We have to ask whether—given some reasonable interpretation of "reflect" and "dominant values"—this premise is true. And our conclusion is that there seem to be some very good reasons for thinking that it is false. For if it were true, then it would follow that regardless of how immoral the dominant values of a society were, schools would be morally required to "reflect" them. But this hardly seems the case.

Moreover, arguing on the basis of a premise such as "Schools should reflect the dominant values of the broader society" is fairly dangerous and may justify a conclusion that even the arguer would not accept. For it is merely a contingent matter that a society happens to have certain dominant values in a certain era. They could have been other than they are, and in the future they may be different. Since this is so, this premise could at that time justify just the opposite conclusion from the one that the arguer is presently attempting to establish. For instance, suppose that one of the "dominant values" was that all social institutions should have affirmative action policies. What would this imply when taken in conjunction with the other premise that schools should reflect the dominant values of the broader society (given some reasonable interpretation of *reflect*)?

This particular criticism of the third premise presents the author of the argument with a problem. Does he want to maintain the premise and possibly have to deny his conclusion at a later date? Or does he want to maintain that his conclusion is true regardless of the dominant values that society might possess at a given time? Moreover, given our previous criticisms of the first two premises, it appears that the "broader society" does not have the "dominant values" that the arguer seems to think it has. And if we are correct, it is conceivable that the actual facts of the matter along with the third premise would imply that the conclusion is false.

The premises of the argument do not measure up very well in terms of truth. How do they fare in terms of relevance? Clearly, the first two premises, taken together or separately, are not obviously relevant to the conclusion. However, they are relevant if the third premise is true—that is, if it really is the case that schools should reflect the dominant values of the broader society. However, our earlier criticism of the third premise suggested that it was false. And if it is false, we have no apparent reason for thinking that the first two premises are relevant to the conclusion. That is, if the third premise is false, the truth or falsity of the first two premises appears to have no bearing on the truth of the conclusion. Hence, in terms of relevance as well as truth, the argument must be judged a poor one.

Finally, we need to consider the argument's strength, given the assumption that all of its premises are true and relevant. That is, we will suppose that the premises are true and relevant—even though we have very good reasons for believing that they are not.

It is obvious that this first argument is not valid. We can easily imagine a situation in which the premises of this argument are all true and its conclusion false. For instance, it is conceivable that American society might have among its dominant values the belief that women and minorities should be represented in colleges in proportion to their numbers in the society. At the same time, it could be an empirical fact that (for some unexplainable reasons) American society as a whole is fast becoming a meritocracy—even though the change is not valued. In addition, colleges might be (valiantly and properly) resisting this trend by having affirmative action admissions policies. In such a situation, it would *not* be the case that colleges should take immediate steps to change their resistance to the social mainstream and eliminate affirmative action admissions policies.

For these reasons, it seems clear that this first argument is not valid. But what of its inductive strength? Even though it is not deductively valid, it may nevertheless be inductively strong.

In assessing the inductive strength of the argument, we have to determine to what degree the premises support the conclusion *assuming* that they are all true. Little examination is required to see that, as it stands, the argument is not a strong inductive one. Even if all of its premises were true, they would not confirm the conclusion to a high degree. The major reason for this is that there is no obvious connection between the first two premises and the conclusion. As we have seen, that American society is becoming a meritocracy and that colleges are resisting are contentions that have no obvious relationship to what colleges should or should not do regarding admissions. And the third premise, even if it were true, does not establish a strong relationship. Hence, we have to conclude that, as it stands, this first argument is very weak and would not be a good argument even if its premises were all true.

In summary, our assessment of this first argument is that it contains key terms which are unclear in many respects. When we assign—as reasonably and fairly as we can—clear meanings to these terms, we find that there are better reasons for thinking that the premises of the argument are false than there are for thinking them true. And if this is so, the premises do not afford adequate support to the conclusion. Moreover, it is highly questionable whether the first two premises—even if they were true—are relevant to the conclusion. And finally, on the matter of strength, the argument is not valid and does not appear to be a strong inductive argument. Overall, then, it is a very poor argument.

In assessing the author's first argument, however, you have done only part of what needs to be done: You next need to consider the second argument; for although the first argument is weak, the second may not be. We will not examine the second argument here, but you should assess its strength yourself, using the procedure that was applied to the first argument. Outlined below, this procedure should also be applied to your own arguments.

A PROCEDURE FOR ASSESSING
EDUCATIONAL ARGUMENTS

1. *Identify the premises and conclusion of the argument and arrange them in schematic form for analysis.*

    If it is your own argument, you should have no problem here. Just be sure that you list all of your reasons for your conclusion.

    If it is someone else's written argument, you might number the various sentences to help in identifying the premises and conclusion. Eliminate any sentences that are not actually part of the argument or that merely restate propositions already identified as premises or conclusion.

2. *Examine the key terms in the argument for clarity.*

>If it is your argument, you should be able to give reasonably clear definitions of the key terms.

>If it is someone else's argument and some of the key terms are unclear, ask for clarification or, if the arguer is not present, assign the most reasonable, clear meaning possible.

>An argument that contains unclear key terms is not a good one.

3. *Check the truth of the premises.*

>If the argument is yours, you should be prepared to defend your claim that the premises are true.

>If the argument is someone else's, the arguer must defend any questionable premises with another argument.

>Obviously false premises are not good reasons.

>If there are better reasons for thinking a premise false than for thinking it true, the premise is not a good reason for accepting the conclusion.

4. *Check the relevance of the premises.*

>If the argument is yours, you should be prepared to show the relevance of your reasons.

>If someone else is offering the argument, that person must show the relevance of any premise whose relevance you find questionable.

>Premises may be true but irrelevant.

>Irrelevant reasons are not good reasons.

>You cannot merely declare that a premise is irrelevant. You must have good reasons for your claim.

5. *Check the strength of the argument.*

>Assess the argument's strength, given the assumption that its premises are true.

>>Is it valid?

>>Is it inductively strong?

>>If it is neither valid nor inductively strong, then even if all of its premises are true and relevant it is not a good argument.

>>Is there a stronger counter-argument? If there is, you have better reason for thinking the conclusion false than for thinking it true.

>Assess the argument's strength using only those premises that you have good reasons for considering both true and relevant.

>If this argument is valid or inductively strong, the original argument is a good one. If it is neither valid nor inductively strong, this and the original argument are poor ones.

Consider the following statement on the effects of the 1954 landmark Supreme Court decision in *Brown* vs. *The Board of Education of Topeka, et al.*

> It is . . . clear that many of the policies formulated to take account of the integration decision have consequences diametrically opposed to its sense. They are so much at variance that one is tempted to believe that the policies have been dictated not by good sense, but by guilt feelings and desperate grasping after symbols, which testify to an effort at atonement. Instead of making education of the appropriate quality available to students, Black or white, they tend to deprive some children of educational opportunity, thus leading to deep resentment, and to impose discomfort, frustration, and a sense of failure on other students, thus leading, again, to deep resentment and loss of educational opportunity. . . .
>
> Such a policy, instituted merely in guilty retrospect and not with forethought about consequences, is bound to lead to disintegration and disruption of educational opportunity. The handicapped child entered in such a program encounters bewildering and incomprehensible problems and assignments. Or he innocently assigns to questions and problems the meanings that his inadequate preparation leads him to, only to discover in the next day or hour that to his advantaged fellows and the teacher his assigned meanings are, at best, wrong and, at worst, absurdly wrong.
>
> At the same time, the disadvantaged child encounters what he thinks is a community of his peers, only to see them transformed into a community of far outdistancing competitors, some of them jeering or patronizing competitors, most of them something worse—pitying or embarrassed competitors. The outcome of such experience can rarely be other than an abiding sense of inadequacy, a retreat from what is unfamiliar and challenging, a deep and justified sense of injury, and a smoldering hatred of those who injured him. (Joseph J. Schwab, "Integration and Disintegration of Education," in *Education and Urban Renaissance,* ed. Roald F. Cambell et al. [New York: Wiley, 1969], pp. 37–39.

Assess the argument contained in the statement using the procedure suggested in the main discussion.

Review

1. Define each of the following terms used in this chapter.

    Reconstructed argument

    Relevant reason

    Informal test of validity

    Informal test of inductive strength

2. Explain how a lack of clarity of key terms is a deficiency in an argument.
3. Show how false premises weaken an argument.
4. Explain why it is important to consider the relevance of premises when assessing an argument.
5. Describe how to informally test the validity of an argument.
6. Explain why, in assessing an inductive argument, it is important to consider evidence that could count against the conclusion of the argument.
7. Apply the procedure for assessing arguments to actual educational arguments.

Copi, Irving. *Introduction to Logic.* 5th ed. New York: Macmillan, 1978.
    A good introduction to aspects of logic, including deductive and inductive arguments, fallacies, and the uses of language.

————. *Symbolic Logic.* 4th ed. New York: Macmillan, 1973.
    An advanced, in-depth examination of logic in deductive arguments.

Engel, S. M. *With Good Reason.* New York: St. Martin's Press, 1976.
    An easy-to-read introduction to informal fallacies, with a section on the uses of language.

Fogelin, R. J. *Understanding Arguments.* New York: Harcourt Brace Jovanovich, 1978.
    A good introduction to logic—especially the informal assessment of arguments—and to some of its practical applications.

Foster, Marguerite, and Martin, M. L., eds. *Probability, Confirmation, and Simplicity.* New York: The Odyssey Press, 1966.
    A collection of advanced essays dealing with major philosophical problems surrounding inductive logic.

Hamblin, C. L. *Fallacies.* London: Methuen, 1972.
    An in-depth examination of logical fallacies.

Komisar, B. P., and Macmillan, C. J. B., eds. *Psychological Concepts in Education.* New York: Rand McNally, 1967.
    A collection of essays that analyze various educational terms and the degree to which ambiguity, vagueness, and other sources of confusion are inherent in educational language.

Munson, Ronald. *The Way of Words.* Boston: Houghton Mifflin, 1976.
    An introduction to logic, with an emphasis on the analysis of language and the informal assessment of arguments.

Peters, R. S., ed. *The Concept of Education.* London: Routledge & Kegan Paul, 1967.
    A collection of essays that examine the meanings of basic educational terms.

Scheffler, Israel. *The Language of Education.* Springfield, Ill.: Charles C. Thomas, 1978.
    A systematic study of the meanings of important educational terms and the role of slogans and metaphors in teaching.

Skyrms, Brian. *Choice and Chance: An Introduction to Inductive Logic.* 2nd ed. Belmont, Calif.: Dickenson Publishing Company, 1974.
    A worthwhile introduction to inductive logic that includes a discussion of the justification of induction.

Soltis, J. F. *An Introduction to the Analysis of Educational Concepts.* 2nd rev. ed. Reading, Mass.: Addison-Wesley, 1978.
    An examination of fundamental terms and concepts in education, including *subject matter, teaching, learning,* and *knowledge.*

PART THREE

Ethics

and Educational

Decision-Making

T*here are few circumstances among those which make up the present condition of human knowledge more unlike what might have been expected, or more significant of the backward state in which speculation on the most important subjects still lingers, than the little progress which has been made in the decision of the controversy respecting the criterion of right and wrong.*

—*John Stuart Mill*

Assessing Educational Decisions from Different Normative Points of View

In the last chapter of Part Two, we identified a procedure for assessing educational arguments. In this chapter, we will see that, with some important additions, the same basic procedure may also be used to assess how rationally educational decisions have been made.

The chapter begins by making a distinction between having reasons for a belief and having reasons for a decision. This is followed by a discussion of the different kinds of normative judgments that can be made concerning educational decisions. This discussion shows how the rationality of a decision depends upon various *normative* judgments concerning the decision and the degree of rationality with which they are made.

DECISIONS AND BELIEFS

To begin, we have to make a distinction between holding a belief rationally and making a decision rationally. As we have seen, to hold a belief rationally a person must have some good reasons for thinking that the belief is true. And we can assess how rationally a person holds a belief by employing the procedure for assessing arguments. However, when it comes to assessing how rationally a person has made an educational decision, the situation is somewhat more complicated. Initially, the complication stems from the fact that a decision is not a proposition, whereas a belief is a proposition.

In order to better understand this problem, consider the following comparison between beliefs and decisions:

Beliefs	*Decisions*
Beliefs are propositions and hence are true or false.	Decisions are *not* propositions and hence are *not* true or false.
To hold a belief rationally, you must have good reasons for the belief, that is, you must offer an argument.	To make a decision rationally, you must have good reasons for the decision, that is, you must offer an argument.
The conclusion of your argument is the belief (the proposition) for which you have reasons.	The conclusion of your argument is *not* the decision *per se,* because a decision is *not* a proposition.

Since a decision is not a proposition, you cannot, strictly speaking, offer an argument for a decision. Rather, what is needed is the formulation of *some proposition concerning the decision.* And then, an argument offered for a decision turns out to be an argument offered for a proposition concerning the decision.

So, when we talk of making an educational decision rationally, we are—strictly speaking—talking of having good reasons for some belief concerning the decision. However, not just any belief concerning the decision is sufficient. The required belief must be a *normative* one. More specifically, it must be a proposition such as:

The decision is a good one.
The decision is better than some other decisions that could have been made.
The decision is one that ought to be made.

The distinction between having reasons for a decision and having reasons for a belief is an important one. It is especially important for assessing how rationally educational decisions are made. However, before we examine the issue further, we must consider some of the different kinds of normative beliefs that someone might have concerning educational decisions and some of the different points of view from which educational decisions can be considered.

MORAL EVALUATIONS

When you contemplate an educational decision, you may be judging it in terms of its moral value. For example, suppose that you are considering the decision to allow your students to set their own learning goals. You may believe that from the moral point of view this is a good decision; thus, you have made a moral value judgment concerning it. Clearly, people make many different moral evaluations concerning education; the following are typical:

> Hitting students with a ruler is bad.
>
> There is value in understanding American History.
>
> Studying subjects you will use is much better than studying subjects you will never use.
>
> Mr. Calder, the art teacher, is a wonderful person.
>
> Teaching tolerance for homosexuals is evil.
>
> Your new reader contains stories of people who led exemplary lives.
>
> It is only moral to allow students to decide whether to learn what adults have to teach them.

Sometimes moral evaluations include no explicit use of moral terms. But in order to keep the discussion from becoming unnecessarily complex, we will henceforth deal only with moral evaluations expressed by sentences that contain the words *good, bad,* and their cognates. With appropriate transformations, what will be said about such evaluations is applicable to all moral evaluations regardless of the terms used to express them.

A *moral evaluation*, or value judgment, is a proposition that involves the ranking of something on a moral good-bad scale. For example, consider the proposition

> It is good to teach children to respect their parents.

This proposition ranks an activity—teaching children to respect their parents—on the "good" side of the moral good-bad scale. Whereas the proposition

> Teaching children to lie is bad

ranks an activity on the "bad" side. The moral good-bad scale may be represented as follows:

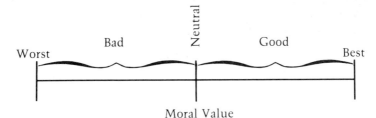

Moral Value

If something is morally good, then it is properly located to the right of the center point on the scale. But just where it is located on this portion of the scale depends upon exactly how good it is. Similarly, if something

---

Some people have maintained that the criterion of moral worth is pleasure or pain. Specifically, they have claimed that "morally good" means "pleasurable" and that "morally bad" means "painful." One of the well-known critics of this position is the British philosopher G. E. Moore:

> It may be true that all things which are good are *also* something else, just as it is true that all things which are yellow produce a certain kind of vibration in the light. . . . But far too many . . . have thought that when they named those other properties they were actually defining good; that these properties, in fact, were simply not 'other,' but absolutely and entirely the same with goodness. This view I propose to call the "naturalistic fallacy". . . .
>
> There is no meaning in saying that pleasure is good, unless good is something different from pleasure. . . .
>
> It is very natural to make the mistake of supposing that what is universally true is of such a nature that its negation would be self-contradictory. . . . And thus it is very easy to conclude that what seems to be a universal ethical principle is in fact an identical proposition; that if, for example, whatever is called "good" seems to be pleasant, the proposition "Pleasure is the good" does not assert a connection between two different notions, but involves only one, that of pleasure, which is easily recognized as a distinct entity. But whoever will attentively consider with himself what is actually before his mind when he asks the question "Is pleasure (or whatever it may be) after all good?" can easily satisfy himself that he is not merely wondering whether pleasure is pleasant. (G. E. Moore, *Principia Ethica* (1903; Cambridge: Cambridge University Press, 1968), pp. 10, 14, 16.)

Assess the argument offered by Moore. Has he shown that "good" does not mean "pleasurable"?

What do you consider the criteria of moral worth? Justify your beliefs in this regard. How strong is your argument?

is morally bad, it is properly located to the left of the center point, where the distance from the center depends upon just how bad it is. And if something is neither morally good nor morally bad, that is, if it is morally neutral, it is located precisely at the center point of the scale.

Not all moral evaluations designate a particular portion of the scale. Some involve only a comparative ranking of two or more things. In a comparative moral evaluation, there is no necessary reference to the actual moral value of either of the things compared. That is, the proposition does not rank either thing as morally good or bad in itself. One thing is merely ranked morally better or worse than the other.

For any two things X and Y, if X is morally better than Y, then X is properly located to the right of Y on the scale of moral value. However, the proposition, "X is morally better than Y" does not imply that X is located to the right of the center point, that is, that X is morally good. Indeed, X may be morally bad, just not as bad as Y. Similarly, if X is morally worse that Y, X is properly located to the left of Y on the scale of moral value. And, as above, even if X is morally worse than Y, X may nevertheless be morally good—just not as good as Y.

Finally, you should note that the negation of a moral evaluation is itself a moral evaluation. For it is a proposition concerning the moral worth of something. For instance, "It is not the case that X is morally good" is a proposition concerning the moral worth of X. It is the claim that X does not have positive moral value. It is important to recognize that "It is not the case that X is morally good" does *not* imply that X is morally bad. Rather, it implies that *either* X is morally bad *or* X is morally neutral.

THE MORAL WORTH OF AN EDUCATIONAL DECISION

It should be clear that an educational decision may be considered and questioned from the point of view of its moral worth. For example, in some school systems the decision has recently been made to require competency testing. In these systems, students may not graduate from high school unless they can pass competency tests in reading and mathematics. Such a decision can be criticized in terms of its moral worth. It might be claimed, for instance, that this is a morally bad decision, because such competency testing unfairly penalizes students who have little or no natural ability for reading or mathematics.

The fact that educational decisions may be questioned from the point of view of their moral worth has an important consequence. For example, suppose that you have decided to hold a class discussion on the uses of marijuana and to present the class with a study that finds marijuana neither addictive nor harmful to health. Now, from the point of view of its moral worth, you will have made this decision rationally only if you have some good reasons for believing that the decision is a morally good one or that it is morally better than any other decision you could have made. If you did not have such a belief or if you did not have some reasons to support the belief, then from the point of view of its moral worth, you would not have made the decision rationally.

Moreover, when your decision is considered from the point of view of its moral worth, it would make no sense to claim that you made the decision rationally but believed that is was a bad decision. For if you believed it was a bad decision, that fact in itself would have been a reason for *not* making it. Similarly, it would make no sense to claim that you made the decision rationally but believed that there was a better decision you could make. For if you knew a better decision you could make, you

---

One educator's set of criteria for determining the worth of educational activities includes the following:

All other things being equal, one activity is more worthwhile than another if it asks students to engage in inquiry into ideas, applications of intellectual processes, or current problems, either personal or social.

An activity that directs children to become acquainted with ideas that transcend traditional curricular areas, ideas such as truth, beauty, worth, justice, or self-worth; one that focuses children on intellectual processes such as testing hypotheses, identifying assumptions, or creating original pieces of work which communicate personal ideas or emotions; or one that raises questions about current social problems such as pollution, war and peace, or of personal human relations is more worthwhile than one that is directed toward places (Mexico or Africa), objects (birds or simple machines), or persons (Columbus or Shakespeare). . . .

All other things being equal, one activity is more worthwhile than another if it requires students to examine topics or issues that citizens in our society do not normally examine—and that are typically ignored by the major communication media in the nation.

An activity that deals with matters of sex, religion, war and peace, the profit motive, treatment of minorities, the working of the courts, the responsiveness of local governments to the needs of the people, the social responsibilities of public corporations, foreign influences in American media, social class, and similar issues is more worthwhile than an activity which deals with mundane "school topics" such as quadratic equations or short stories—topics usually considered safe and traditional. (James D. Raths, "Teaching Without Specific Objectives," *Educational Leadership* 28, no. 7 [April 1971], pp. 717–18.)

What are your beliefs concerning the usefulness of these criteria in determining the moral worth of educational decisions? Assess the strength of your argument in accordance with the procedure developed in previous chapters.

had (and ignored) a good reason for not making the decision you did make. And hence, you did not make your decision as rationally as you could have.

NONMORAL EVALUATIONS

A moral evaluation is not the only kind of evaluation, or value judgment, that can be made concerning educational decisions. Some evaluations of a decision have nothing to do *per se* with its morality. For instance, consider the propositions "This is a good wine" and "Stanford is a good school." Clearly, each of these is an evaluation; in each, something is being ranked on a good-bad scale. Yet just as clearly, neither of these propositions involves a moral evaluation. That is, there is no claim concerning the "morality" of either the wine or Stanford. Each proposition is an example of a *nonmoral evaluation,* a proposition concerning the worth or value of something exclusive of its moral value. In this context, you should be careful to avoid confusing "nonmoral" with "immoral." As it is typically used, "immoral" means morally bad or morally ought not to be done. "Nonmoral," on the other hand, has no connotation one way or the other regarding the morality of anything.

In a nonmoral evaluation, something is claimed to have a certain value *as a thing of a particular sort.* In other words, the claim is that X (the thing being evaluated) is a good or bad Y. For instance, in the proposition

Tim is a good baseball pitcher

Tim is the "thing" being evaluated (X), and the thing he is being evaluated as (Y) is a baseball pitcher.

Making a nonmoral evaluation amounts to ranking the thing evaluated on a particular nonmoral good-bad scale. "Tim is a good baseball pitcher" is essentially the claim that Tim ranks in the "good" portion of the good-bad scale that applies to baseball pitchers:

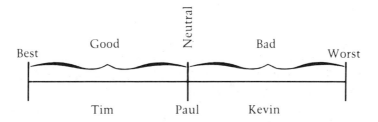

If Tim is a good pitcher, then he is properly located to the left of the center point on the scale. Exactly where he is located on this portion of the scale depends upon just how good a pitcher he is. Likewise, if Kevin is a bad pitcher, he is properly located to the right of the center point—the

distance depending upon just how bad a pitcher he is. And if Paul is neither good nor bad as a pitcher, he is properly located at the center point on the scale.

Any nonmoral good-bad scale has limits. These limits identify the best and the worst of things of the sort to which the particular scale applies. Such limits are comprised of criteria or conditions that a thing must satisfy to be the best or worst of things of that sort. On the good-bad scale for baseball pitchers, for example, the "best" limit includes the following criteria:

Earned-Run Average $= 0$
Ratio of Walks to Strike-outs $= 0$
Ratio of Hits to Batters Faced $= 0$
Ratio of Strike-outs to Batters Faced $= 1$

If these are all the criteria that comprise the "best" limit of the good-bad scale for baseball pitchers, and if Tim satisfies all of them, then he is one of the best pitchers. That is, Tim is properly located at the left-hand limit of the good-bad scale that applies to baseball pitchers.

On the other hand, if Tim has an earned-run average of 2.31, a ratio of hits to batters faced of 2:7, a ratio of walks to strike-outs of 1:3, and a ratio of strike-outs to batters faced of 1:5, then, though he is a good pitcher, he cannot be properly placed at the left-hand limit of the scale. In general, given a particular scale, a thing has a certain value depending upon the *degree* to which the limiting criteria of that scale are satisfied by that thing. As the degree to which the limiting criteria of the positive extreme of the scale are satisfied decreases, the value of the thing evaluated decreases.

So far we have considered the nonmoral evaluation of things in relation to one good-bad scale. However, as may be obvious, there are countless nonmoral good-bad scales; there are good-bad scales for the nonmoral evaluation of teachers, textbooks, wines, cars, carving knives, and so on. As suggested earlier, this multiplicity does not hold for moral evaluations: moral evaluations all involve the same moral good-bad scale.

Moreover, a certain thing may have a positive value given one nonmoral scale and a negative value given another. For instance, a wooden stick may be a bad baseball bat (say, because it is cracked) yet still be a good weapon. Likewise, a person could be a good English teacher but a poor mathematics teacher. Each of these cases involves the ranking of the same thing on two nonmoral good-bad scales. It is also important to recognize that something may be nonmorally good in terms of a particular nonmoral good-bad scale and yet morally bad. For example, McX may be a very good (nonmoral value) assassin but a very bad (moral value) person. Or someone may be a good (moral value) person but a bad history teacher. In general, the nonmoral worth of something does not imply its moral worth; nor does moral worth imply nonmoral worth.

A newspaper article on the problem of educating gifted children notes that

> Educators debate the best way to aid the gifted, if they are to be served at all. One basic approach is called "acceleration"; another is "enrichment." There is an inevitable overlap between the two. Acceleration involves letting a student work at a higher grade level—for example, giving sixth-grade books to a fourth grader or even advancing him into a sixth-grade class. Enrichment calls for keeping a student on grade level, but giving him assignments and experiences that enable him to go into greater depth on subjects than his less gifted peers. (Gene I. Maeroff, "The Unfavored Gifted Few," *New York Times Magazine,* 21 August 1977, pp. 72–73.)

Identify some reasons that would justify the claim that a program of acceleration is (nonmorally) better than enrichment for gifted children. Identify some reasons for the claim that from another point of view a program of enrichment is better for gifted children than acceleration.

Finally, as was the case with moral evaluations, there are comparative nonmoral evaluations. That is, many nonmoral evaluations compare the relative nonmoral value of two or more things without implying the actual nonmoral value of either. In such comparative nonmoral evaluations, the rankings must always be effected in terms of the same nonmoral good-bad scale.

THE NONMORAL WORTH OF AN EDUCATIONAL DECISION

Educational decisions can be evaluated not only in terms of their moral worth but also in terms of their nonmoral worth. In this section, we will consider two common types of nonmoral evaluations of educational decisions.

Frequently, educational decisions are judged in terms of their effectiveness. Did the decision get the job done? Did it produce the desired result? For example, suppose that you are a math teacher who has decided to give surprise quizzes throughout the year. Your intention is to make your students study harder. But in fact just the opposite happens. They complain a great deal but study very little. With such results, you might conclude that you had not made a very good decision. Your conclusion would constitute a nonmoral evaluation of your decision in terms of its effectiveness.

In general, when you make a nonmoral evaluation of a decision in terms of effectiveness, you rank the decision on a nonmoral good-bad scale. And the "best" limit of this scale has only one criterion: effectiveness. The more effective the decision is, the better it is.

Another common nonmoral evaluation of an educational decision is the one made in terms of aesthetic value. For example, you might say, "What a beautiful decision; I wish I had thought of that." In general, such an evaluation is concerned with the "artistic" merit of a decision. Hence it may be labeled "beautiful," "clever," "well-conceived," "elegant," and so on; or, if viewed negatively, "clumsy," "muddled," and the like.

An aesthetic evaluation, like an evaluation of effectiveness, ranks a decision on a good-bad scale. However, the criteria of this scale are not nearly as clear as are the criteria of the effectiveness scale. Indeed, there are many philosophical issues that need to be resolved with regard to aesthetic evaluations. In attempting to make sound aesthetic evaluations of educational decisions, you will ultimately have to deal with many of these issues. For present purposes, however, it is sufficient to recognize that educational decisions may be evaluated aesthetically and to note that such evaluations are nonmoral ones.

THE WORTH AND RATIONALITY OF EDUCATIONAL DECISIONS

Now that we have established that educational decisions may be evaluated in terms of moral worth and nonmoral worth, let us consider how making such evaluations is related to making educational decisions rationally.

Sometimes when you make an educational decision, you are primarily concerned with its nonmoral value. For example, suppose you are trying to determine what to do to get your students to enjoy learning French. After considering the various alternatives, you decide to use a mixed-media approach, combining films, records, and little plays acted by the students. This, it seems to you, is the best decision that you can make. You, have, in essence, made a nonmoral evaluation of the decision in terms of its effectiveness.

But how rationally have you made this decision? If we limit ourselves to the point of view of the nonmoral worth (effectiveness) of the decision, we first must identify your reasons for thinking that the proposition—*This is the best decision (in terms of its effectiveness) that I can make*—is true. Then, we would have to assess the resulting argument in accordance with the procedure identified in Chapter 8.

However, this assessment would show only how rationally you hold the *belief* that the decision is the best (in terms of its effectiveness) that you could have made. It would not necessarily show how rationally you made the *decision.* The reason for this incompleteness is the fact that we have considered the decision only with respect to its nonmoral worth. Consequently, determining how rationally you hold this belief shows only how rationally you have made the decision *from the point of view of its nonmoral worth (effectiveness)*.

This is a very important qualification, for a decision may be made quite rationally from one point of view but not very rationally from another point of view. For example, while you may have strong reasons for thinking that a decision is a good one in terms of effectiveness, you may have no reason for thinking that it is aesthetically good. Thus it could be said that you made the decision rationally with regard to effectiveness, but irrationally with regard to its aesthetic value. The point here is that in some cases the claim that a decision was made rationally is legitimate only with qualification. The assessment is actually in terms of how rationally it was made from a particular point of view.

In order to properly make an unqualified claim about how rationally a decision was made, we must take into account all the points of view relevant to the decision. For instance, suppose it were decided that corporal punishment is to again be allowed in the public schools. Clearly, it would be relevant to question this decision nonmorally, to evaluate how effective it would be in maintaining school discipline, increasing learning, and so on. Yet, it is just as clearly relevant to question its moral worth. Would such a decision be in keeping with the rights of students and parents?

Suppose that a state legislature actually decided to reinstitute corporal punishment. How might we assess (in an unqualified sense) how rationally the decision was made? First, we would have to identify the different points of view that are relevant to the worth of this decision. As suggested earlier, these include (1) nonmoral worth in terms of effectiveness in maintaining school discipline, (2) nonmoral worth in terms of effectiveness in increasing learning, and (3) moral worth. (There are certainly other points of view relevant to this decision; but, in the interest of brevity, we will consider only these three.)

Now suppose that we find that the state legislature has good reasons for believing each of the following propositions:

> In terms of effectiveness in maintaining school discipline, the decision to reinstitute corporal punishment is a good one.
>
> In terms of effectiveness in increasing learning, the decision to reinstitute corporal punishment is a good one.
>
> The decision to reinstitute corporal punishment is morally good.

If we determine that the legislature's reasons for believing each proposition are strong ones (and if the legislature has strong reasons for accepting similarly positive propositions related to all other relevant points of view), then we have determined that the legislature made its decision quite rationally.

Other conclusions are possible. If we were to find that the legislature had strong reasons for believing some of the propositions and only weak reasons for believing others, then their decision was not as rational as in the previous case.

Should reading instruction be offered in nursery school/kindergarten, or delayed until first grade? Before you answer, consider the following position:

> Reading in the public schools has long been a subject of controversy. But the press and public, in their continuing criticism of reading instruction, are working on a new problem. Despite the faults they have found in our reading practices, the hue and cry now is to place children in that questionable situation at least one year earlier than is necessary or recommended. As a first grade teacher, I most seriously challenge the advisability of such precipitate action. . . .
>
> One has only to teach in different states across the country to run the gamut of reading philosophies. In one area phonics is in, in another area phonics is out. Some prefer teaching by the whole word method, others refuse to allow any part of this method. As pressure is applied changes are made. Are these changes made to alleviate the problem or to alleviate the pressures? Constant evaluation is needed in the educational process, but changes must be made for growth and progress. Herein lies my contention in opposing the lowering of the beginning reading age. . . .
>
> . . . more children are attending nursery school, and attending for a longer period of time. The nursery schools, perhaps to justify facing the child for a longer period of time, have started the teaching of reading. It must be admitted that it adds to the status of the nursery school. I do not believe that the extent or results of their program have been studied, but many children from nursery schools have been formally exposed to reading. In retrospect, children who begin reading in first grade seem to have much greater interest and motivation than those who have had prior reading experience. This will vary according to ability in all cases. (Nancy McCormick, "The Countdown on Beginning Reading," *The Reading Teacher* 20, no. 2 [November 1966], pp. 115, 117.)

Choose a point of view and supply some reasons which, if true, show that the decision to begin reading instruction in nursery school is quite rational from that point of view. Then choose another point of view and supply some reasons which, if true, show that the decision to begin reading instruction in the first grade is quite rational from that point of view. Could either decision be shown to be unqualifiedly rational? Explain your answer.

Given the argument in the passage, do you believe that the author made a very rational decision in deferring reading instruction until the first grade? Why?

MORAL OBLIGATION

Educational decisions can also be considered from the point of view of a person's moral obligations. Was the person under a moral obligation to make that decision? Was there some other decision that should have been made? From the point of view of the person's moral obligations, a decision can be made rationally only if the individual holds some beliefs concerning his or her moral obligations in relation to the decision. In other words, the person must believe that certain moral "ought" propositions are true.

A *moral "ought" proposition* is a proposition concerning what morally ought (or ought not) to be done or occur. For example:

> Teachers ought to respect their students.
>
> Educators ought to try to bring about a well-ordered society.
>
> Public schools ought not to include sex education in their curriculum.
>
> Elementary schools ought to stress the basics.
>
> There ought not to be compulsory education for all children.

In each case, the "ought" used here is the "ought" of morality. That is, the claim is that from the point of view of morality something ought (or ought not) to be done or occur.

Like moral evaluations, moral "ought" propositions are usually expressed by means of particular words and phrases. These include *should, must,* and *moral obligation.* Sometimes, however, a moral "ought" proposition does not contain such easy clues. For instance, consider the sentence

> The aim of education is the full development of each child's potential.

Although the sentence contains no specific terms of obligation, it frequently is used to express a moral "ought" proposition. When you first look at the sentence, it appears to be an empirical one to the effect that as a matter of descriptive fact the aim of education *is* the full development of each child's potential. Yet in many cases, closer examination will show that the proposition actually being expressed by the sentence is that the aim of education *ought* to be the full development of each child's potential.

It is also important to recognize that "It is not the case that X ought to do Y" does not imply that X ought not to do Y. In other words, it may well be the case that X is under no moral obligation to do Y, but clearly this does not in itself imply that X is morally obligated to not do Y. For example, it may be that it is not the case that teachers ought to meet every need of their students. However, this does not imply that teachers ought not to meet every need of their students—only that they are not under any moral obligation to do so. Indeed, they may be under a moral obligation to meet some, but not all, of the needs of their students. Similarly, "It is not the case that X ought not to do Y" does not imply that X ought to do Y.

MORAL OBLIGATIONS AND EDUCATIONAL DECISIONS

We can now see how educational decisions can be considered from the point of view of a person's moral obligations. Suppose that you have decided to allow your class to discuss the advisability of unmarried males and females living together as sexual partners. Someone might very well criticize your decision by claiming that as a teacher you have a moral obligation to advocate and foster the values of the community; and that since the community at large does not value—indeed, is opposed to—un-

---

The following passage argues that the schools (teachers?) are under a moral obligation to teach certain matter and to produce a particular outcome:

> The fact of world interdependence needs no further demonstration. But we need a great deal of experimentation and innovation in teaching world history and world affairs. Our young people are going to be citizens of the world. They are going to help decide major questions concerning the relations of the United States to South America, to Africa, to China, and to Russia. They are going to help decide how we should use our armed forces in relation to the rest of the world. They are going to help decide on momentous changes in the character and functions of the United Nations Organization. We have to use all of our imagination and understanding in the choice of what and how we should teach about the world community.
>
> Social change is producing a new material and social setting for Americans with such speed that the schools cannot keep abreast of them by sheer teaching of knowledge. Therefore, we must help boys and girls become independent and self-directing learners, equipped with the basic skills and the interest in learning that will enable them to become life-long learners. Our educational research workers have given us valuable assistance during the past decade with this task. At the same time, we should give priority in our teaching of social studies to the kind of content that provides a base of knowledge for citizenship in the metropolitan community and citizenship in the world community. (Robert J. Havinghurst, "The Challenge of Social Change to Education," in *Educational Imperatives in a Changing Culture,* ed. William B. Brickman, [Philadelphia: University of Pennsylvania Press, 1966], p. 20.)

What matter does the writer of the passage believe ought to be taught to children? What are some of the outcomes the writer believes ought to occur? How strong are the arguments presented? Do you agree or disagree with the writer's position concerning what the matter and outcomes of education ought to be? What reasons do you have for your position? How strong are your arguments?

married adults living in the manner of husband and wife, you ought to avoid doing anything that might lead your students to accept such a living arrangement.

The moral point of view may also come into play when you are trying to determine what decision to make. When you are examining the alternatives open to you, you may wonder, "Am I morally obligated to pursue any of these alternatives?" "Are some of these alternatives ones which I ought not to pursue?"

In some cases, you may come to the conclusion that there is a certain decision that you are morally obligated to make. That is, given the alternatives which are open to you, there is one which you ought to pursue. On the other hand, there may be other circumstances in which you determine that, although you have to make a decision, there is no particular decision that you ought to make. In other words, it is not the case that you ought to pursue one or another of the alternatives. And, of course, there may be still other situations in which you find that there are certain decisions that you ought *not* to make. In such a case, you would believe that you have a moral obligation to not pursue one or another of the alternatives open to you.

In cases in which this point of view is relevant, we can inquire about how rationally an educational decision was made by asking, "Did the person have good reasons for thinking that he or she was morally obligated to make this particular decision?" How well those reasons support this belief will determine just how rationally (from the point of view of moral obligations) the person made the decision.

NONMORAL OBLIGATION

Another way of assessing a decision is in terms of nonmoral obligations. Frequently, we say, "You ought to do this" or "You ought not to do that" without meaning that the person being addressed is under any moral obligation to do what we recommend. For example, someone might say, "You ought to get a new television set; the sound on yours is terrible." Clearly, there is no claim that you are under a moral obligation to get a new television. The point is merely that, if you want to hear television programs as they are meant to be heard, you will need a new television. Such a statement expresses a *nonmoral "ought" proposition*, that is, a proposition to the effect that something ought (or ought not) to be done or occur if (or only if) something else is to occur, where the "ought" in the proposition does not imply that something morally ought (or ought not) to be done or occur. A nonmoral "ought" proposition has one of the following forms:

(1) If S is to occur, then X ought (or ought not) to do Y.

(2) If S is to occur, then Z ought (or ought not) to occur.

(3) X ought (or ought not) to do Y, only if S is to occur.

(4) Z ought (or ought not) to occur, only if S is to occur.

In the discussion that follows, we will concentrate on propositions that have form 1 and form 3. But most observations concerning these sorts of propositions can be easily applied to propositions that have form 2 or 4.

When a nonmoral "ought" proposition has form 1, the implicit claim is that X's doing Y is *necessary* for the occurrence of S. For instance, the proposition

> If you want your students to learn the multiplication tables, then you ought to give them a great deal of drill

involves the claim that your giving your students a great deal of drill is necessary if a certain goal is to be realized, namely, their learning the multiplication tables. The claim here, then, is conditional. You ought to give students drill *if* (that is, on the condition that) your "want" is to be realized.

A proposition having form 1 does not imply that someone morally ought to do something. For instance, consider the proposition

> If your students are to become adept criminals, then you ought to teach them to lie and steal.

This proposition may be true, but it may also be true that you morally ought not to teach your students to lie and steal.

Whereas nonmoral "ought" propositions of form 1 involve claims concerning necessary conditions, those of form 3 involve claims concerning *sufficient* conditions. For instance, the proposition

> You ought to let students read that book only if you can withstand a lot of complaints from their parents

involves the claim that letting students read a particular book is sufficient for generating a lot of complaints from their parents. Notice that this proposition does not imply that letting students read the book is necessary for generating parental complaints; it leaves open the possibility that they could be generated in other ways. Also notice that, as with propositions having form 1, the "ought" here is not the moral "ought." The proposition does not imply that you are morally obligated to let students read the book. Indeed, it contains no implications whatsoever with regard to moral obligations.

Nonmoral "ought" propositions, then, are prescriptive—they prescribe that someone do something—but they are conditionally prescriptive. In this respect, nonmoral "ought" propositions are different from moral "ought" propositions, which are all unconditionally prescriptive. There are no conditions attached to moral prescriptions.

The education of disadvantaged children presents continuing problems. Some people maintain that one way to solve them is through special training for teachers:

> Needless to say, the teacher should be the focal point of programs designed to improve the learning experiences for disadvantaged youngsters. Teachers must be trained to provide them with the respect they crave, to be less judgmental, to understand their language and approach to life, to know which values and customs to select for change, and to know how children learn best. Then, too, a thorough study of the urban inner city community—the customs, the family life, and the institutions of importance in the lives of these children and their families—is another means of destroying the invisible iron curtain between the school and the home. Above all, a training program for teachers of the culturally different should provide opportunities for teachers to develop a warm, friendly, firm attitude and consistent behavior. (Nancy L. Arnez, "The Effect of Teachers' Attitudes upon the Culturally Different," *School and Society* 94 [19 March 1966], p. 151.)

The quoted paragraph includes several nonmoral "ought" propositions. Identify each of these propositions and tell whether it involves a claim concerning necessary conditions or sufficient conditions. Justify your interpretations.

Are these nonmoral "ought" propositions true, or false? What reasons do you have for your beliefs here? How strong are your arguments?

NONMORAL "OUGHTS" AND EDUCATIONAL DECISIONS

When we consider whether, from a nonmoral point of view, a particular educational decision ought to have been made, we have to be clear as to the kind of nonmoral "ought" we have in mind. For example, suppose that you are wondering whether you (nonmorally) ought to grade your students according to very high standards. The question that immediately arises is, What sense of the nonmoral "ought" is being used here? Are you wondering whether

> You ought to grade your students according to very high standards *if some particular thing is to happen*

or whether

> You ought to grade your students according to very high standards *only if some particular thing is to happen*.

If your original formulation has the first meaning, your problem is quite different from what it would be if the formulation had the second meaning.

An educational decision may be criticized with respect to a person's nonmoral obligations. For example, suppose that a teacher has made the decision to be uncompromisingly firm with his students. Moreover, he believes that this is something that he ought to do. Specifically, his nonmoral "ought" belief is

> If my classes are to be well-disciplined, I ought to be uncompromisingly firm with my students.

One way to criticize this decision is to show that the teacher's nonmoral "ought" belief is false. To do this, you would have to argue that his being uncompromisingly firm is not a necessary condition for having well-disciplined classes.

On the other hand, suppose that a teacher decided to allow her students to set their own learning goals on the grounds that she ought to only if they are to become responsible adults. You can criticize this decision by showing that this nonmoral "ought" belief is false. To do so, you would argue that allowing students to set their own learning goals is not a sufficient condition for their becoming responsible adults.

There is one more point that needs to be made here. We have seen that a person may believe that she or he (nonmorally) ought to make a certain decision but that she or he may be mistaken. However, whether the person is mistaken depends not just upon the point of view of his nonmoral obligations, but also upon the particular conditions that are part of certain nonmoral "ought" propositions. In other words, we cannot properly criticize the decision from the point of view of what the person nonmorally ought to do unless we specify the particular conditions built into the corresponding nonmoral "ought" propositions. For, as we have seen, a nonmoral "ought" proposition is always a conditional proposition. It is not possible to properly consider such a proposition without at the same time considering the conditions that are a part of it.

DIFFERENT POINTS OF VIEW AND RATIONAL EDUCATIONAL DECISIONS

We have made a distinction between how rationally a person holds a normative belief about a decision and how rationally the decision has been made. This distinction implies that the person may hold a belief quite rationally but at the same time may not have made a decision very rationally at all. We can now understand this distinction better.

Since educational decisions may be considered from several points of view, a particular decision may be fairly good from one point of view but quite poor from another point of view. For example, the decision to require all children to follow the same curriculum may be a very good decision with respect to (nonmoral) economic value but a bad one with respect to moral value.

A question arises here for most decision-makers: If from one point of view a decision is good and from another point of view it is bad, what should I do? Unfortunately, there are no pat answers to this critical question. There are, however, some guidelines that help to answer it in particular cases.

When contemplating a decision, you should begin by considering it in terms of your moral obligations. The major reason for this is that if in fact you are morally obligated to make a particular decision, then you ought to make it. No other conditions can alter this imperative. That is, if you morally ought to make a certain decision, then you ought to make it even though in terms of its nonmoral worth (whatever the nonmoral good-bad scale) it is a bad decision. Given a moral obligation to make a particular decision, all nonmoral considerations are fundamentally irrelevant to whether you should make that decision. So, if you could determine that you morally ought to make a particular decision, you need not consider that decision from any other points of view.

The problem, of course, is that it may not be possible for you to conclusively determine that you morally ought to make a certain decision. At best, you might only be able to offer a strong inductive argument for thinking that you have such a moral obligation. In such a case, it is usually helpful to consider the decision from other points of view. For instance, is it morally good? What is its nonmoral worth, in terms of several nonmoral good-bad scales? Do you have equally strong reasons for believing that there is a decision that you ought to make instead? If so, is that decision nonmorally better or worse than the first alternative? It is especially helpful to consider whether there is something that (morally) ought or ought not to happen and for which making a particular decision is a necessary or sufficient condition.

Considering the decision from these different points of view may result in your identifying even stronger reasons for making that decision. Or, in some cases, you may find that these different points of view help you to uncover some reasons against the belief that you are morally obligated to make the decision.

For example, suppose that when you initially considered a decision from the point of view of your moral obligations, you thought that you had some good (but not conclusive) reasons for making it. Then, you consider it with respect to its consequences and determine that making that decision would be sufficient to cause something (say, S) to happen. That is, you nonmorally ought to make the decision, only if S is to occur. But, suppose that at the same time you have very good reasons for believing that S (morally) ought *not* to occur. If your reasons for believing that S ought not to occur are stronger than your reasons for initially believing that you are morally obligated to make the decision, then you will have uncovered a stronger argument for *not* making the decision.

This gives rise to another question: If I have good but not conclusive reasons for thinking that I morally ought to make a certain decision, from how many other points of view should I consider it? Considering it from every other relevant point of view is, of course, ideal; but it is often unrealistic. Sometimes there may be hundreds of other relevant points of view. (Of course, in certain cases there may be only a few.) What you need to do is to consider the decision at least from those points of view that are *most* relevant.

Some points of view are obviously more relevant to certain decisions than are others. For instance, consider the decision to prohibit smoking in elementary schools. This may be a nonmorally bad decision in terms of the local cigarette dealer's income. But this particular point of view does not seem especially relevant here. And unless some strong reasons are offered to show its relevance, it need not be taken into consideration. On the other hand, the decision's nonmoral worth with regard to the health of students does seem relevant.

In general, how relevant a point of view is to a particular decision is determined in the first instance by reference to some ethical theory. We will have more to say about ethical theories in the next chapter. For now, we will say only that, when you consider a decision in terms of its moral worth or your moral obligation, you do so in terms of some ethical theory. If you determine that one (or both) of these moral points of view is relevant, the ethical theory that you employ will indicate nonmoral points of view that are relevant.

But there may be cases in which you determine that the moral point of view is itself not relevant to determining which decision to make. For example, suppose that you have to make a decision concerning whether to teach badminton or volley ball to your gym class. Good reasons could be given for believing that, from the moral point of view, it does not matter which of these you teach—that you have no moral obligation to teach either sport. In such a case, you must consider the decision in terms of relevant nonmoral values and obligations. Just which ones are relevant depends upon the decision under consideration and the purposes for which the decision is to be made. If you think that a certain point of view is relevant, you must have reasons for this belief.

Review

1. Define each of the following terms used in this chapter:

Moral evaluation	Nonmoral evaluation
Comparative moral evaluation	Comparative nonmoral evaluation
Moral "ought" proposition	Nonmoral "ought" proposition

2. Explain the difference between "having reasons for a decision" and "having reasons for a belief."
3. Discuss how the rationality of a decision may be judged from different points of view.
4. Discuss the fact that something may be good given one nonmoral good-bad scale and bad given another nonmoral scale.
5. Explain how a decision may be made quite rationally from one point of view but not very rationally from another point of view.
6. Compare moral "ought" propositions and nonmoral "ought" propositions.

Selecting
A Reasonable
Ethical Theory

We have seen that making a rational educational decision requires that reasons be given for various normative beliefs concerning the decision. In general, the better your reasons for these normative beliefs, the more rationally you have made your decision. And the weaker your reasons, the less rationally you have made your decision. In this chapter, we will examine the importance of an ethical theory in choosing strong reasons for educational decisions. We will also see how an ethical theory is used in assessing the strength of arguments offered in support of such decisions.

RELEVANT REASONS FOR
NORMATIVE BELIEFS

As we saw in Chapter 8, the degree to which reasons support a belief depends in part upon whether the reasons are relevant. And since making an educational decision rationally requires having some normative beliefs concerning the decision, the question that arises is, What kinds of reasons are relevant reasons for normative propositions? (This is not the same as asking, What points of view are relevant to a certain decision?)

We have already explored part of the answer to this question. If the proposition is a nonmoral evaluation, reasons for it derive their relevance from the particular nonmoral good-bad scale being employed. If it is a nonmoral "ought" proposition of the sort

If S is to occur, then X ought (or ought not) to do Y

relevant reasons are those concerning the necessity of X's doing Y in order for S to occur. And if it is a nonmoral "ought" proposition of the sort

X ought (or ought not) to do Y, only if S is to occur

relevant reasons are those concerning the sufficiency of X's doing Y for S's occurrence.

So, the problem of what kind of reasons are relevant reasons for normative propositions has been reduced to: What kind of reasons are relevant reasons for *moral* propositions? This issue is a very significant one in making educational decisions intelligently.

As we saw in Chapter 9, you can always consider your educational decisions in terms of your moral obligations. And in certain respects, this point of view has a kind of primacy over other points of view. For if you were to determine that you are morally obligated to make a certain decision, other points of view become fundamentally irrelevant. Consequently, it is critical that in a decision-making situation you have some good reasons for thinking that your judgments concerning your moral obligations are true. And this requires that you have some idea of the kinds of reasons that are relevant to moral propositions.

Understanding what kinds of reasons are relevant to moral propositions is also important for assessing your own or someone else's arguments for educational decisions. As we have seen, in order to properly assess an argument, you have to determine whether the premises are relevant—in addition to determining whether they are true. So for these purposes—choosing your reasons for educational decisions and assessing arguments for educational decisions—you need to have some way of determining what kinds of reasons are relevant to the justification of moral propositions. And this is where ethical theories are involved.

An *ethical theory* is a position concerning what is morally obligatory, right or wrong, good or bad. As such, an ethical theory purports to identify certain basic principles in terms of which a person can determine what he or she should and should not do. But this is not all that ethical theories do. They also claim to identify the kinds of reasons that are *relevant* to deciding what should be done and what should not be done.

Many people find talk of "giving reasons" for moral propositions confusing. To them, all moral propositions are merely "personal opinions." Believing that moral propositions are not "facts" like non-normative propositions, they contend that it is not possible to give reasons for moral and other normative propositions. The following excerpt addresses this belief:

> It is customary to distinguish statements of fact from expressions of opinion. While this distinction is quite legitimate, it is important that you realize the difference between it and the normative/non-normative distinction. . . . When we distinguish statements of fact from matters of opinion, we have in mind that the statements of fact are known to be true whereas the matters of opinion are statements that nobody is now in a position to know. For example, someone might believe that soccer will have more fans in the year 2000 than football will. Since no one today can know whether this will prove true, this assertion about the future popularity of soccer is a matter of opinion.
>
> Whether a given normative statement should be regarded as a matter of opinion is, in the first place, a question of whether any reasons can be given in support of it. If a person asserts a normative statement without having any reasons for it, the assertion might be called a matter of opinion. Normative assertions, however, can be backed by reasons. Moreover, there are several well-accepted standards by which the relevance and the strength of those reasons can be evaluated. Ethics and social philosophy are in large part attempts to define the relevance and strength clearly. Accordingly, we should not assign all normative statements to the category of matters of opinion. In contrast to normative opinions we should be aware of reasoned, normative assertions. . . .
>
> Arguments in support of normative statements attempt to demonstrate, in nontrivial and nonfallacious ways, that their normative conclusions are true. Proofs offered in support of statements, either normative or non-normative, are basically arguments; their premises can be listed, they can be examined for logical correctness, their premises can be evaluated as true or false. (Peter A. Facione, Donald Scherer, and Thomas Attig, *Values and Society* [Englewood Cliffs, N.J.: Prentice-Hall, 1978], pp. 8–9.)

Why do you agree (or disagree) with the position stated above? How strong is your argument for your position? What other problems can you identify in the position that reasons cannot be given for moral propositions?

For example, consider the following argument:

Emphasizing the basics in school will result in children getting into a prestigious college.

Emphasizing the basics in school will result in children getting a high paying job.

Teachers ought to emphasize the basics in school.

Obviously, this argument is invalid. But how strong an inductive argument is it? That is, how much bearing does the truth of these premises (assuming that they are true) have on the truth of the conclusion? Does their truth have *any* bearing on the truth of the conclusion? In other words, are the premises of this argument relevant to the conclusion? We can ask this question in another, more general, way. Are the consequences of a course of action relevant to whether or not that course of action ought to be pursued? That is, do the ends justify the means? Some ethical theories maintain that they do, while others maintain that they do not.

In the following passages on the nature of an ethical theory, the word *opinion* is used as we have used the word *belief* and the word *statement* as we have used the word *proposition*.

> We may reasonably ask about ethical statements, "Which ethical statements are true . . . ?" And "Why?" A person's answer to these questions may be called his "normative ethical theory." Everybody, of course, accepts some ethical statements, and will, when pressed, offer some kind of defense of them. To this degree, everybody has a "normative ethical theory" of a sort. A philosopher's normative ethical theory is thus essentially of the same nature as the opinions, on these points, of everyone. . . .
>
> Part of a person's normative ethics, . . . is the *reasoning* or *defense* he gives of his ethical principles or statements. Obviously, just as a principle in physics must be supported by experimental evidence or otherwise, so the assertion of ethical principles must be supported. Providing this support is a part of normative ethics. . . . It should be stressed that unsupported ethical statements are no better than unsupported physical theories. As a part of one's normative ethics, one will do *something* to support one's ethical assertions: perhaps deduce a given statement from more general and already well-supported principles, in some cases; perhaps something entirely different in other cases. To have a normative ethics is to be prepared to do something—and the more forceful and systematic the defense one is prepared to give, the more developed his normative ethics.
>
> Normative ethics, then, as a philosophical study, is an inquiry aiming to state and defend as . . . true a complete and economic set of general ethical principles, and also some less general principles that are important for what we may call "providing the ethical foundation" of the more important human institutions. (Richard B. Brandt, *Ethical Theory* [Englewood Cliffs, N.J.: Prentice-Hall, 1959], pp. 4, 7.)

Are there any claims in these passages with which you disagree? If so, what are they? What reasons do you have for *your* position?

Can you identify some of the basic principles that are included in your ethical theory?

One of the fundamental sources of disagreement over what educational decisions ought to be made is the fact that people subscribe to different ethical theories. As a result, they frequently have different beliefs about what ought to be done. But more importantly, because they hold different ethical theories, they have different beliefs about the kinds of reasons that are relevant to determining what should or should not be done.

TYPES OF ETHICAL DISAGREEMENT

In order to more clearly understand the nature of such disagreements and their relationship to ethical theories, certain distinctions must be kept in mind. First, two people may subscribe to the same ethical theory but disagree on what should be done in a particular situation. The source of their disagreement is not rooted in any disagreement about basic ethical principles. Nor does it stem from a disagreement about what evidence is relevant. They agree on both of these. Rather, their disagreement is likely to be due to a disagreement about certain empirical facts.

For example, while two individuals may agree that people have a moral obligation to help achieve racial integration throughout society, they may disagree on whether the law should require racial balancing in student enrollments. One might believe that required racial balancing in schools is necessary for promoting racial integration in the larger society; the other might believe that such a requirement is not only unnecessary but counter-productive, working against broader integration. In such a case, these individuals do not disagree about the relevance of any of the reasons nor do they disagree about basic moral principles. Their initial disagreement is an empirical one and this leads them to a moral disagreement about whether racial balancing in schools ought to be required. The way to resolve such a disagreement is to gather more evidence to determine which of the empirical claims is most likely true.

On the other hand, people in complete agreement as to the empirical facts in a particular situation may still disagree on what decisions should be made. The source of this kind of disagreement is usually the fact that the people subscribe to different ethical theories.

For example, two people who agree that required racial balancing of school enrollments is necessary if there is to be racial integration throughout the larger society may disagree about whether schools have a moral obligation to promote racial integration. For the person who believes that schools do not have such an obligation, the empirical fact that balancing enrollments promotes integration is irrelevant to what schools should or should not do. And hence, that person would not accept that fact as a good reason for a decision to racially balance school enrollments. Of course, the other person would consider it a relevant reason. Their basic disagreement, then, is at the theoretical level.

When two people have this sort of disagreement, searching for additional empirical evidence is usually pointless. What is actually at issue is not the conclusiveness of the empirical evidence, but rather the relevance of that evidence. The parties to the dispute must shift their attention from the particular issue—should there be required racial balancing of schools—to a consideration of the ethical theories to which they subscribe. Each of these theories must then be examined in terms of its reasonableness.

Finally, you should note that it is possible for two people to disagree about what moral principles are really fundamental and what kinds of reasons are relevant in particular cases, but nevertheless agree that certain decisions ought to be made. For example, they may agree that we should require the racial balancing of schools—that this would be a morally good decision—but they have different reasons for thinking that we should. One may believe that in the long run it will make more people happier; the other may consider it a correction of social injustice, the long-range (and short-range) happiness of people being irrelevant by comparison. In such cases, the impartial third party may wonder which ethical theory is more reasonable. Or perhaps, is there another theory that is more reasonable than either of these, and hence should be used by both individuals?

One philosopher offers the following concerning ethical disagreements:

> Very often when one is puzzled about what he or someone else should do in a certain situation, what one needs is not really any ethical instruction, but simply either more factual knowledge or greater conceptual clarity. Certainly, a large part of the debate about what to do about drugs, pollution, or war arises because we are ignorant of much of what bears on these problems. On these issues and on many others, most of us would probably be clear about what should be done if only we knew all of the relevant facts. Again, in the field of education, much of our difficulty about decisions of policy is due to unclarity about what intelligence is, what liberty is, and so on. I stress these points because I think that moral philosophers cannot insist too much on the importance of factual knowledge and conceptual clarity for the solution of moral and social problems. The two besetting sins in our prevailing habits of ethical thinking are our ready acquiescence in unclarity and our complacence in ignorance. . . . (William K. Frankena, *Ethics,* 2nd ed. [Englewood Cliffs, N.J.: Prentice-Hall, 1973], p. 13.)

What empirical facts are relevant regarding drugs? pollution? war? Why are they relevant? Is it possible to answer these questions without reference to some ethical theory?

Can you think of two different ethical theories such that a certain empirical fact would be relevant to what should be done given one of the theories but would be irrelevant given the other theory?

THE REASONABLENESS OF
AN ETHICAL THEORY

The notion of one ethical theory being "more reasonable" than another is an important one. For centuries, people have argued about ethical theories. But so far, no one has been able to conclusively prove that any ethical theory is the "true" or "correct" one.

Nevertheless, the fact that no such conclusive proof has yet been offered is not a good reason to conclude—as unfortunately many people do—that all ethical theories are equally "true," "correct," or "valid." For while we may not be able to offer conclusive deductive "proofs" for any ethical theory, we can offer very strong inductive arguments for some eth-

---

One of the major ethical theories to which people subscribe is called *utilitarianism*. Often invoked by people giving reasons for their moral "ought" beliefs concerning education, utilitarianism is also often criticized as being not very reasonable:

> Utilitarianism proposes to judge the rightness of an act by reference to its consequences. An act ... is right if, and only if, it contributes more to the greatest happiness of the greatest number than any other act possible under the circumstances. Does Utilitarianism mean actual consequences or intended consequences? If actual consequences, then it is letting the notion of the accidental, the unintended, become ingredient in the notion of rightness. This is to part company with much legal and common sense thinking, a somewhat paradoxical business for a moral philosophy which, historically at least, was generated by concern for just such considerations. Common sense and the law distinguish between what a man intends and what, in point of fact, sometimes happens. We may regret unintended consequences as unfortunate, but we do not condemn them as wrong. ...
>
> If actual consequences are to be retained as alone decisive, we are threatened with skepticism. We do not know all, perhaps not even most, of the actual consequences of any act. The consequences of an act ramify in ever widening circles. If we guess, we may guess wrong. If we try to find out, we set ourselves a seemingly endless task. If we do neither, we admit that we cannot say whether the act was right or wrong, and this is to admit ethical skepticism. ... (Alburey Castell, *An Elementary Ethics* [Englewood Cliffs, N.J.: Prentice-Hall, 1954], pp. 63–64.)

Does this argument show that utilitarianism is an unreasonable ethical theory? How strong is the argument?

What defenses are there for utilitarianism? That is, what good reasons are there for believing that it is correct or nearly correct? If you believe that there are none, explain why you think so. How strong is your argument?

ical theories. That is, we can show that some ethical theories are more reasonable than others. To say that an ethical theory is reasonable is only to say that there are some good reasons for believing that the theory is correct (or nearly correct). In this respect, some ethical theories are more reasonable than others. And some are not at all reasonable.

There are basically two ways in which an ethical theory may be considered an unreasonable one. First, the arguments that have been offered in support of it may all be weak arguments; no good reasons may have been given for thinking that it is correct. Second, although some arguments may have been offered in its support, there may be much stronger counter-arguments against the theory. That is, there may be better reasons for thinking that the theory is incorrect than there are for thinking that it is correct.

Since ethical theories play a key role in the making and assessing of educational decisions, it is most important to hold a reasonable one. That is, you should have some good reasons for holding and applying your theory. You should also have some assurance that there are no stronger arguments for thinking that it is not correct or that another theory is more reasonable than yours. Checking the reasonableness of your ethical theory, then, involves your assessing your own arguments and arguments of others.

In the following sections, we will examine two ethical theories held by many educators. This examination of these theories will illustrate how you can proceed in determining the reasonableness of any ethical theory, particularly the theory you hold. It will also illustrate how one ethical theory may be more reasonable than another and show in more detail the ways in which an ethical theory embodies certain fundamental moral principles and criteria for the relevance of reasons in moral arguments.

ETHICAL RELATIVISM

There is a group of ethical theories that are called "relativistic." Each of these theories makes the claim that no one set of moral standards, principles, rules, or values is superior to or more correct than another. That is, when it comes to morality—what is right or wrong, good or bad, ought or ought not to be done—everything is relative. There is no "absolute" good or bad, right or wrong, and there are no "absolute" moral obligations. Relativists do not contend that nothing is good or bad, but rather that things are good or bad only in relation to some set of moral standards or values.

One of the more popular forms of relativism, *cultural relativism,* is the position that what a person ought or ought not to do depends completely upon the standards of that individual's culture. What is right in one culture may be wrong in another.

For instance, suppose that you are a member of a cannibal tribe and that one of the standards of your culture is that one ought to consume human flesh at least once a month. In such a case—according to cultural relativism—you are morally obligated to practice cannibalism at least once a month. To refuse to engage in the practice would be to do something that you ought not to do. On the other hand, if you are a member of contemporary American culture, then you ought not to engage in the practice of cannibalism. For to do so would be to engage in an activity that is proscribed by the standards of your culture. In short, what you ought to do if you are a member of one culture is not necessarily what you ought to do if you are a member of a different culture.

The following paragraph identifies some reasons that have been used against absolute ethics and in support of ethical relativism. It is an argument based upon the (claimed) empirical fact that there are no moral principles that have been accepted by all cultural groups.

There have been, as a matter of fact, a great many different moral standards both in the past and at the present day, and any attempt to say that one is better than another may be due to bias or prejudice in favour of our own. The duel which was considered the only right way of settling disputes by men of honour in the seventeenth century is now everywhere considered to be wrong. The sati or widow who burned herself on her husband's funeral pyre did an act that was regarded as good by Hindus of a former age, but was regarded as bad by the British invaders of India. (William Lillie, *An Introduction to Ethics* [London: Methuen, 1961], p. 102.)

Assuming the truth of the empirical claim that there are no moral principles accepted by all cultural groups, does it follow that there are no absolutely true moral propositions? Explain your answer. If the empirical claim were false, would this fact count as a reason against ethical relativism? Why?

Is it possible that while the empirical claim is true, some version of ethical absolutism is also true?

Although cultural relativism is a fairly popular ethical theory, it may not be a very reasonable one. First of all, notice some of the implications of the theory. If cultural relativism is correct, then we would have to say that the brutal murder of millions of Jews, Poles, and Russians by the Nazis was not only all right but morally commendable because the Nazis did just what their (Nazi) cultural standards mandated. In an educational context, we would be forced to conclude that educational policies should be racist.and sexist as long as the broader culture holds standards and values that are racist and sexist. The point here, then, is that if we accept cultural relativism, we become logically committed to other beliefs that most of us would rather not accept. To be consistent—and rationality requires consistency—you either have to reject cultural relativism or accept all of its implications.

Another problem with cultural relativism is that it appears to be self-contradictory. While maintaining that no moral claim or standard is absolute, the theory itself seems to suggest some absolutes: "You ought to do whatever is required by the moral standards of your culture" and "You ought not to do whatever is proscribed by the moral standards of your culture." Cultural relativism must maintain that these two moral "ought" propositions are absolutely true. For if it is not the case that you ought to do whatever is required by the moral standards of your culture, then it follows that cultural standards are not the sole moral determinants of what you morally ought to do. And if this is so, then the essence of the theory is essentially denied.

Consider one well-known sociologist's argument in support of cultural relativism:

> The folkways are the "right" ways to satisfy all interests, because they are traditional and exist in fact. They extend over the whole of life. There is a right way to catch game, to win a wife, . . . , to treat comrades or strangers, to behave when a child is born, on the warpath, in council, and so on in all cases which can arise. The ways are defined on the negative side, that is, by taboos. The "right" way is the way which the ancestors used and which has been handed down. The tradition is its own warrant. It is not held subject to verification by experience. The notion of right is in the folkways. It is not outside of them, of independent origin, and brought to them to test them. In the folkways, whatever is, is right. This is because they are traditional, and therefore contain in themselves the authority of the ancestral ghosts. When we come to the folkways we are at the end of our analysis. . . . "Rights" are the rules of mutual give and take in the competition of life which are imposed on comrades in the in-group, in order that the peace may prevail there which is essential to the group strength. Therefore rights can never be "natural" or "God-given," or absolute in any sense. The morality of a group at a time is the sum of the taboos and prescriptions in the folkways by which right conduct is defined. (William Graham Sumner, *Folkways* [1906; New York: Dover, 1959], pp. 28–29.)

Assess this argument using the procedure developed in Part Two.

A third problem with cultural relativism stems from the fact that the usual statement of the position involves the claim that you cannot make "cross-cultural" moral judgments. That is, you cannot use the standards of one group in judging the behavior of members of another group. At first glance, this seems to be a proposition concerning the abilities of people. In particular, it seems to be a proposition to the effect that people do not have the ability to ("cannot") make cross-cultural moral judgments. Yet as an empirical proposition concerning people's abilities, this is obviously false. For people do in fact make such cross-cultural moral judgments. Indeed, in many instances, the proponent of cultural relativism advances the theory in order to get people to refrain from making cross-cultural moral judgments.

Now if the sentence

> You cannot use the moral standards of one culture in making moral judgments concerning the actions of a member of a different culture,

is false as an empirical proposition, what proposition might it reasonably express? Perhaps a moral proposition:

> You *ought not* use the moral standards of one culture in making moral judgments concerning the actions of members of a different culture.

But putting this moral proposition forward as being true, that is, absolutely true, contradicts the part of the theory that maintains that *no* moral proposition is absolutely true. And if the proposition is not put forward as being absolutely true, a significant part of the theory is lost. In other words, the theory maintains that moral standards are always relative and never absolute; but the very statement of this position lays down an absolute moral standard that presumably applies to all people regardless of their culture.

The last problem we will consider is the following. On the one hand, the theory maintains that the *only* moral standards relevant to determining what a person ought or ought not to do are the moral standards of the person's culture. Yet an analysis of the notion of "cultural membership" shows that cultural standards *per se* are actually irrelevant with regard to what a person should or should not do. And this is implicit in the theory itself.

Consider how a person's cultural membership is determined. Are people members of a culture because they live in a certain geographical region? For instance, is the missionary who lives in an area dominated by an aboriginal tribe a member of that tribe's culture? Clearly, not. Indeed, the aim of most missionaries is to change someone else's culture.

If sharing territory is not enough, what does make for membership in a particular culture? One of the basic determinants of cultural membership is whether the individual shares the standards and values of the culture. That is, the missionary is not a member of the aboriginal tribe's culture primarily because he does not have the same moral standards and values as the members of the tribe. But if membership in a given culture depends upon personal moral standards, then in order to identify a person's cultural membership, we must *first* identify that individual's personal moral standards.

In other words, even a brief analysis of what is commonly meant by "cultural membership" shows that cultural relativism actually implies that it is the moral standards of the individual and not the standards of the culture that are of ultimate relevance in determining what a person ought or ought not do. But this contradicts the part of the theory that maintains that *only* cultural standards are relevant to determining what one ought or ought not to do.

These and other problems presented by cultural relativism strongly suggest that it is a very unreasonable position. Not only is it inconsistent

---

Many educators who advocate "multi-cultural" education or "cultural pluralism" in education base their beliefs on cultural relativism:

> Much of the problem of discontinuity experienced in school exists because the middle-class runs the school. They operate it on the idea that the middle-class existence, as they experience it, is superior to the lower-class way of life. . . .
> This is especially true in urban areas whose slums are made up of a coalition, or at least a collocation, of minorities. Simply stated, a "natural" superiority over minority groups is assumed by many of those of the middle-class. Functioning with this point of view in mind, it becomes evident that middle-class people can perceive that the school . . . has no obligation to meet the irrelevant expectations of the lower class. . . .
> If, on the other hand, along with Ruth Benedict, A. L. Kroeber, Franz Boas, and Melville Herskovits, one can assume that no particular way of life is superior, but rather that all culture is functional in nature (including lower-class or minority group culture), it is legitimate to expect, nay insist, that the public school of America meet the expectations of the youth of any given social class. . . . If the life styles of minority groups and the lower class are granted functional validity, and if the school as a social institution creates programs based on the environmental and motivational correlates of this culture, then by this action the school would truly reflect the most cherished wishes of an operational democracy. (Maurie Hillson, "The Reorganization of the School: Bringing About a Remission in the Problems Faced by Minority Children," *Phylon* 28 [1967], pp. 231–32.)

In what respect does the argument above depend on the correctness of cultural relativism? If cultural relativism is false, how strong is the argument? Does the argument in any way assume that democracy is the best way of life, regardless of what certain cultures (or subcultures) might think? If so, does this assumption contradict some of the overt claims in the argument? Assess the strength of the argument using the procedures developed in Part Two.

with other beliefs, but it also seems to be self-contradictory. Anyone sub-
scribing to this theory and expecting similar adherence from others seems
obliged to show that such objections are somehow mistaken and to offer
a strong argument in support of the theory.

Another popular kind of relativism, one that appears to be even more
unreasonable than cultural relativism, is *individual relativism,* the position that what anyone ought or ought not to do depends completely upon
his or her own personal moral standards. What is right for one person may
be wrong for another. More specifically, any moral proposition to the
effect

McX ought (or ought not) to do Y

is true or false relative only to the moral standards of McX. In other
words, no individual is under a moral obligation to do anything that is
not required by his or her own moral standards. Likewise, a person is under a moral obligation to avoid doing *only* what is proscribed by his or her
own moral standards. In addition, one person cannot use his or her personal moral standards in making or justifying moral judgments concerning the actions of another person. For, no one person's standards are any
better than another person's. This sentiment is often expressed in such
statements as:

Who are you to say what's right for me?
You have no right to force your values on me or anyone else.
Different strokes for different folks.
To each his own.

As a theory of ethical justification, individual relativism is perhaps even
more popular among many educators than is cultural relativism. However, there are as many serious objections to this theory as there are to cultural relativism.

The first major problem is that, like cultural relativism, individual relativism appears to be self-contradictory. On the one hand, it maintains
that

No moral proposition is absolutely true.

On the other it implies that

There is at least one moral proposition that is absolutely true, namely,
"You ought to do whatever is required by your own personal moral standards."

Since these two propositions cannot both be true, individual relativism
appears to be self-contradictory and hence false.

Individual relativism also appears to be self-contradictory in another respect. The position maintains that

> You cannot use your own personal moral standards in making moral judgments concerning the actions of another person.

But, as we saw in our discussion of cultural relativism, as an empirical proposition, the statement is false. And if it is not an empirical proposition, it can only be a moral proposition to the effect that

> You *ought not* to use your own personal moral standards in making moral judgments concerning the actions of another person.

But if this moral proposition is put forward as being only relatively true, it has no significant prescriptive force. Moreover, to offer it as only rel-

Individual relativism is often used as the theoretical basis for justifying educational decisions. Among those who clearly appeal to this theory are some advocates of the use of "values-clarification" in the public schools:

> The values-clarification approach tries to help young people answer [ethical] questions and build their own value system. . . .
> The values-clarification approach does not aim to instill any particular set of values. Rather the goal . . . is to help students utilize the . . . processes of valuing in their own lives. . . .
> The teacher should participate in the exercises and discussions wherever possible. The best time for the teacher to give his view is toward the end, after the students have had a chance to think things through for themselves and to express their own points of view. The teacher should present himself as a person with values . . . of his own. Thus the teacher shares his values, but does not impose them. . . . The teacher gets a chance to share his actual values as does any other member of the class. The particular content of his values holds no more insight than would anyone else's. . . . (Sidney B. Simon, Leland W. Howe, and Howard Kirschenbaum, *Values Clarification: A Handbook of Practical Strategies for Teachers and Students* [New York: Hart Publishing Company, 1972], pp. 18, 20, 26–27.)

What are some of the problems inherent in this position? Do you believe that teachers should not teach their moral beliefs to their students? Justify your answer. Is it possible to use individual relativism as the theoretical foundation for a strong argument in support of the belief that teachers *should not* impose their values on others and at the same time not contradict yourself? What exactly does it mean to "impose one's values"?

atively true seems pointless given the theory. If, on the other hand, it is put forward as being absolutely true, it contradicts the other part of the theory, which maintains that *no* moral proposition is absolutely true.

A related problem is just as damaging. If it is true that you ought to do whatever is required by your own personal moral standards, then it is possible that you are morally obligated to use your standards in making moral judgments concerning the actions of others. This would be the case if one of your moral standards were

> I ought to always employ my own moral standards in making moral judg-
> ments concerning the actions of other persons.

If you have this particular moral standard, the theory implies that you both ought and ought not to use your moral standards in making moral judgments concerning the actions of others. And this is a contradiction. For these reasons, individual relativism appears to be a very unreasonable ethical theory.

ETHICAL EGOISM

More plausible than ethical relativism is *ethical egoism*, the position that a person ought to do that which will maximize his or her own well-being and ought not do that which will create his or her disadvantage. In other words, whether an action is right or wrong depends exclusively upon the value of the consequences of the action for the actor.

For example, a teacher might make a decision simply because it will help him to gain tenure. The decision may not be in the best interests of his students. But reasoning in accordance with ethical egoism, he may consider this fact irrelevant. All he is concerned with is how the decision affects him personally. His guiding principle is "take care of number one." In most versions of ethical egoism the value produced for others is relevant to whether or not you ought to do something only if it will ultimately have some bearing upon the amount of good produced for you.

In addition, most versions of ethical egoism maintain that the rightness or wrongness of an action depends upon the value it actually produces, not the value you believe it would produce. What you believe to be good for you may not actually be so. You can make mistakes and hold false beliefs. Hence, your beliefs *per se* are not the criteria for determining what you ought to do. The only proper criterion is the value of the actual consequences.

This also helps to explain a difference between egoism and individual relativism. People frequently confuse these two positions even though they are quite different. Whereas individual relativism claims that personal moral standards are the sole measure of what an individual should do, egoism maintains that personal standards are not at all relevant. You might act on your personal standards and produce bad consequences for yourself.

If ethical egoism seems somewhat more reasonable than the version of ethical relativism we have considered, one of the major reasons may be that we expect a moral action to benefit the actor in most cases. It seems inconceivable that anything approaching a correct theory of morality would consistently be to the disadvantage of the individual. In this respect, egoism may seem more reasonable, but it too has difficulties.

One difficulty involves not so much the position itself, but rather an argument that is frequently offered in its support. This argument is based upon the psychological claim that people always act in ways that they believe will—all things considered—benefit themselves. That is, people always act selfishly. The argument, then, is basically that since as a matter of fact egoism is the theory that people use in making decisions, it is the proper one for them to use.

Such an argument is not very convincing. The way people act is not necessarily the way they should act. Even if the psychological claim is true, it is not, by itself, a very good reason for thinking that egoism is the proper theory to employ in justifying moral judgments.

Moreover, it is not at all clear that the psychological claim is true. There seem to be many instances in which people have done things contrary to any conceivable self-interest. The firefighter who risks serious burns and disfigurement in order to save a child's life seems to be knowingly acting for the good of the child and not for his or her own good. Physicians who treat a patient who has a life-threatening, contagious disease appear not to be concerned only with their own good but rather with the good of the patient. Indeed, the more we think about it, there appear to be countless instances of people doing things that they could not in any reasonable sense consider to be in their own self-interest. Hence, the psychological claim appears to be false, and this seriously weakens this particular argument in support of egoism.

In addition, there seem to be several serious problems with the theory itself. One of these problems is that egoism requires that you identify the actual consequences of your actions in order to determine whether they are right or wrong. And "the actual consequences" means *all* the consequences, not merely the immediate or the most lasting ones. Nor, as we have seen, does it mean what you *believe* the consequences will be. Therefore, it seems humanly impossible to actually apply the theory to any given act—when does the last consequence occur?—and certainly impossible to do so before the act is performed.

This, of course, does not mean that the theory is incorrect. But it does identify a problem with which advocates of the position should be expected to deal. And if they cannot deal with it satisfactorily, we have some reason for thinking that egoism is not a very reasonable ethical theory, for it seems that it cannot be applied to any real action.

A second problem, one that the egoist may find more difficult to deal with than the first, arises from the claim that the morality of an action depends upon the value of its consequences. How do we properly determine how valuable a certain consequence is? Moreover, does the value produced have to be a moral value or could it be a nonmoral value?

Complicating this problem is the fact that several different theories of value have been advocated. It is important to remember here that ethical egoism is a theory of moral obligation and not a theory of value. Some people have maintained that in the final analysis the value of anything is properly determined only in terms of the amount of pleasure it produces. But even among those who agree on this point, there is disagreement about whether it is the quantity or the quality of the pleasure that is significant. For example, some claim that only the amount of physical

---

An interesting strain of ethical egoism, the "superman" theory of morality, was given one of its earliest statements in a speech by Thrasymachus in Plato's *Republic:*

> What I say is that "just" or "right" mean nothing but what is to the interest of the stronger party. . . .
> In every case the laws are made by the ruling party in its own interest; a democracy makes democratic laws, a despot autocratic ones, and so on. By making these laws they define as "right" for their subjects whatever is for their own interest, and they call anyone who breaks them a "wrongdoer" and punish him accordingly. That is what I mean: in all states alike "right" has the same meaning, namely what is for the interest of the party established in power, and that is the strongest. So the sound conclusion is that what is "right" is the same everywhere: the interest of the stronger party. . . .
> Despotism . . . uses force or fraud to plunder the goods of others . . . and to do it in a wholesale way. If you are caught committing any one of these crimes on a small scale, you are punished and disgraced. . . . But if, besides taking their property, you turn all of your countrymen into slaves . . . your countrymen themselves will call you the happiest of men and bless your name . . . for when people denounce injustice, it is because they are afraid of suffering wrong, not of doing it. . . . Injustice, on a grand enough scale, is superior to justice in strength and freedom and autocratic power; and "right," as I said at first, means simply what serves the interest of the stronger party; "wrong" means what is for the interest and profit of oneself. (*The Republic of Plato,* trans. Francis MacDonald Cornford, [New York: Oxford University Press, 1966], pp. 18, 25–26.)

Why does this position seem correct (incorrect) to you? How strong is your argument for your position? In what respects is the "superman" theory a type of ethical egoism?

pleasure is relevant; others maintain that physical pleasures are qualitatively inferior to the pleasures of the mind. In the latter view, pleasures of the mind must be given greater weight in determining how much value an action produces.

Beyond "pleasure" theories, there are value theories that maintain that human excellence, self-realization, union with God, or love is the only ultimate good. And still others endorse several of these and claim that they are equally good.

The second problem for ethical egoists, then, is identifying from among the many different theories of value the most (or one of the most) reasonable ones. And whatever the value theory to which he or she subscribes, the egoist should be expected to have devised arguments in support of the value theory that are at least as strong as the strongest arguments others offer in support of their value theories.

HOW TO ASSESS THE REASONABLENESS OF AN ETHICAL THEORY

In examining ethical relativism and ethical egoism, our purpose has not been to "prove" that one is "correct" and the other "incorrect." We have not attempted to offer full critical analyses of these theories. Nor, clearly, have we tried to provide a systematic overview of the many different ethical theories that people have proposed; such a task lies beyond the scope of this text. Rather, our primary purpose has been to provide a better understanding of how you can proceed in assessing the reasonableness of an ethical theory. A summary of the steps followed in the preceding assessments may be helpful.

As a first step in assessing the reasonableness of an ethical theory, you should consider the theory with regard to clarity. Is it clear as to precisely what the theory maintains? Our examination of cultural relativism, for example, showed that theory to be less than clear. And when we sought clarification, we found the theory to be self-contradictory and, therefore, quite unreasonable.

Now suppose you find that the ethical theory under consideration is sufficiently clear. The next step is to determine whether the theory has implications that are either contradictory or obviously false. If, as in the case of cultural relativism, we find that an ethical theory implies a contradiction, then the theory can be reasonably considered false. Moreover, we can have no good reasons for holding it.

If the theory does not seem self-contradictory, you should proceed to determine whether it has any implications that are obviously false. If a theory implies a statement that is obviously false, then the theory itself must be false, and it would be unreasonable to hold it. If you find that the theory under consideration does not contain any contradictory or obviously false implications, this would not be a positive confirmation of its reasonableness.

Thus, if the theory passes these negative tests, the next step is to assess the arguments that have been offered in its support. If none of these arguments are strong ones—that is, if no good reasons are given for the theory—then it would be unreasonable for you to hold the theory. For example, we found an argument that is frequently offered in support of egoism to be a very weak one, because one of its major premises is false. If this were the only argument given for egoism—but it is not—then egoism would not be a reasonable ethical theory.

Now suppose that after assessing the various arguments for a particular theory, you determine that at least some of them are fairly strong arguments. You are still not justified in concluding that the theory is a reasonable one; there may be some stronger arguments against the theory. So, you have to assess the strength of the counter-arguments. And if you find that some of the counter-arguments are stronger than the strongest arguments in favor of the theory, then you have to conclude that, at this time, it is more reasonable to *not* hold the theory than to hold it.

If a theory passes these tests, *and* if you have some good positive reasons for holding it, then you can conclude that it is a reasonable theory and that it is reasonable for you to hold it. This, of course, is not to say that you will have "proven" that the theory is correct. A proof would be much more difficult. Rather, it is only to say that you will have determined which ethical theory is the most reasonable one for you to hold as of the time of your assessment. Obviously, you should reassess your ethical theory from time to time. In the face of new evidence, you may find that some other theory is more reasonable than the one you previously held.

Before we leave this topic, it is important to understand that we are *not* recommending that you reassess your ethical theory every time you apply it. Rather, we are suggesting that you occasionally reconsider your ethical theory when you are not pressured to make a decision. If you wait until you have to make a decision based on your ethical theory, then your reassessment may be less objective and less thorough than it might otherwise be. Thinking out your ethical theory as much as possible in advance of any need to apply it allows you to use it with greater confidence that it is a reasonable one.

Clearly, you should try to hold the most reasonable ethical theory possible. And you should try to avoid holding an unreasonable one. The more unreasonable your ethical theory, the greater the probability that it is mistaken. And if it is mistaken, you will probably judge reasons to be relevant when in fact they are not. In such a case, your moral arguments will be weakened because they will contain irrelevant reasons. And your chances of making the decisions that ought to be made will be decreased. One of the best ways of refining and perfecting your ethical theory is by considering the different ethical theories which have been advanced by various philosophers. As you deepen your understanding of the issues involved in ethical reasoning, you will undoubtedly formulate a more and more reasonable ethical theory.

Review

1. Define each of the following terms used in this chapter:

   Ethical theory   Individual relativism
   Cultural relativism   Ethical egoism

2. Explain the ways in which an ethical theory is important in making an educational decision intelligently.

3. Describe how an ethical theory must be used in assessing the strength of an argument offered in support of an educational decision.

4. Explain how two people may subscribe to the same ethical theory and yet disagree about what ought to be done in a particular situation.

5. Explain how it is possible for two people to subscribe to different ethical theories and yet agree that certain educational decisions ought to be made.

6. Identify and discuss two ways in which an ethical theory can be unreasonable.

7. Discuss the ways in which cultural relativism appears to be an unreasonable ethical theory.

8. Discuss the ways in which individual relativism appears to be an unreasonable ethical theory.

9. Identify and discuss some difficulties inherent in ethical egoism.

10. Explain how to proceed in assessing the reasonableness of an ethical theory.

Brandt, Richard. *Ethical Theory.* Englewood Cliffs, N.J.: Prentice-Hall, 1959.
A somewhat advanced study of aspects of ethical theory, including ethical relativism, moral "ought" propositions, moral value, and justice.

Broad, C. D. *Five Types of Ethical Theory.* London: Routledge & Kegan Paul, 1930.
A critical examination of the ethical theories of Spinoza, Butler, Hume, Kant, and Sidgwick.

Frankena, William K. *Ethics.* 2nd ed. Englewood Cliffs, N.J.: Prentice-Hall, 1973.
A good introduction to ethics, with valuable discussions of ethical relativism, egoism, utilitarianism, and deontological ethical theories.

Hospers, John. *Human Conduct.* New York: Harcourt Brace Jovanovich, 1972.
A critical examination of ethical language and the bases of ethical theories.

MacIntyre, Alasdair. *A Short History of Ethics.* New York: Macmillan, 1966.
A work that presents, in historical context, the ethical theories of Plato, Aristotle, Kant, Hegel, Marx, Kierkegaard, Nietzsche, and others.

Melden, A. I., ed. *Ethical Theories.* 2nd. ed. Englewood Cliffs, N.J.: Prentice-Hall, 1967.
A collection of essays that provides an introduction to the ethical theories of Plato, Aristotle, St. Augustine, Hobbes, Bentham, Mill, and Moore, among others.

Sellars, Wilfrid, and Hospers, John, eds. *Readings in Ethical Theory.* 2nd ed. New York: Prentice-Hall, 1970.
A collection of writings by many ethical theorists of the modern era.

Warnock, G. J. *Contemporary Moral Philosophy.* New York: St. Martin's Press, 1967.
An examination of intuitionism, emotivism, prescriptivism, and naturalism.

PART FOUR

Educational Decisions

Since the development of human capacities
does not take place of its own accord, all
education is an art. Nature has bestowed no
instinct for that. The origin, as well as the
progress, of this art is either mechanical,
without plan . . . , or rational. . . . Every art of
education which arises merely mechanically
must carry with it many faults and
deficiencies, since it has no plan for its
foundation. The art of education, or pedagogy,
must therefore become rational if it is to
develop human nature so that it attain its
goal. . . . In order to improve children, it is
necessary that pedagogy become a study,
otherwise there is nothing to hope from it. . . .

—*Immanuel Kant*

CHAPTER

11

The Matter and
Manner
of Education

To this point we have examined in a general way how a philosophy of education and thinking philosophically about education are involved in the making of intelligent educational decisions. We have seen how central an ethical theory is to identifying relevant reasons for educational decisions and why it is important to continually try to develop the most reasonable theory possible. We have also considered some fundamental points of logic and have developed a procedure for assessing educational arguments. These understandings provide us with a general framework for making intelligent educational decisions. In this final section of the book, we will attempt to refine that framework by directly examining in more depth the different kinds of educational decisions that must be made.

As a first step toward providing this specificity, the present chapter will examine the central notions of the matter and manner of education. We will begin with an examination of the nature of teaching and the kinds of things that can be taught, namely, propositions, skills, and dispositions.

We will then make a distinction between the matter of education in general and the matter of a person's education.

Finally, we will consider the manner of education and how decisions concerning it are related to decisions concerning the matter and the outcomes of education.

TEACHING AND THE MATTER OF EDUCATION

We have previously defined "the matter of education" as that which could be taught. There is, however, a potential problem with this definition because in ordinary language the word *taught* and other forms of the verb *to teach* are vague. In order that our definition of "the matter of education" not be affected by this problem, we shall define "teach" as follows.

If someone (X) teaches, he or she must teach something (C) to someone (Z). Now there are two different—but related—senses in which X can be said to teach C to Z. First, we can mean that X behaves in certain ways with the *intention* that his or her behavior will result in Z's acquiring C. For example, Mr. Stone sits before Johnny saying various things to him while periodically showing him diagrams drawn on a piece of paper— all with the intention that as a result of these actions Johnny will come to acquire the belief that the bisector of the vertex angle of an isosceles triangle bisects the base of that triangle.

Second, we can mean by "X teaches C to Z" that X behaves in certain ways that *actually result* in Z's acquiring C. Notice that in this second That is, X teaches C to Z in this second sense if and only if X's behavior actually results in Z's acquiring C. Whether or not X has any intention that Z acquire C is *irrelevant*. So, for instance, if Ms. Myer regularly yells at the students in her biology class, and if as a result of this behavior they acquire a dislike for biology, then Ms. Myer has taught them to dislike biology. Of course, this may not have been her intention. But her intention is irrelevant with regard to this second sense of "teach."

The major difference between these two senses of *teach*, then, is that the first depends upon the intentions of the "teacher," while the second depends upon the actual results of the "teacher's" behavior. Thus, it is possible for a person to teach C to Z in both of these senses or in only one. For instance, suppose that Mr. Wicks intends that, as a result of his behavior, Tim will acquire the belief that table salt is comprised of sodium and chlorine and that as a result of the teacher's behavior Tim does acquire that belief. In this case, Mr. Wicks has taught this belief to Tim in both senses of the word *teach*. On the other hand, if Mr. Wicks intends that Tim acquire the belief but Tim does not acquire it as a result of Mr. Wicks' behavior, then he has taught the belief to Tim in the first sense of *teach* but not in the second. Similarly, if Tim acquires the belief as a result of Mr. Wicks' behavior, but there was no intention on the part of Mr. Wicks that Tim acquire it, then Mr. Wicks has taught the belief to Tim in the second sense of the term but not in the first.

Both of these senses of "teaching" involve the notion of X's behavior resulting in Z's acquiring C. Saying that "X's behavior *results in* Z's acquiring C" means that X's behavior is sufficient either by itself or in conjunction with some other conditions for Z's acquiring C. However, since it is quite unlikely that a teacher's behavior is ever sufficient by itself for students to learn something, we will consider "X's behavior results in Z's acquiring C" only in the sense of "the conjunction of X's behavior and some other conditions being sufficient for Z's acquiring C."

Saying that "the conjunction of X's behavior and some other conditions is sufficient for Z's acquiring C" means, in turn, that if X behaves in a certain way and certain other conditions hold, then Z will acquire C. For example, a teacher's reading a particular poem aloud in English may be sufficient for his students acquiring the belief that metaphor is an effective literary device, *given that* those students understand English. On the other hand, if the students did not understand English, then reading the poem aloud in English would not be sufficient for their acquiring that belief.

Finally, the conjunction of a teacher's behavior and certain other conditions is sufficient for students' learning something only if those other conditions are not sufficient by themselves for their learning. For example, consider Dr. Weinberg's tendency to pat her hair every minute or so when she lectures. This behavior may occur in conjunction with certain other conditions—such as her writing on the chalkboard, her saying certain things, the room's being relatively quiet, and so on. If these latter conditions by themselves are sufficient for her students' acquiring certain beliefs, then her patting her hair is irrelevant to their acquiring those beliefs. That is, this behavior is not necessary for her students' learning, given that the other conditions hold.

While no one seriously contends that patting one's hair results in students' learning mathematics or history, it is important to recognize that a teacher may do certain things with the intention of teaching that have as little relation to students' learning such subjects. For instance, some teachers may think that they are teaching reading (in the result sense) when in fact what they are doing may be irrelevant to their students' learning how to read. That students learn what a teacher intended to teach them is not by itself a good reason for believing that the teacher taught it to them in the result sense.

As we said above, since it is unlikely that a teacher's behavior is ever sufficient by itself for students' learning something, we will consider "X's behavior results in Z's acquiring C" only in the sense of X's behavior being sufficient in conjunction with some other conditions for Z's acquiring

Many educators use the phrase *hidden curriculum* to refer to what is actually taught in the result sense, implying that it can be significantly different from what everyone involved intends:

> Kohlberg speaks of the influence of the "hidden curriculum"—all the ways the teachers and other adult authorities transmit, usually unwittingly, moral lessons to children. Most students, for example, must compete for grades with their classmates; helping another person may be defined as cheating. Most kids go to schools in which rules are laid down by authority; children never have a chance to participate in formulating, revising or enforcing moral requirements, and they're expected to obey without question the adult in charge.
>
> I recently came across [a story] about an incident in which a student called the teacher an obscene name. . . . [A] second grade boy called his teacher a "son-of-a-bitchin' whore." The teacher marched the boy down to the principal's office and demanded that the child be expelled, which he was. The lesson that student learned was almost surely: the only reason to respect others is to avoid punishment. (Thomas Lickona, "How to Encourage Moral Development," *Learning,* March 1977, p. 42.)

Identify two cases in which something was taught in the result sense but not intended. Why is it important for teachers to be aware of the "hidden curriculum" they may be teaching?

C. But it is unnecessarily complicated to continue to say "sufficient in conjunction with some other conditions." Consequently, we will shorten this phrase to read simply "sufficient."

With this stipulation, we can summarize this discussion by saying that "X teaches C to Z" means either

> (1) X behaves in a certain way with the *intention* that this behavior is sufficient for Z's acquiring C.

or

> (2) X behaves in a certain way and X's behavior is *actually* sufficient for Z's acquiring C.

Yet this is not the complete definition of "teach." For although we have specified what the variables X and Z represent, we have not yet indicated the possible replacements for C. This we must now do.

In the formula X teaches C to Z, X and Z represent persons and C represents either

- a proposition or set of propositions
- a skill or set of skills
- a disposition or set of dispositions

That is, the matter of education is comprised of propositions, skills, and dispositions. In the following sections, we will examine each of these components. Our uses of the word *teach* in these discussions will deal only with actual results, not with intentions.

PROPOSITIONS AS PART OF THE MATTER OF EDUCATION

There are two senses in which a proposition can be taught to someone. First, it can be taught in such a way that the person comes to *believe* that it is true. Second, it can be taught so that the person comes to *understand* the proposition but does *not* then believe that it is true. In other words, teaching someone a proposition amounts to teaching that person that something is the case.

Suppose that X teaches proposition P to Z and Z comes to believe that P is true. If Z believes that P is true, he or she is affording a certain degree of psychological assent to P (see Chapter 4). Z may believe P very strongly, moderately, or only weakly, but some degree of psychological assent to P is present. If Z did not believe that P is true prior to X's behavior and if he or she acquired this belief as a result of X's behavior, then X taught P to Z. Indeed, even if Z already believed that P is true prior to X's behavior, it is still possible that X taught P to Z. X's behavior may have increased the strength of Z's belief concerning P. In general, then, teaching a person a belief, whether or not that person already possesses it, amounts to increasing the degree of psychological assent that he or she affords the proposition.

The second sense in which a proposition can be taught to someone involves that person understanding the proposition, but not believing it. More specifically, X can teach proposition P to Z such that Z understands P but does not believe that P is true. For example, a person might understand the proposition "Stanton planned and paid for the assassination of Lincoln" but afford no psychological assent to it. Here you should remember that "affording no psychological assent" does not imply that Z believes that P is false. Rather, it means that Z has no belief at all with regard to the truth of the proposition.

Truth is often suggested as the criterion for determining what beliefs should be taught:

> Formal education not only has an obligation to educate learners as total organisms, but, at such time as they are ready for the exposure and when contextually appropriate, to reveal life to them as it is—not as dreamers would like it to be. The thesis is that improvement in the society will take place only when its members, old and young alike, see it realistically for what it is. Accordingly, if it can be substantiated beyond reasonable doubt that corruption in high places is rampant, if . . . tax legislation is habitually slanted to favor some more than others, if materialism is a dominant national trait, if ghettos are repellently subhuman, if racism prevails, and if our basic national documents grossly fail the test of implementation, formal education is remiss when sweeping unsavory facts such as these under the table. We emphasize once more, however, the importance of relating the "teach it like it is" approach to the stipulations cited at the paragraph's beginning. (Gail M. Inlow, *Values in Transition* [New York: Wiley, 1972], p. 196.)

Can the truth of a proposition reasonably be used as a sufficient condition for determining whether the proposition ought to be taught? Can it reasonably be used as a necessary condition?

Do schools have a moral obligation to teach true beliefs, that is, beliefs about life as it is? Why? How strong is your argument?

Do you believe that teachers could ever be under a moral obligation to teach some false beliefs? Explain and justify your answer.

SKILLS AS PART OF THE MATTER OF EDUCATION

As mentioned earlier, the matter of education also includes skills, a *skill* being the ability to do something—ride a bicycle, play the piano, read, write, reason logically, and so on. Having a skill is not simply having a potential, say, in the sense that a newborn baby has the potential to walk. If someone has a skill, then he or she must actually be able to demonstrate it. For instance, if a person has the skill of bicycle riding, then when placed on a bicycle he or she must actually be able to ride it. If the person falls off the bicycle every time he or she attempts to ride it, there is a good reason for believing that he or she does not have the skill.

However, while having a skill requires that a person be able to demonstrate it, this does not mean that he or she must actually demonstrate it. It simply means that, given the absence of external constraints that would prevent the exercise of the skill, the person could demonstrate it. So, for example, although you have not been on a bicycle for years, you may still possess the skill of bicycle riding. Moreover, you may possess some skills that you will never exercise. The skills of a hurdler, murderer, or thief might be included in this category.

People possess skills to different degrees. For instance, some people are more proficient than others at playing the piano. In addition, the degree of proficiency with which a person demonstrates a skill can increase or decrease over a period of time. Once a person has acquired a certain degree of proficiency at certain skills, regular exercise of the skill is often necessary to retain that degree of proficiency.

Teaching a person a skill, then, amounts to teaching *how to* do something. Compare this with teaching a person a proposition, which amounts

---

Many people argue that children should be taught the "basic" skills of reading, writing, arithmetic. By this, they usually mean that the child's proficiency in these skills should be progressively increased:

> Communication in written and spoken language should have equal stress with mathematics. Both the use of language and its development should be emphasized, so that we constantly seek improvement in communication and never look on the job as completed. Certainly not to be duplicated is the policy adopted by one American state where university professors urged high schools to teach "honors" programs in English, by which they meant literature. Under this stimulus the programs of the better pupils were altered to stress great literature and to go light on composition. The decision to read rather than write is, I suspect, a direct cause of the inadequacies in composition of which these same professors complain when the students come to the university. From the point of view of educational policy, it cannot be wise. There should be continuous practice in writing English at every level, and the standards should be progressively higher as time passes. There is no year in either elementary or secondary schools when this job should be regarded as done.
>
> We need to accept it as a fact that what are called the basic skills are not misnamed; they are basic. Anything a school does later hinges upon success in developing these skills. We ought, therefore, to act accordingly. (James E. Russell, *Change and Challenge in American Education* [Boston: Houghton Mifflin, 1965], pp. 56–57.)

Assess the argument's claim that "we ought, therefore, to act accordingly." Is the "ought" here the moral "ought" or a nonmoral "ought"?

What do you consider the proper grounds for determining the proficiency high-school students must demonstrate at writing English? For instance, should the required degree of skill vary with the student's probable occupation? Justify your position.

to teaching *that* something is the case. Teaching skill S to Z amounts to behaving in such a way that Z acquires the ability to do S. That is, assuming there was no previous possession of the skill, Z's degree of proficiency at S is increased from none at all to some. If, however, Z already possessed skill S to some degree, then teaching skill S to Z amounts to increasing Z's proficiency to a higher level. In general, then, if X teaches skill S to Z, then Z comes to acquire skill S with a certain degree of proficiency as a result of X's behavior.

DISPOSITIONS AS PART OF THE MATTER OF EDUCATION

Along with propositions and skills, the matter of education also includes dispositions. A *disposition* is a tendency to do something. For example, some children have the disposition to suck their thumbs. And certain people have the disposition to be nasty to others. Saying that Z has a disposition to do D does not necessarily mean that he or she always does it. Rather, it means that under certain conditions, Z does D more often than not.

In order to fully describe a particular disposition of a person, you have to specify not only what is done but the conditions under which it is done and the regularity with which the person does it under those conditions. For example, John may have the disposition to consider a problem analytically and critically, if the problem has been assigned to him for homework. This means that under the conditions of having a problem assigned for homework, John will more often than not consider that problem analytically and critically. Just *how often* he does this when those conditions hold determines the strength of his disposition.

"Z has the disposition to do D under certain conditions" means then that whenever Z is in a situation where those conditions hold, he or she does D more often than not. If Z has a strong disposition to do D under those conditions, then when in a situation where they hold, Z will usually do D. On the other hand, if Z's disposition to do D under those conditions is not very strong, then under those conditions Z does D little more than half the time. If Z does not have the disposition to do D under those conditions, then either Z never does D when those conditions hold or when they hold Z does D less than half of the time.

There are three major kinds of dispositions: (1) dispositions of thought, (2) dispositions of behavior, and (3) dispositions of emotional attachment. A disposition of thought is a tendency to think in a certain way. For instance, a person may have the dispositions to be analytical, look for causes, and to offer reasons for beliefs. Another person may have the dispositions to accept beliefs uncritically or to accept them on the basis of fallacious arguments.

It is important to differentiate here between believing and the disposition to accept beliefs (whether critically or uncritically). When a person has a belief, he or she affords some degree of psychological assent to a proposition; whereas, having a disposition to believe is a tendency to assent, not actually assenting. Just as the tendency to go swimming once a week is not the same as actually swimming, so the tendency to accept beliefs uncritically is not the same as believing that a proposition is true.

The second kind of disposition, a disposition of behavior, is a tendency to behave in a certain way. For example, a person might have the disposition to drink two martinis before dinner each night. He might have the disposition to bully smaller children. Or he might have the disposition to be kind to animals. Some people have the disposition to pout or cry if things do not go as they want them to. In general, a disposition of behavior is a tendency to exhibit some form of overt behavior under certain conditions.

Just as dispositions of thought should not be confused with believing, dispositions of behavior should not be confused with either an instance of behavior or with a skill. If a person behaves in a certain way under certain circumstances, this may be indicative of that person's having a disposition. However, the behavior is not the same as the disposition. For

---

One of the major concerns of many teachers is classroom discipline. The following paragraph suggests that how a student generally behaves in the classroom is a learned disposition:

It is extremely easy to make-believe, to pretend that behavior is mystical and that somehow children will learn the opposite of what they are taught. Are the fine, gifted students direct products of our inspired teaching, while the slow, mischievous or dull students products of someone else? If we are honest, we must take our share of the grief as well as the joy. Perhaps the most frightening aspect of teaching is that behavior is most certainly learned, and, for this, we as teachers must take full responsibility. Pretending is easier, for discipline is an awesome challenge. We prefer to believe that the deviant child will somehow change—that his bad behavior is just a stage, or if only he could work it out of his system everything would be all right. We hope, but hope wears thin without positive signs of improvement. We struggle, we wait, we often become discouraged, and finally we realize that it is indeed a cause-and-effect world—in the long run we do "reap that which we sow." (Charles H. Madsen, Jr., and Clifford K. Madsen, *Teaching/Discipline* [Boston: Allyn and Bacon, 1970], p. 41.)

Classroom discipline clearly involves dispositions of behavior. But does it involve dispositions of thought? Explain your answer. How strong are your arguments?

Are there any moral issues associated with attempting to maintain classroom discipline? Explain.

similar reasons, dispositions of behavior are not skills. A behavioral skill is an ability to behave in a certain way, but it is neither the behavior itself nor the disposition to behave in that way. Indeed, one may have a particular skill but not be at all disposed to exercise it.

Finally, there are dispositions of emotional attachment. A disposition

Many people criticize the American economic system for its dependence upon aggressive competition. Indeed, they argue, the economic system makes it necessary for the schools to teach children some otherwise undesirable dispositions: to care only for oneself, to expect to be a winner, and to derive pleasure from others' losses.

In an indictment of many dispositions of emotional attachment taught in American schools, one writer describes the situation of Boris, a fifth-grader, who has been asked by his teacher to reduce a certain fraction to its lowest terms but is unable to answer correctly. Other children in the class, however, energetically attempt to get the teacher's attention so that they might correct Boris. The teacher disregards their raised hands and continues to press Boris for the answer. After prolonging this situation, thereby causing Boris much anguish, the teacher finally calls on another student, Peggy, who provides the correct answer:

> Thus Boris' failure had made it possible for Peggy to succeed; his depression is the price of her exhilaration; his misery the occasion for her rejoicing. This is the standard condition of the American elementary school, and is why so many of us feel a contraction of the heart even if someone we never knew succeeds merely at garnering plankton in the Thames; because so often somebody's success has been bought at the cost of our failure. To a Zuñi, Hopi, or Dakota Indian, Peggy's performance would seem cruel beyond belief, for competition, the wringing of success from somebody's failure, is a form of torture foreign to those non-competitive redskins. Yet Peggy's action seems natural to us; and so it is. How else would you run our world? And since all but the brightest children have the constant experience that others succeed at their expense they cannot but develop an inherent tendency to hate—to hate the success of others, to hate others who are successful, and to be determined to prevent it. Along with this, naturally, goes the hope that others will fail. (Jules Henry, *Culture Against Man* [New York: Random House, 1963], pp. 295–96.)

What are the emotional dispositions identified in the quote? Do you agree that these dispositions are taught in most American schools? What are your reasons? How strong is your argument?

What are some of the dispositions of emotional attachment that should be taught to children? Offer the strongest arguments you can for your claims here. Assess the strength of those arguments.

of emotional attachment is a tendency to attach certain emotions to certain things. For example, some people regularly derive enjoyment from watching basketball games. These people have the tendency to attach certain positive emotions to the viewing of such games. Others tend to attach no particular emotions to watching basketball games. That is, they have no emotional dispositions with regard to viewing them. Still others find viewing basketball games uninteresting and even unpleasant. These people tend to attach certain negative emotions to the viewing of basketball games. To say, then, that a person has a particular emotional disposition is to say that under certain conditions that person will more often than not experience certain emotions.

Like beliefs and skills, dispositions can be strengthened. For example, a person may have the disposition to be honest in dealings with others. Yet this disposition may be a weak one, that is, the person behaves honestly in just over 50 per cent of the cases. The disposition could be strengthened so that the person behaves honestly in, say, over 80 per cent of the cases. If the person's disposition is increased as a result of someone else's behavior, then the second person has taught that disposition.

Teaching a disposition amounts to teaching a person *to* do something (which is not the same as teaching a person *that* something is the case or *how to* do something). If Z does not possess disposition D, teaching disposition D to Z amounts to behaving in such a way that Z acquires the tendency to do D under certain conditions more often than not. The strength of Z's disposition to do D under those conditions may be increased from none at all (that is, 50 per cent or less) to a weak, moderate, or strong disposition; or, from a weak or moderate disposition to a moderate or strong one.

THE MATTER OF A PERSON'S EDUCATION

The matter of education includes all of the alternatives from among which a teacher must make decisions concerning what to teach. In this sense, the matter of education is different from *the matter of a particular person's education*, which includes only those propositions, skills, and dispositions that have *actually* been taught to the individual. Consequently, we cannot properly ask what the matter of education in general ought to be. For the matter of education is simply all propositions, skills, and dispositions that could be taught. But it does make sense to ask what the matter of a *person's* education ought to be. For although at a given time the matter of a person's education is what it is, it could have been, and may one day be, otherwise. The matter of a person's education may not be what it ought to be. Perhaps different propositions, skills, and dispositions should have been taught.

Making a decision concerning the matter of education, then, amounts to deciding to teach this proposition, or that skill, or this disposition to a particular person or group of persons. Any determination as to whether you have made a good decision concerning the matter of education must always take into account both what you have decided to teach and to whom you have decided to teach it. It is possible that what ought to be taught to one person ought not to be taught to another. And what might be a very good decision with regard to one group may be a very bad decision with regard to another.

THE MANNER OF EDUCATION

In addition to making decisions concerning the matter of a person's education, teachers have to make decisions concerning *the manner of education,* the ways in which any matter could be taught. Decisions of manner involve more than just deciding on what is commonly called a "teaching method." Certainly, decisions about teaching method are important and have to be made; but they do not take place in a vacuum. There are many aspects in the educational environment that contribute to or work against the success of a teaching method. And frequently, many of these environmental aspects are the result of other decisions we have made.

For example, consider the common situation of schools whose students are divided into grades. In these schools, teachers have to make decisions concerning such things as how to teach reading to the second graders and how to teach multiplication to the third graders. But how good their decisions are is in many instances seriously affected by the fact that they are made within the context of a graded situation.

The school graded mainly according to age creates many problems for teachers. For instance, how do you teach multiplication to a group of children who come to your class with very different skills, understandings, and dispositions. Should you aim your teaching at the most ill-prepared members of the group and risk boring the others? Or should you divide the class into achievement groups—top, middle, and low—and risk problems of discipline and perhaps the reinforcement of feelings of negative self-worth among members of the "lower" groups? These are only a few of the significant problems faced by teachers in graded schools. And the point to recognize here is that such difficulties result from the policy decision to have a graded school.

Faced with such difficulties, a teacher is likely to make the decision that will make things easiest for him. Although he should, he is unlikely to call into question the assumption that having a graded school is desirable. That is, the problems of making a good decision about teaching method may be due to the limited range of alternatives established by the earlier decision to have a graded school. There may be much better ways to structure a school. The teacher in such a situation should examine the reasons for having graded schools and assess those arguments with the in-

Ability grouping, a manner of education used in many schools, is criticized by some for both its educational ineffectiveness and its psychological and social side-effects:

> To a very large extent, ability or homogeneous grouping based on intelligence and/or achievement scores is still widely practiced in the public schools of this country. This practice rests on the assumption that bright children learn more when they are separated from their slower peers and grouped for instructional purposes with other bright children. . . . The argument for ability grouping is that if we narrow the range of ability and achievement within an individual class we can increase the quantity and quality of learning in that class. . . .
>
> I think that most teachers and administrators would agree that when a child is confined to a particular ability group he is committed, whether we like to admit it or not, to an education of very definite caliber. The student who has been placed in a slow class quickly learns that he is in the "stupid" class. . . .
>
> There is also overwhelming sociological evidence that ability grouping offers a way in which we can create *de facto* segregation in the classroom after we have integration of the schools. Low-income children are almost always assigned to the lower-ranking groups, and upper-income children to higher-ranking groups. . . .
>
> In addition, the better teachers are usually assigned to the better classes, with the result that those children who most need the best teaching do not receive it. . . . It would seem that simple justice and common sense would dictate that the lower-ability classes would get the best teachers so that they would have the best teaching available to compensate for their academic deficiencies. . . .
>
> Ability grouping does not solve [the problem of meeting individual differences]. What we must do is *construct a program which makes it possible for teachers to individualize instruction* on the following levels: the content of learning, the level of content, the kind of methodology, and the speed of learning. (James Olsen, "Should We Group by Ability?" *The Journal of Teacher Education* 18, no. 2 [Summer 1967], pp. 201–03.)

How strong is this argument? Is any emotive language used in stating it? Do you believe that ability grouping is undesirable? What are your reasons for your position? How strong is your argument?

tention of determining whether there are better reasons for *not* having graded schools.

Yet there is even more to be considered here, for the manner of education is not comprised only of school structure and teaching method. It also includes such things as the books and materials that are used. And, importantly, it includes curriculum design, that is, the order in which things are taught. Should we teach science in the elementary school, or should science be deferred until junior high or high school? Should we try to teach all children how to read beginning in the first grade, or are there some good reasons for choosing another time?

DECISIONS CONCERNING MANNER AND MATTER

Certainly, many of the things that affect the education of individuals cannot reasonably be changed at the present time. However, within the parameters established by such conditions there exists a wide range of alternatives.

Too often, poor decisions concerning manner are made because people have not seriously and rationally considered other alternatives. They accept the greater part of the current manner of education—graded schools, standardized curricula, and so on—as a given. They uncritically assume that these aspects of the manner of education cannot be changed or that they are the best decisions that could have been made. The first of these assumptions is clearly false, and the second ought not to be accepted unless one has some very good reasons for considering it true. Both assumptions severely restrict the range of further decision-making.

A similar situation holds with regard to the matter of education. It is interesting to ponder how many teachers ever seriously consider whether there are good reasons for teaching what they teach. Should all of the students in French II really learn French? Are there good reasons for requiring every student in a school to do gymnastics? What justification is there for requiring every student preparing for college to learn algebra? Are there strong arguments against these requirements?

As with the manner of education, there are any number of alternatives concerning the matter of education. The fact that certain decisions have been made does not necessarily mean that they were the best decisions possible. And even if they were good decisions when they were made, changes in society may have made them obsolete. We should not let decisions made in the past unreasonably restrict the range of alternatives we examine in confronting the present and the future.

Decisions concerning the matter or manner of education should be reviewed regularly. The teacher needs to consider not only the "new" decisions that he or she makes but also "old" decisions that may still influence effectiveness. Most importantly, individual teachers should not focus only on the decisions that they personally make. For in many cases, to do so would be to uncritically accept the decisions of others as establishing proper limits to the alternatives open to teachers and their students. Teachers need to engage in rational dialogue among themselves and with others concerning the broad decisions that tend to limit the range of possibilities open to them and their students individually.

Finally, in coming to understand what needs to be considered in making intelligent decisions concerning the matter and manner of education,

it is important to understand that decisions concerning matter are logically prior to decisions concerning manner. That is, making an intelligent decision concerning how to teach something presupposes that you have
already determined that that thing should be taught.

For example, suppose that you have decided to use the inquiry approach to teach your class that Paul Revere was not—as they have been
taught—a selfless hero of the American revolution. This decision to use
the inquiry approach is a good one, only if the decision to teach your students that Paul Revere was not a selfless hero is a good one. In other
words, if you ought *not* to teach them this matter, then there is *no* manner that you ought to use in teaching them this. The decision to use this
manner to teach this matter cannot be a good one if the decision to teach
that matter is not a good one.

While it is true that decisions concerning matter should be made before
decisions concerning manner, decisions concerning matter are not the
first educational decisions that have to be made. As we will see, decisions
concerning the outcomes of education must precede decisions concerning
either matter or manner.

Review

1. Define each of the following terms used in this chapter:

   Matter of education   Disposition

   Teaching   Manner of education

   Skill

2. Identify and contrast the two different meanings of "teach."
3. Discuss the two senses in which a proposition can be taught
   to someone.
4. Explain what is meant by "teaching a person a skill."
5. Identify and discuss three different kinds of dispositions.
6. Compare and contrast teaching a proposition, teaching a skill,
   and teaching a disposition.
7. Differentiate between the matter of education and the matter
   of a person's education.
8. Explain how decisions of manner may involve more than deciding upon "teaching method."
9. Show how some decisions of manner may be affected by other decisions of manner.
10. Explain how a decision of manner may be a good one from
    one point of view but a bad one from another point of view.
11. Discuss how certain decisions of manner and matter can limit
    the range of educational alternatives in the future.
12. Explain why decisions of matter should occur prior to deci-
    sions of manner.

The Outcomes of Education

In addition to decisions concerning matter and manner, decisions must be made concerning the outcomes of education. This chapter will examine the notion of educational outcomes and differentiate between the outcomes of education for an individual person and outcomes of education for a group. The chapter will conclude with a discussion of why decisions concerning outcomes should be made prior to decisions concerning matter or manner.

THE OUTCOMES OF EDUCATION

An outcome of education is any result of education or, more specifically, any result of teaching* some matter in some manner. If Laura has come to understand Einstein's theory of relativity as a result of someone's

*In this chapter, we will continue to use "teach" in the result sense only. However, with some minor modifications what we say here also applies in the intention sense.

having taught her the theory, her understanding is an outcome of education. And if Jane learns how to use an electron microscope as a result of someone's teaching, her possessing this skill is an outcome of education.

More precisely, O is an outcome of education if and only if

(1) O is someone's having a belief, understanding, skill, or disposition as a result of its having been taught to him or her,

or

(2) O is something for the occurrence of which someone's having been taught a belief, understanding, skill, or disposition is sufficient either by itself or in conjunction with some other conditions.

With regard to the first of these conditions, it is important to recognize that a person may have a belief, for example, that is not an outcome of education. The belief is an outcome of education only if it was taught to the person. It is at least logically possible for a person to possess a belief without its having been taught. In such a case, having that belief would not be an outcome of education.

Moreover, an educational outcome is not a belief, understanding, skill, or disposition *per se*. Rather, it is a person's possession of a belief, understanding, skill, or disposition. For instance, suppose that McX teaches John that two plus two equals four by showing him a movie. In this case, the manner of education is McX's showing John the movie; the matter of education is the proposition "Two plus two equals four"; and the outcome of education is John's having the belief that two plus two equals four.

With regard to the second condition above, suppose that something O has occurred. In order for O to be an educational outcome, some person (or persons) must possess some particular beliefs, understandings, skills, or dispositions. And they must have acquired those beliefs, understandings, skills, or dispositions as a result of their having been taught to them. Finally, that person's (or those persons') possession of those beliefs, understandings, skills, or dispositions must have been sufficient either by itself or in conjunction with some other conditions for the occurrence of O.

For example, suppose that Dr. McAndrew operates on Jill and thereby saves her life. Dr. McAndrew is able to perform this operation because he has certain medical skills and beliefs. These skills and beliefs were taught to him by the faculty of his medical school. Notice that although Dr. McAndrew's having these medical skills is not sufficient by itself for the saving of Jill's life, it is sufficient in conjunction with certain other conditions—such as the existence of surgical instruments, the availability of an appropriate operating room, antibiotics, and so on. In this example, the matter of education is the beliefs and skills taught to Dr. McAndrew about such an operation. The manner of education is the sum of the techniques used at the medical school in teaching Dr. McAndrew those beliefs and skills. The outcomes of education are the doctor's proficiency and the saving of Jill's life.

In considering what outcomes of education ought to occur, it is important to understand that some outcomes are possible but others are not. Moreover, what is possible today may not have been possible at an earlier time. For instance, two thousand years ago, learning microsurgery would have been impossible. No one possessed the knowledge and instruments necessary to teach it.

In order to make an intelligent decision concerning an educational outcome, you must presuppose that the outcome is possible. It would be contradictory for you to claim that you can make an intelligent decision to produce a certain educational outcome and also that you believe that outcome cannot actually occur. In the next chapter we will examine the question of how to make intelligent decisions concerning the outcomes of education. But before we do that, we need to consider two important kinds of educational outcomes: individual outcomes and social outcomes.

For many years, there has been controversy concerning what the outcomes of education ought to be. Even with regard to reading—an area that at first glance may seem clear-cut—there is a great deal of disagreement. Many people believe that educational outcomes ought to include more than increases in the student's ability to decode written symbols:

> It has become clear that various means may be used to establish and improve reading skills. Although reading skills may be achieved by different approaches, we should observe that there are different outcomes and relationships associated with each. Increasingly, educators are recommending a comprehensive program of instruction which stresses meaningful reaction and reading as thinking. Accordingly, greater recognition is being given to the effects of reading experience upon the pupil. In efforts to provide a more valid evaluation than that reflected only by the acquisition of skill, teachers are asking questions such as: Do pupils read more widely? Are they more interested in and better able to read the materials of the subject fields? Have they obtained competency in using the library to satisfy interests and meet recurring needs? Have they developed, as a result of instruction, a strong interest in reading and independence in the selection of materials? (Paul Witty, "Reading Instruction—A Forward Look," *Elementary English* [National Council of Teachers of English], March 1961, p. 156.)

What educational outcomes are recommended in the quoted passage? Categorize each as the acquisition of a skill, disposition, belief, or understanding. Are any of the key terms in the passage ambiguous or vague? Explain.

INDIVIDUAL EDUCATIONAL OUTCOMES

An *individual educational outcome* is an outcome of education for an individual. More specifically, I is an individual outcome of education for a person Z if and only if

(1) I is an outcome of education

and

(2) Z's having been taught some belief, understanding, skill, or disposition was sufficient either by itself or in conjunction with some other conditions for I

and

(3) the occurrence of I implies a true description of Z.

Any belief, understanding, skill, or disposition that is taught to a person is an individual educational outcome for that person. For instance, if Tim was taught that democracy is the best form of government and hence acquired this belief, then an individual outcome of education for Tim is his believing that democracy is the best form of government. Of course, this is not necessarily an individual outcome for Tim's foreign pen-pal David or for Michael, the royal heir who is an exchange student in Tim's class. What is an individual educational outcome for one person is not necessarily that for another.

Individual educational outcomes are not limited to having beliefs, understandings, skills, or dispositions. For example, being employed as a computer programmer is an individual outcome of education for Deb. She was taught certain propositions, skills, and dispositions related to programming, and these were sufficient in conjunction with some other conditions—such as the existence of computers and a demand for computer programmers, and so on—for her being a computer programmer.

The various individual outcomes of education for a person involve many—and perhaps most—of the aspects of that person's way of life: attitudes, occupation, personal relationships, emotions, dreams, and so forth. For a person does not merely live. Living as an aborigine in a primitive village in New Guinea is quite different from living in a contemporary technological society. Certainly the biological processes in each case are similar. Yet unless one has only a simple biological existence, as does an individual in a coma, a person always lives a certain kind of life—has a certain way of life.

The unique way of life of an individual, in turn, depends upon two basic factors: the person's own beliefs, understandings, skills, and dispositions and the existing external conditions. These two factors establish parameters for the individual. That is, they serve to set limits on the way of life an individual can actually have.

For example, there are many things that a person living in a contemporary technological society can do that were not possibilities even a hundred and fifty years ago. Driving an automobile, going to a movie, or being an astronaut depend upon recent developments. That certain things exist (or do not yet exist) sets limits on the ways of life that are possible for any group of people at a given time and place. In addition, each person's own set of beliefs, understandings, skills, and dispositions further delimit the possibilities for that person. For instance, you cannot drive a car unless you possess the necessary skills—even now that cars exist.

When we ask what the individual outcomes of a person's education ought to be, we are essentially inquiring into what some of the characteristics of that person's way of life ought to be. For example, suppose that you determine that Joe ought to be taught to respect the members of his government. The individual educational outcome that you have identi-

---

The following have been offered as educational outcomes that ought to be produced:

1. Education should aim to develop the powers of critical, independent thought.

2. It should attempt to induce sensitiveness of perception, receptiveness to new ideas, imaginative sympathy with the experiences of others.

3. It should produce an awareness of the main streams of our cultural, literary, and scientific traditions.

4. It should make available important bodies of knowledge concerning nature, society, ourselves, our country, and its history.

5. It should strive to cultivate an intelligent loyalty to the ideals of the democratic community and to deepen understanding of the heritage of freedom and the prospects of its survival.

6. At some level, it should equip young men and women with the general skills and techniques and the specialized knowledge which, together with the virtues and aptitudes already mentioned, will make it possible for them to do some productive work related to their capacities and interests.

7. It should strengthen those inner resources and traits of character which enable the individual, when necessary, to stand alone.

—Sidney Hook, *Education for Modern Man: A New Perspective*
(New York: Knopf, 1966), p. 55

Which of the educational outcomes listed above are *individual* educational outcomes? Explain. Should these outcomes be produced for everyone? How strong is your argument for your position?

fied is Joe's possessing the disposition to respect the members of his government. But you have also identified a characteristic of Joe's way of life: respect for the members of his government.

It is also important to recognize that the occurrence of certain individual educational outcomes requires that other persons have distinct ways of life. For example, suppose that you determine that Marty should have a way of life characterized by watching ball games on television every weekend, that is, that he have this disposition.* Now if in fact Marty's way of life is to have this characteristic, some other people must necessarily have certain ways of life. Specifically, there must be some persons who play ball games, some who work in the television industry, and so on. Assuming that particular things must be taught to these other people to enable them to do what they do, it becomes clear that certain individual educational outcomes must have occurred with regard to these people as well. In other words, in order for a particular educational outcome to occur with regard to Marty, certain other educational outcomes must occur for some other people.

In general, then, making a decision concerning the outcomes of education for a particular individual many times involves making a decision concerning the outcomes of education for other people. Certain individual educational outcomes have implications for other people. And this is to say that they have implications for the social outcomes of education.

SOCIAL OUTCOMES OF EDUCATION

Teaching something to someone always has individual educational outcomes and sometimes it has social outcomes. A *social outcome of education* is a result of education that pertains to a group of persons. In particular, S is a social outcome of education for a group of persons G if and only if

(1) S is an outcome of education

and

(2) Some member(s) of G having been taught some belief, understanding, skill, or disposition was sufficient either by itself or in conjunction with some other conditions for S

and

(3) The occurrence of S implies a true description of the group G.

*For purposes of this example, we will assume that if Marty has this disposition, it must have been taught to him.

For example, the fact that most Americans have televisions is a social outcome of education. Many Americans have been taught certain things that, given certain other conditions, result in this outcome's occurrence.

The following passage advocates two major social outcomes of education for the United States:

1. To channel the energies of education toward the reconstruction of the economic system—a system which should be geared with the increasing socializations and public controls now developing in England, Sweden, New Zealand, and other countries; a system in which national and international planning of production and distribution replaces the chaotic planlessness of traditional "free enterprise"; a system in which the interests, wants, and needs of the consumer dominate those of the producer; a system in which natural resources, such as coal and iron ore, are owned and controlled by the people; a system in which public corporations replace monopolistic enterprises and privately owned "public" utilities; a system in which federal authority is synchronized with decentralized regional and community administration; a system in which social security and a guaranteed annual wage sufficient to meet scientific standards of nourishment, shelter, clothing, health, recreation, and education are universalized; a system in which the majority of the people is the sovereign determinant of every basic economic policy.

2. To channel the energies of education toward the establishment of genuine international order—an order in which national sovereignty is always subordinate to international authority in all crucial issues affecting peace and security; an order therefore in which all weapons of war (including atomic energy, first of all) and police forces are finally brought under that authority; an order in which international economic planning of trade, resources, labor standards, and social security, is practiced parallel with the best cooperative practices of individual nations; an order in which all nationalities, races, and religions receive equal rights in its democratic control; an order in which "world citizenship" thus assumes at least equal status with national citizenship.

These two great guiding principles involve a multitude of specific educational tasks to which the profession should now devote itself. (Theodore Brameld, *Ends and Means in Education: A Midcentury Appraisal* [New York: Harper and Brothers, 1950], pp. 190–91.)

What are some of the beliefs, understandings, skills, and dispositions that Americans would have to be taught in order for these outcomes to occur? How would the occurrence of these social outcomes of education change the American way of life?

Do you believe that these outcomes ought to occur? Why? How strong is your argument?

Questions concerning the social outcomes of education must always be considered with regard to a specific group. That is, you cannot properly ask, "What ought the social outcomes of education be?" Rather, you must ask, "What ought the social outcomes of education be for group G?" So, for example, you can ask what the social outcomes of education ought to be for Americans. Or for middle-class women. Or for athletes. You can also ask what the social outcomes of education ought to be *for everyone.* Whatever the case, you must always identify the particular group for which social outcomes are to be considered.

The social outcomes of education for a particular group will have bearing on the characteristic way of life of that group. For example, the way of life of the Hopi Indians was in large measure a function of their education. If the adult members of that community had not transmitted certain beliefs, understandings, skills, and dispositions to the younger generation, the Hopi way of life would not have continued.

Or consider mainstream America's way of life. Some of its more striking characteristics are its mass media, material goods, and geographical mobility. The last involves a high dependence on the automobile, which, in turn, requires a high level of technological achievement in hundreds of areas—finding and refining petroleum, mining and processing ores, designing and machining components, and so on. Clearly, the American transportation system depends upon many people having many different beliefs, understandings, skills, and dispositions. And this, in turn, depends upon some matter's having been taught in some manner.

The way of life of any group is a function not only of the beliefs, understandings, skills, and dispositions of its members but of various conditions external to the group. Both factors set limits on the way of life the group can have. For instance, consider again the highly mobile way of life of most Americans. If the external conditions of, for instance, large territory and iron ore did not exist, then even if most Americans had all of their present beliefs, understandings, skills, and dispositions, their present degree of mobility would not exist.

RELATIONSHIPS BETWEEN SOCIAL AND INDIVIDUAL OUTCOMES OF EDUCATION

In order to better understand what social and individual outcomes of education are and how they are related, consider the following. Imagine that you have complete authority over the education of all the children in a particular society (group). These children will be taught only what you want and allow them to be taught. And the manner employed in teaching them will be whatever you want and allow to be used.

In order for you to intelligently decide what the matter and manner of these children's education ought to be, you must first determine what the outcomes of their education ought to be—individual and social. (The reasons for this will be explained later in the chapter.)

Thus, for this group of children—and for simplicity we will further suppose that they are all infants—you must ask yourself, "What should the social outcomes of education be for these children?" This question, however, is connected with another: "What way of life should these individuals come to have?" The reason for this is that the social outcomes of their education will comprise a major part of their way of life. If you could determine what the way of life of this group should be at some time in the future, then you could examine that way of life with the intention of determining what the social outcomes of their education ought to be.

For instance, suppose that you determine that these children ought to come to have a way of life characterized by (among other things) every member of the group having all of the necessities of life. But what are the necessities of life? Clearly, they include food, water, adequate clothing, and shelter. Yet what of medicine and physicians? It seems that under certain conditions these are as "necessary" for preserving a person's life as are food and water. Let us suppose, then, that you determine that food, water, clothing, shelter, medicine, and physicians are necessities of life, and that your group's way of life should be characterized by an adequate supply of each for every member.

Depending upon where the group is to live, the existence of enough water may or may not require that some of the members of the group have certain beliefs, understandings, skills, or dispositions. For instance, in parts of the southwestern United States there are not enough naturally occurring water supplies to keep a large number of people alive. If your group is to live in such an area some of the members of the group will have to be taught certain things about building and maintaining reservoirs, purifying the water, and so on. On the other hand, if your group is to live in an area in which plentiful and pure water supplies exist naturally, these particular teachings will not be required.

Satisfying the condition with regard to clothing and shelter is somewhat different. Whereas water occurs naturally in many areas, adequate clothing and shelter do not. Usually, people must produce them. And, for the most part, the production of clothing requires that certain beliefs, understandings, skills, and dispositions be taught.

Similarly, some medicines may occur naturally—such as the roots of certain trees or herbs—but the majority of medicines necessary to the continuation of human life do not. They must be produced by individuals who have been taught certain beliefs, understandings, skills, and dispositions. In addition, physicians do not occur naturally. In order for a person to acquire the beliefs, understandings, skills, and dispositions necessary for being a good physician, he or she must be taught.

Thus, when we consider the condition that everyone possess the necessities of life, we begin to see that meeting it will, in turn, require that other conditions be satisfied. That is, we see that this one condition implies other things concerning the way of life of this group: some members must become collectors and purifiers of water, some makers of clothes, some builders of shelter, some producers of medicine, and some physicians.

At mid-century, psychologist Eric Fromm argued that human society had reached a watershed in its development:

> Our dangers are war and robotism. What is the alternative? . . . We must take the responsibility for the life of all men, and develop on an international scale what all great countries have developed internally, a relative sharing of wealth and a new and more just division of economic resources. . . . We must retain the industrial method. But we must decentralize work and state so as to give it *human proportions.* . . .
>
> Our only alternative to the danger of robotism is humanistic communitarianism. The problem is not primarily the legal problem of property ownership, nor that of sharing *profits;* it is that of sharing *work,* sharing *experience.* Changes in ownership must be made to the extent to which they are necessary to create a community of work, and to prevent the profit motive from directing production into socially harmful directions. Income must be equalized to the extent of giving everybody the material basis for a dignified life, and thus preventing the economic differences from creating a fundamentally different experience of life for various social classes. Man must be restored to his supreme place in society, never being a means, never a thing to be used by others or by himself. . . . Capital must serve labor, things must serve life. (Erich Fromm, *The Sane Society* [1955; New York: Fawcett World Library, 1968], p. 313.)

If the society that Fromm advocates is to exist, what beliefs, understandings, skills, and dispositions will have to be taught to individuals? Do you agree or disagree with Fromm that we ought to work to produce such individual outcomes? Should we produce the social outcomes Fromm identifies? Offer the strongest argument you can to support your position.

And if the group's way of life is to continue from one generation to another, some members of the group must become teachers.

The point here is that in order for a group's way of life to possess certain characteristics, there may be any number of other characteristics which it must also possess. Moreover, it may be necessary for some members of the group to have rather different individual ways of life. For instance being a physician entails a way of life significantly different from that of a maker of clothes.

In the preceding example, we began with a consideration of the characteristics that the group's way of life ought to have. However, we could have begun our inquiry by considering individual members of the group. That is, instead of asking, "What characteristics should the way of life of the group possess?", we could have asked, "What characteristics should the way of life of this individual member of the group possess?" When we begin with this question, we ultimately come to identify some of the characteristics that the group's way of life should possess.

For example, suppose that for one member of the group you determine that one of the characteristics of his way of life ought to be his being able to drive his automobile wherever he wants. In order for his way of life to actually possess this characteristic, he must have an automobile. And unless he has the requisite skills to manufacture his own automobile, someone else must be a maker of automobiles. In addition, there must be producers and suppliers of fuel. But perhaps most importantly, the other members of his group must be disposed to not do anything that would interfere with his driving his automobile wherever he wanted to. Clearly, each of these required conditions relates to the way of life of the group as a whole and thus represents characteristics that the group's way of life should include. It should also be obvious that each of these required conditions is an outcome of education.

DECISIONS CONCERNING OUTCOMES, MATTER, AND MANNER

As a general rule, decisions concerning outcomes should be made before decisions concerning either matter or manner. Suppose that you have made a decision to teach arithmetic to David. As you think about it, it should be clear that this decision includes within it the decision that David acquire the understandings and skills of arithmetic. That is, it includes a decision concerning an outcome of education. In general, any decision concerning matter contains a decision concerning outcomes.

A similar conclusion follows from a consideration of decisions concerning manner. As we have seen, you cannot just teach; rather, if you teach you must necessarily teach something to someone. Consequently, it makes no sense to talk about a decision to *just* use a certain manner. Any decision to use a manner must always be a decision to use that manner to teach something to someone.

Consider the decision to use the phonics method to teach John how to read. It is obvious that this decision includes two other decisions. It contains a decision concerning matter—the skill of reading—and a decision concerning outcome—that John acquire the skill of reading. In general, any decision concerning manner contains a decision concerning matter and a decision concerning outcomes.

Since both decisions concerning matter and those concerning manner include decisions concerning outcomes, making a rational decision about either requires that you have also made a rational decision concerning the included outcomes. For example, suppose that you made the decision to use the discovery approach in teaching general science to your class. In order to have made this decision rationally, you must have some reasons for believing either that this is a good decision or that it is one that you ought to make. In either case, one of your reasons must be that your students ought to learn general science or that it is good for them to learn general science. And these are beliefs about an educational outcome.

Hence, it is generally better to make your decisions concerning outcomes before making decisions concerning either matter or manner. And likewise, it is usually better to make decisions concerning matter before making decisions concerning manner. In the following chapters we will consider some strategies for making each of these kinds of decisions intelligently.

Review

1. Define each of the following terms used in this chapter:

   Outcome of education
   Individual outcome of education
   Way of life of an individual
   Social outcome of education
   Way of life of a group

2. Explain why in making an intelligent decision concerning an educational outcome you must presuppose that the outcome can actually occur.
3. Identify and discuss some different kinds of individual outcomes of education.
4. Discuss what is meant by a person's way of life and show how individual outcomes of education are related to that way of life.
5. Explain how a person's beliefs, understandings, skills, and dispositions along with external conditions establish parameters for the person.
6. Show how deciding upon certain outcomes of education for one person may entail decisions concerning the outcomes of education for other people.
7. Explain how the social outcomes of education for a group have bearing upon its characteristic way of life.
8. Identify and discuss the relationships between social and individual outcomes of education.
9. Explain why decisions concerning outcomes should usually be made prior to decisions concerning matter or manner.

13

Making Intelligent Decisions Concerning the Outcomes of Education

We are now in a position to directly consider some strategies for making intelligent decisions concerning the outcomes of education. Clearly, there are many strategies that you might profitably employ in trying to make educational decisions intelligently. However, the effective ones will all rest on the same basic foundation: they will provide help in uncovering good reasons for the decision. Equally important, any effective strategy will provide a way of uncovering reasons that might count *against* the decision.

In this chapter, we will discuss two strategies for making intelligent decisions concerning the outcomes of education. One relates to social outcomes, and the other to individual outcomes. Each of these strategies will be considered from the point of view of moral obligations. We will then consider how such decisions can be made intelligently with regard to moral and nonmoral worth and nonmoral obligations.

A STRATEGY FOR DECIDING ON SOCIAL OUTCOMES

In trying to make intelligent decisions concerning the social outcomes of education, it is helpful to begin by considering your society as it actually exists. What are some of its good characteristics? What things are wrong with it? What sort of way of life should your society have in five, ten, or twenty years from now? What should the characteristics of that way of life be?

For example, consider the fact that so many Americans get divorced. Is this a good characteristic of American society? Is it something that should be changed? Does it matter one way or the other? Likewise, is the existence of mammoth corporations and conglomerates important to American life? Is there anything wrong with this aspect of society? Is it a characteristic that should be preserved? Should the entire economic system be changed?

In general, you should examine your society as it is and consider how it ought to be. In doing this, however, it is important to realize that you are dealing with *real* issues and trying to identify *realistic* answers. Done properly, such an examination is not an exercise in idle speculation resulting in impossible solutions. Rather, it identifies some beliefs that you have concerning the society in which you live.

Another way of saying this is that you need to identify some reasonable beliefs about your society. Specifically, you should attempt to determine the most rationally defensible position possible with regard to the characteristics that society ought to possess and realistically could possess.

Clearly, this examination will require that you think philosophically about education and produce the strongest arguments for your beliefs that you can. It will also involve your assessing those arguments. Of course, you should not expect to achieve a final resolution of these topics. Over a period of time, as you read and learn more, as you reexamine your own arguments and the arguments of others, you may find good reasons to change some of your beliefs. Moreover, as you continue to reassess the ethical theory that you hold, you may find that it would be more reasonable to give up some or all of that theory in favor of another. And this in turn may result in your changing some of your beliefs concerning what your society should be.

Some people never seriously try to identify rational beliefs concerning their society because they feel that they will not be able to get "final" or "conclusive" answers to their questions. But theirs is the wrong way to look at the situation. What you need is not "final" answers but the most rationally defensible ones that you can find. The hope is that by striving

Psychologist B. F. Skinner has identified conditions that he considers characteristic of a strong society:

> We do not need to predict the future to see some of the ways in which the strength of a culture depends upon the behavior of its members. A culture that maintains civil order and defends itself against attack frees its members from certain kinds of threats and presumably provides more time and energy for other things (particularly if order and security are not maintained by force). A culture needs various goods for its survival, and its strength must depend in part on the economic contingencies which maintain enterprising and productive labor, on the availability of the tools of production, and on the development and conservation of resources. A culture is presumably stronger if it induces its members to maintain a safe and healthful environment, to provide medical care, and to maintain a population density appropriate to its resources and space. A culture must be transmitted from generation to generation, and its strength will presumably depend on what and how much its new members learn, either through informal instructional contingencies or in educational institutions. A culture needs the support of its members, and it must provide for the pursuit and achievement of happiness if it is to prevent disaffection or defection. A culture must be reasonably stable, but it must also change, and it will presumably be strongest if it can avoid excessive respect for tradition and fear of novelty on the one hand and excessively rapid change on the other. Lastly, a culture will have a special measure of survival value if it encourages its members to examine its practices and to experiment with new ones. (B. F. Skinner, *Beyond Freedom and Dignity* [New York: Knopf, 1971], pp. 152–53.)

Why do you agree (or disagree) with Skinner regarding the characteristics of a strong society? Does contemporary American society possess some of these characteristics? Should it possess all of them? Why? What implications, if any, do your answers have for education? What ethical theory does your argument presuppose?

for the more realizable goal of holding rational beliefs, you will come to hold more and more true beliefs and fewer false ones. And absolute conclusive "proof" is not necessary for this.

Now, suppose that, on the basis of the strongest evidence of which you are currently aware, you have identified some characteristics that you believe your society ought to possess and which you believe it realistically could possess. You should next examine each of those characteristics to determine which, if any, are social outcomes of education.

For example, suppose that you have good reasons for believing that society should be characterized by adequate medical care for everyone. Clearly, this characteristic would be a social outcome of education, because some of the members of your society would have to be taught certain things in order for it to occur. And their having been taught these things, along with other conditions that prevail, would bring about adequate medical care for everyone. In other words, having this characteristic satisfies the definition of a social outcome of education.

In attempting to determine whether a social characteristic is (or could be) a social outcome of education, it is important to recognize that there are two different ways in which it may be one. The first is that someone's having been taught something may be both necessary and sufficient* for the society's possessing that characteristic. And the second is that someone's having been taught something is sufficient *but not* necessary for the society's possessing the characteristic.

Thus, for instance, teaching some people certain beliefs, skills, and dispositions would be both necessary and sufficient (along with other conditions) for there being adequate medical care for everyone. More specifically, there are certain beliefs, understandings, skills, and dispositions that a person must possess in order to be a good physician. Enough people will acquire these beliefs and understandings *only if* they are taught to them. Hence, teaching this matter is a necessary condition for having a society characterized by adequate medical care for everyone. The teaching of these beliefs, understandings, and so on (along with other conditions) is also sufficient for the society's possessing this characteristic.

Sometimes, however, teaching some matter to some people may be sufficient but not necessary for society's having a certain characteristic. For instance, teaching some people about plastics may be sufficient, along with certain other conditions, for society's having many different games and entertainments. Yet clearly, this teaching is not *necessary* for the existence of games and entertainments.

Now if you have good reasons for believing that your society ought to possess a certain characteristic, and if it is reasonable to believe that teaching some matter to some people is both necessary and sufficient for that characteristic, you thereby have good reasons for believing that this is a social outcome of education that ought to occur.

This conclusion does not follow, however, if teaching some matter is sufficient but not necessary for society's having that characteristic. For if teaching some matter is sufficient but not necessary, it is possible for society to have the characteristic without teaching anyone some matter. And if this occurs, the characteristic will *not* be a social outcome of education. Consequently, knowing only that society ought to have the characteristic is not by itself a good reason for believing that society's having that characteristic is a social *outcome of education* that ought to occur. Of course, you could strengthen such an argument by identifying some other reasons for teaching that matter.

---

*As in Chapter 11, we will continue to use "sufficient" to mean either "sufficient by itself" or "sufficient in conjunction with some other conditions."

In the following excerpt, Admiral Hyman Rickover suggests that the outcomes of schooling ought to be primarily "intellectual":

> In my opinion our "professional" educators have a wrong idea of what is the proper function of a school in a modern industrial country that is also a democracy. When they engage in "whole" child education they invade the domain of home, church, and community. Besides there just isn't time for the schools themselves to do the whole education job. What the child learns at school can never be more that a *part* of his education. . . . A school system performs its proper task when it does a first-rate job of equipping children with the requisite knowledge and intellectual skill for successful living in a complex modern society.
>
> It is civilization that makes school a necessity for the continuance of social life. . . .
>
> If we adult Americans are not intelligent enough to figure out a way to improve American education, we cannot hope that our children will be intelligent enough to keep our Nation strong and prosperous and capable of living up to its task of leading the free world.
>
> I do not wish to deprecate the importance of high moral standards, of good character, of kindliness, of humaneness, of ability to get along well with fellow citizens—there are innumerable virtues I should like to see inculcated in American youth. But the one thing which I believe will be of the greatest importance for the future of our Nation and of the free world, the one *indispensable* thing, is to bring all our children to markedly higher intellectual levels. (H. G. Rickover, *American Education—A National Failure* [New York: Dutton, 1963], pp. 120–21, 307.)

What are some of the social outcomes of education that Rickover believes ought to occur? Why do you agree, or disagree? Are there good reasons for believing that schools should not be especially concerned with the "whole" child? Explain.

What reasons could be given to support the claim that increased intellectual knowledge is necessary for the realization of the social outcomes Rickover believes ought to occur? Is it necessary that *everyone* acquire this sort of knowledge, or need it be acquired by only some people? Explain.

We can summarize this strategy for making intelligent decisions concerning the social outcomes of education as follows:

1. Consider a given society with the intention of identifying some characteristics that it ought to possess.

   You may find that a characteristic it currently has should be preserved, modified, or eliminated.

   You may find that there are some characteristics that it ought to have but does not.

2. After you have identified a characteristic that you have good reasons for believing the society ought to have, determine whether the characteristic must be a social outcome of education or whether it could have another origin. (That is, determine whether teaching some matter to someone is both necessary and sufficient *or* sufficient but not necessary for society's having that characteristic.)

The following excerpt provides an important perspective for considering what the social outcomes of education ought to be.

The most controversial issues of the twenty-first century will pertain to the ends and means of modifying human behavior and who shall determine them. The first educational question will not be "What knowledge is of most worth?" but "What kinds of human beings do we wish to produce?" . . .

The nerve cells of the brain, far more than muscles or any other organs, are highly sensitive to small electric currents, to a variety of chemicals, and to changes in blood supply. Sedatives, barbituates, tranquilizers, and various psychedelics provide powerful ways of controlling behavior by direct action on the brain. Similarly, we can manipulate behavior by applying electric currents to regions of the brain. Experiments are now under way with drugs and brain extracts designed to enhance learning or memory.

Aldous Huxley long ago introduced us to the possibilities of genetic selectivity through the availability of sperm and ovum banks. The means of drastically altering the course of human development through artificial insemination, chemical treatment, and electric manipulation are with us. We are already tampering with human evolution. The possibilities for further doing so will be enormously enhanced and refined as we move into the twenty-first century.

We of the teaching profession have tended to get bogged down in the narrow details of our calling, in details pertaining primarily to means: buildings, classrooms, textbooks, and so on. We have seldom gone beyond these trivialities to recognition of the fact that education and teaching are much bigger than schools. Schools are only a convenient means to more important ends, means that may no longer be relevant several decades from now. . . .

We must raise the level of the dialogue to the truly significant questions of educational ends. . . .

"*What kinds of human beings do we wish to produce?*" (John I. Goodlad, "The School of Tomorrow," *NEA Journal,* February 1968, p. 51.)

Of course, the critical question is *not* "What kinds of human beings *do we wish* to produce?", but rather, "What kinds of human beings *should be* produced?" Explain why this latter question is the significant one. What rationally defensible answer can you give to this question in terms of the kind of society we ought to produce?

3. If you have good reasons for believing

(a) that teaching some matter to someone is both necessary and sufficient for the society's coming to possess a certain characteristic

and

(b) that the society ought to possess that characteristic,

then you have good reasons for the belief that the characteristic is a social outcome of education that ought to occur.

4. If you have good reasons for believing

(a) that the society ought to have that characteristic

but

(b) that teaching some matter to someone is sufficient but not necessary for society's coming to have that characteristic,

then you do *not necessarily* have good reasons for the belief that the characteristic is a social outcome of education that ought to occur.

In such a case, you must have other reasons for believing that the possession of the characteristic is a social outcome of education that ought to occur.

5. From time to time, reexamine your decisions and beliefs concerning the social outcomes of education by

(a) reassessing your arguments and the arguments of others in the light of additional evidence gathered from reading, continued study, and so on;

(b) reassessing the reasonableness of the ethical theory you hold.

A STRATEGY FOR DECIDING ON INDIVIDUAL OUTCOMES

In making decisions concerning the social outcomes of education, you may also have made some decisions concerning outcomes for certain individuals. This is possible because of the relationship between social outcomes and individual outcomes (see Chapter 12). Of course, whether or not it occurs will depend upon the specific characteristics you believe the society should possess. If, however, you have not identified any individual outcomes in your decisions concerning social outcomes or if you have not as yet considered the question of social outcomes, there is a strategy that you can employ in making rational decisions concerning individual outcomes of education. As you will see, this strategy closely parallels that for making decisions concerning social outcomes.

Since you are now concerned with the outcomes of education for an individual, you should begin by making a serious study of that particular individual. In other words, you should deal with the real person and not some hypothetical construct. What beliefs should this person come to possess? Are there any beliefs that he or she should not have? For example, should the person acquire some scientific beliefs? If so, what kinds? And how sophisticated should the person's understanding of science become?

We can ask similar questions with regard to skills. Are there any specific skills that this person ought to have? Are there certain kinds of skills (such as musical skills, reasoning skills, or reading skills) that he or she ought to have? And if so, to what degree should the person acquire them?

Next, there are decisions to be made regarding dispositions. Are there any particular dispositions that the person ought to acquire? For instance, should he or she develop the disposition to question things and demand reasons? Or should the person become more accepting and intellectually docile? And what are the appropriate dispositions of emotion? Are there certain things to which the person should attach positive emotions—such as honesty, kindness, and courage—or negative emotions? Finally, you must consider dispositions of behavior. What, if any, behavioral dispositions ought the person to have? Are there any that he or she ought not to have? To what degree should each of the desirable dispositions be achieved?

In order to sort out these questions, it is helpful to begin by asking yourself about the person's way of life. Specifically, what should be the characteristics of that person's way of life in, say, five, ten, or twenty years? Should the person become a professional—a physician, an engineer, a business executive, for example? Should he or she appreciate and regularly read good literature? Respect the law? Read and speak more than one language?

As you try to identify the characteristics you believe this person's way of life ought to possess, you need to take into consideration the realities of the world. In particular, you must have good reasons for believing that this particular person's way of life could actually take on that characteristic. For unless you have a reasonable expectation that the person's way of life can actually have that characteristic, you seriously weaken your argument for thinking that it ought to. Moreover, if you have good reasons for thinking that it would not be possible for the person's way of life to have that characteristic, you have good reasons for thinking that it is not the case that his or her way of life *ought* to possess that characteristic. For if something cannot occur, it cannot be the case that it ought to occur.

This observation presents an important problem, however. For instance, suppose that you are trying to make a rational decision concerning Charlie's way of life. And you begin by reasoning that Charlie should be some sort of executive with a large corporation. His scores on aptitude and achievement tests indicate that he is best suited for this kind of occupation. Moreover, your own observations tend to confirm this point. But at the same time, you recognize that Charlie is the son of a coal miner who has contracted black lung disease. Charlie's family's financial situation is such that not only can he not afford to go to college but he is also going to have to drop out of high school in his junior year. He will probably go to work in the mines to support himself and his family, and you have very good evidence for your belief that those who drop out of school to work in the mines do not later complete college and become business executives. Rather, they live out their lives in the coal mines.

When you began your investigation, you determined that, other things being equal, Charlie should become a business executive. But a closer examination of the real world has shown you that other things are *not* equal and that it is not realistic to believe that Charlie might actually become a corporate executive.

The impossibility of Charlie's becoming an executive is due not to the reality of the physical world but to the reality of the social world. If the social world were different, it might be quite possible for him to become an executive. For example, if ill people and their families were given adequate financial support by the government, and if a high-quality college education were available to everyone, and so on, then it would actually be possible for Charlie to become an executive.

Is it the case that Charlie's way of life ought not to include his being a business executive simply because he cannot actually become one given prevailing social conditions? Or should those social conditions be changed so that Charlie can become what you have determined, on the grounds of aptitude and achievement, he ought to become? This problem is clearly a moral one, and a rational solution will require that you determine what morally ought to occur—what is morally better—in this situation. In addition, it should be obvious that dealing rationally with this problem will involve you in a renewed consideration of what the social outcomes of education ought to be.

In more general terms, when you try to make a rational decision concerning the individual outcomes of education for a particular person, you may find that because of certain social conditions it is highly improbable that a certain individual outcome could actually occur. But, at the same time, there may be very good reasons for believing that that particular outcome ought to occur *if* it could occur. And if those social conditions could actually be changed, you are presented with a moral problem that must be resolved: Should those social conditions be changed, or should you not try to produce the individual outcome? Your task is to identify the most rationally defensible position and to make your decisions accordingly.

There is yet another problem that you could encounter. You might identify a characteristic that you believe a person's way of life ought to have. However, closer examination might show that if this characteristic is to occur, someone else's way of life will have to have a characteristic that—on other grounds—you have good reason for believing it ought not to have. This possibility exists because of the relationships we discussed in Chapter 12.

For example, suppose that in thinking about Jane's way of life you identify some good reasons for believing that she should become wealthy and
have many servants. But further consideration leads you to the conclusion that no one should be anyone's servant. Obviously, there is an in-
consistency. The two beliefs cannot both be true. Your problem in such
a case is to determine which of the conflicting positions is the most rationally defensible one and to make your decisions accordingly.

As a general rule, then, you begin your investigation by determining
some characteristics that a person's way of life ought to have. Once this
is done, you can determine which of these are outcomes of education.

First, you should determine whether or not the person's having been
taught something is both necessary and sufficient for the occurrence of
the characteristic being considered. For instance, suppose you have determined that Paul should become an electrical engineer. It is reasonable to
believe that in order for this to occur, Paul must be taught some mathematics and physics, it being highly improbable that he would learn these
subjects if they were not taught to him. That is, a necessary condition for
his becoming an electrical engineer is that he is taught these subjects. If
you also have some good reasons for believing that Paul's acquisition of
these understandings (along with certain other things) is sufficient for his
becoming an electrical engineer, then you have good reasons for believing
that his becoming an electrical engineer is an individual outcome of education. And if his way of life ought to be characterized by his being an
electrical engineer, then, for Paul, being an electrical engineer is an individual outcome of education that ought to occur.

On the other hand, you may find that teaching some matter to a person
is sufficient but not necessary for the occurrence of a certain characteristic. As we saw in our consideration of social outcomes, if this is the case,
then knowing that the person's way of life ought to have the characteristic is not *by itself* a good reason for believing that having that characteristic is an individual outcome of education that ought to occur.
Additional reasons will have to be given if you wish to establish this belief.

We can summarize this strategy for making intelligent decisions concerning the outcomes of education for a particular person as follows:

1. Consider the person with the intention of identifying some characteristics that his or her way of life ought to have.

   > For every characteristic you identify, you must have good rea-
   > sons for believing that the person's way of life can actually
   > come to include it.

   > You may find that while the person's way of life ought to have
   > a certain characteristic, social conditions make its acquisition
   > highly improbable. In such a case, you will have to identify the
   > most rationally defensible position with regard to whether the
   > social conditions ought to be changed.

You may also find that in order for the person's way of life to have one of these characteristics, someone else's way of life must come to include a characteristic that, on other grounds, it ought not to include. In such a case, you will have to determine which of the conflicting positions is the most rationally defensible.

2. After you have identified a characteristic that you have good reasons for believing the person's way of life ought to include, determine whether that characteristic must be an individual outcome of education or whether it could but need not be. That is, determine whether teaching some matter to the person is both necessary and sufficient *or* sufficient but not necessary for the acquisition of that characteristic.

3. If you have good reasons for believing

   (a) that teaching some matter to the individual is both necessary and sufficient for the person's way of life coming to have the characteristic

   and

   (b) that the person's way of life ought to have the characteristic,

   then you have good reasons for believing that having the characteristic is an individual outcome of education that ought to occur.

4. If you have good reasons for believing

   (a) that the person's way of life ought to have that characteristic

   but

   (b) that teaching the person some matter is sufficient but not necessary for coming to have it,

   then you do not necessarily have good reasons for believing that the characteristic is an individual outcome of education that ought to occur.

   In such a case, you must have other reasons for believing that the possession of the characteristic is an individual outcome of education that ought to occur.

5. From time to time, reexamine your decisions and beliefs concerning the outcomes of education for a particular individual by

   (a) reassessing your arguments and the arguments of others in the light of additional evidence gathered from reading, continued study, and so on;

   (b) reassessing the reasonableness of the ethical theory you hold.

Attempting to determine rationally what the individual outcomes of education for a child ought to be requires considering the way of life that he or she ought to have:

> What can a teacher say to a child who has nothing and is nothing? . . . He needs to be convinced of his innate capability. But how? The only plausible approach is to convince him that his inherited disadvantages are really no fault of his own. Rather, he is deprived because his family and friends have long been exploited by those who control the real sources of power. Although his exploiters may possess the best of intentions, he will continue to remain the victim of social injustice until he learns to manipulate American institutions so that in fact he becomes the political as well as moral equal of his oppressors.
>
> In effect the preceding advice advocates social revolution. It asserts that the poor should have more power simply because their poverty indicates a need for it. It contends that the poor and ignorant, whether they perform wisely or not as judged by the standards of more affluent Americans, should be taught in school to manipulate the larger society for their own ends. It assumes that the aspirations and self-respect of the impoverished will not rise until they have been able to participate effectively in decision-making processes. (Richard R. Renner, "Schools and the Poor: The High Cost of Classroom Candor," *Educational Forum*, November 1967, pp. 58–59.)

Why do you agree (or disagree) with this position? What conditions should characterize the way of life of a poor child? Explain. Which of these conditions are individual outcomes of education? Why are they?

MORAL AND NONMORAL WORTH OF DECISIONS CONCERNING EDUCATIONAL OUTCOMES

The two strategies that we have just identified consider decisions concerning outcomes from the point of view of moral obligations. As we saw in Chapter 9, a decision can always be considered and questioned from this point of view. And since it is important to know whether or not you are under any moral obligations to make or not to make a certain decision, these issues should be dealt with first.

If, in a given situation, you find that you have very strong reasons for believing that you morally ought (or ought not) to make a particular decision, then other points of view are more or less irrelevant. However, in many cases, you may determine that the strongest argument supports the belief that you are under no moral obligations to make one decision as opposed to another. In such an event, it would become not only relevant but also important to consider the alternatives from other points of view.

If, in considering educational outcomes, you determine that you are under no moral obligation to make a particular decision, you should next examine the various alternatives from the point of view of their moral worth. Is one outcome morally better than the others? Are there several outcomes that have essentially the same moral worth? Are there some that are morally bad?

Suppose that you have determined that for a given set of outcomes there are no particular decisions that morally ought to be made. You could still make a rational decision by producing a strong argument to the effect that bringing about one of the outcomes would be morally better than bringing about any of the others. The stronger your argument is, the more rational your decision.

But, suppose that there are no good reasons for believing that one outcome is morally better than any of several other alternatives. Instead, you have good reasons for believing that some of the alternatives are of essentially the same moral value. In such a case, you would have good reasons for pursuing all of those alternatives. However, you may also find that it is not possible for you to pursue *all* of them. Limitations of time, labor, resources, money, and so on, may allow you to pursue only one or two, certainly not all.

In other words, the moral evidence, although important, is not sufficient for making a reasoned choice from among the morally good alternatives. It is at this point that nonmoral considerations become significant. Are some of those alternatives *nonmorally* better than some others? Are there certain decisions that you ought to make *if* something is to occur? Are there certain decisions that you ought to make *only if* something is to occur? In trying to determine the alternative that has the strongest nonmoral reasons supporting it, you will have to use different nonmoral good-bad scales and different conditions with regard to your nonmoral "ought" beliefs. In each case, of course, you will have to be able to show that these particular scales and conditions are relevant.

In the final analysis, how intelligently you make your decisions concerning the outcomes of education will depend on the strength of your arguments. And this in turn will depend on how well you meet the criteria considered in previous chapters, most importantly: clarity of key terms, truth and relevance of premises, deductive or inductive strength of the argument, reasonableness of ethical theory, and relevance of any nonmoral points of view.

Review

1. Define each of the following terms used in this chapter:

Outcome of education
Social outcome of education

Individual outcome of education

Necessary and sufficient condition

Sufficient but not necessary condition

2. Explain why in trying to determine what the social outcomes of education ought to be it is helpful to begin by considering your own society and the way of life that it ought to have.

3. Discuss why it is that some people do not seriously try to identify rational beliefs concerning what the social outcomes of education ought to be for their society.

4. Explain why (a) having good reasons for believing that teaching some matter to some people is both necessary and sufficient for your society's coming to have a certain characteristic and (b) having good reasons for believing that your society ought to have that characteristic together amount to having good reasons for believing that having this characteristic is a social outcome of education that ought to occur.

5. Identify and discuss the strategy for making intelligent decisions concerning social outcomes of education.

6. Identify and discuss some moral problems that arise if the actual occurrence of an individual outcome—one that ought to occur if it could occur—is improbable because of certain social conditions.

7. Identify and discuss some moral problems that arise if you initially have some good reasons for believing that someone's way of life ought to have a certain characteristic but then determine that if this occurs, someone else's way of life will have to possess a characteristic that you have good reason to believe it ought not to have.

8. Explain how to determine whether a certain characteristic of a person's way of life must be or could be an individual outcome of education.

9. Identify and discuss the strategy for making intelligent decisions concerning individual outcomes of education.

10. Show under what conditions different nonmoral points of view are relevant to making intelligent decisions concerning the outcomes of education.

Making
Intelligent Decisions
Concerning the
Matter of Education

A s with decisions concerning outcomes, there are many different strategies that you might profitably employ in making intelligent decisions concerning the matter of education. In this chapter, we will consider some of these strategies and see how they can be used in trying to identify a rationally defensible position concerning what to teach to whom. Our examination will proceed primarily from the point of view of what morally ought to be done. The concluding section will review how other normative points of view may be relevant.

REASONING FROM INDIVIDUAL OUTCOMES TO THE MATTER OF EDUCATION

One way of making rational decisions concerning the matter of a person's education involves first showing that certain individual outcomes of education ought to occur, then arguing that the person ought to be taught some particular matter. In other words, this strategy involves reasoning from the fact that certain outcomes ought to occur to the conclusion that certain matter ought to be taught.

For example, suppose that you have good reasons for believing that Tim's way of life ought to be characterized by kindness, that is, that he should have the disposition to be kind. And suppose that you also have good reasons for believing that teaching him this disposition is both necessary and sufficient* for his actually being kind. As we saw in Chapter 13, these would be good reasons for believing that the disposition to be kind is an outcome of education that ought to occur for Tim. But in addition to being good reasons for a decision concerning outcomes, they are also good reasons for a decision concerning matter—for the decision to teach Tim this disposition. Whenever you have good reasons for believing that a certain individual outcome ought to occur for a person and that teaching that person some matter is both necessary and sufficient for its occurrence, you also have good reasons for teaching that matter to the person.

However, a caution is necessary. The reasons will be good reasons only for the decision to teach the precise matter that you have shown to be necessary for the occurrence of the particular outcome. For instance, suppose that you have good reasons for believing that teaching Debbie some mathematics is necessary for her becoming a computer engineer. And at the same time you also have good reasons for believing that she ought to be a computer engineer. These can be good reasons for the decision to teach Debbie some mathematics without necessarily being good reasons for a decision to teach her calculus, for example. Additional reasons will be required if this latter decision is to be made rationally.

This, then, is one strategy that you could use in trying to make rational decisions concerning the matter of someone's education. However, in many cases it may not be possible to identify a strong argument for believing that teaching someone some particular matter is *both* necessary and sufficient for the occurrence of a certain outcome—even though you may have good reasons for believing that it is an outcome of education that ought to occur for the particular person.

For example, suppose that you have determined that David ought to be-

---

*We will continue to use "sufficient" to mean "sufficient by itself or in conjunction with some other conditions."

come a musician. Teaching him to play the piano might be sufficient for this, but it obviously is not necessary. Hence, the argument

> David ought to become a musician.
>
> Teaching David to play the piano is sufficient for his becoming a musician.
> _____
>
> David ought to be taught to play the piano.

is quite weak. In fact, examination will show that it is a version of the invalid argument form "affirming the consequent," which we discussed in Chapter 5. Even if the premises of this argument are true and relevant, they do not supply very good evidence for the conclusion. Consequently, additional reasons are required if you are to rationally make the decision to teach David to play the piano.

Although reasoning from individual outcomes to a conclusion about the matter of a person's education is often an effective strategy for making rational decisions, there is a danger inherent in its use. The danger is the tendency to disregard possible "side consequences" of teaching certain matter to someone.

For example, suppose that, reasoning from individual outcomes to a decision concerning matter, you identify some good reasons for believing that John ought to be taught the disposition to read literature of other countries. In particular, suppose that you identify some good reasons for believing that he ought to become a cultured, sensitive person and that reading literature of other countries is sufficient for the acquisition of this characteristic. If you limit yourself to this line of reasoning, you may not make a very good (or very rational) decision. It may be, for example, that teaching John to read the literature of other countries is sufficient not only for his becoming a cultured, sensitive person but also for his becoming committed to radically revolutionizing your society. Now if he ought *not* to become a revolutionary and if teaching him to read the literature of other countries is sufficient for his becoming one, then you have good reasons for *not* teaching him to read the literature of other countries.

That is, reasoning from certain outcomes that you believe ought to occur, you may appear to have very good reasons for making a certain decision concerning matter. However, this limited perspective may lead you to make an improper decision. For in reasoning from a particular outcome to a decision concerning matter, you may fail to recognize that teaching that matter will have other outcomes, outcomes that ought not to occur.

When you reason from an outcome to a decision concerning matter, you should also reason from teaching that matter to other probable outcomes. More precisely, after you have identified some initial reasons for teaching certain matter to someone, you should consider the probable additional outcomes of teaching the person that matter. Clearly, you will have already identified some good reasons for believing that teaching it will have the original outcome. And you will also have some reasons for thinking that this outcome ought to occur. However, further consideration may uncover good reasons for believing that teaching it will have additional consequences, some or all of which ought not to occur. In such a case, you will have to carefully examine the different arguments and determine which of the conflicting positions is the most rationally defensible. In particular, when other probable outcomes are considered, are there better reasons for teaching or for not teaching that matter to that person? Answering this question will require that you reconsider your decisions and beliefs concerning the outcomes of education (see Chapter 13).

In summary, then, this strategy for making rational decisions concerning the matter of a person's education is as follows:

1. Identify an individual outcome of education that ought to occur.

2. If possible, identify a strong argument that shows that teaching the person some particular matter is both necessary and sufficient for the occurrence of the outcome.

3. Using the beliefs established in steps 1 and 2, argue that the matter identified in step 2 ought to be taught to the person.

    Consider whether teaching the person this matter has additional probable consequences.

    If there might be additional outcomes, consider whether there are good reasons for believing that some or all of them ought *not* to occur. If you find that some of these outcomes ought not to occur, you will have to determine which is the more rationally defensible position: to teach the person that matter and produce some outcomes that ought to occur and some that ought not to occur or to not teach the person that matter and forego the original outcome.

4. If you cannot identify any strong reasons for believing that teaching the person some particular matter is necessary for the occurrence of the outcome identified in step 1, then even though you may have good reasons for believing that it is sufficient, you cannot properly argue that it ought to be taught only on the grounds that it is sufficient for the outcome. (That is, it would not be rational to base a decision to teach certain matter on the fact that teaching it is sufficient—but not necessary—for the occurrence of a particular outcome—even if that outcome ought to occur.)

    To make a rational decision in such a case, you must have reasons in addition to the fact that the outcome ought to occur and teaching some matter is sufficient for its occurrence.

Moreover, you must consider whether there are good reasons for believing that there will be additional outcomes that ought not to occur. If there are, you will have to take these arguments into consideration in determining the most rationally defensible position.

5. As with the other strategies we have discussed, you should, from time to time, reexamine your decisions and beliefs concerning the matter of a person's education by

---

Consider the following example of reasoning from outcomes to decisions concerning the matter of young people's education:

> A knowledge of science is essential for understanding modern society, its achievements and its problems. A certain literacy in science is necessary if young people are to be able to cope with a rapidly changing modern scientific world. Scientists are generating new knowledge at a faster pace than ever before. By the time children, now in the first grade, finish high school, our present knowledge of science will have doubled in amount.
>
> Science education is also becoming increasingly complex. Young people require an education in the sciences which will provide them with the intellectual skills necessary to read and understand the changing content of science. They need to acquire skills that will allow them to keep up in some manner with new knowledge as it is generated throughout their lifetimes. . . .
>
> The experimental and conceptual methodology of science provides the source for one major goal. This goal is characterized in terms of the processes of science, systematic inquiry, experimental investigation, and intellectual-cognitive skills. It appears reasonable that if a person is to cope with the problems of today as well as tomorrow, he will need to be capable in the ways of knowing and in critical reflection. He needs to know something of the methods of inquiry practiced in science investigations. Acquisition of knowledge is also a goal of science teaching, the kind of knowledge that may be organized into testable ideas, and from which generalizations and hypotheses may be abstracted for seeking insight into new problems and appreciating new developments. (Paul DeHart Hurd, "New Directions in Science Teaching: K-College," *Education,* December 1966, pp. 210–11.)

What individual outcomes of education does the statement suggest ought to occur for young people? What does it suggest young people should be taught? Are good reasons given for teaching the matter recommended? Explain. Is this matter necessary and/or sufficient for the occurrence of the outcomes?

Why do you agree (or disagree) with the statement concerning the matter that should be taught?

(a) reassessing your arguments and those of others in the light of new evidence;

(b) reassessing the reasonableness of the ethical theory you hold.

REASONING FROM SOCIAL OUTCOMES TO THE MATTER OF EDUCATION

You can also reason from social outcomes to decisions concerning the matter of education. If you have good reasons for believing that a society ought to have a certain characteristic and if you have good reasons for believing that teaching someone some particular matter is both necessary and sufficient for this, then you have some good reasons for thinking that the particular matter ought to be taught.

For example, suppose that you have some good reasons for believing that your society should be technologically advanced. You might then reason that in order for this to occur, some of its members must be taught certain things, such as mathematics, physics, chemistry, biology, and so on. As we have seen, this would be a strong argument for deciding to teach that matter.

However, it is important to recognize that such an argument could establish only that *some* members of the society ought to be taught those things. It would not in itself provide good reasons for teaching any of that matter to a *particular* person. That is, having good reasons for believing that some people ought to be taught physics is not the same as having good reasons for believing that Sam or Joan ought to be taught physics. And this fact points out a significant difference between arguing from individual outcomes to decisions concerning the matter of a person's education and arguing from social outcomes.

Nevertheless, it is possible to make a rational decision to teach some matter to a particular individual and to base that decision on the fact that certain social outcomes ought to occur. However, this will necessitate your having some additional reasons that support the belief that this particular person ought to be taught that matter.

For example, you might argue that since your society should continue to develop its technological capacity, mathematics and physics ought to be taught to some of its children. Then, on other grounds—such as a moral principle of fairness—you might argue that these subjects ought to be taught to all children: it would not be fair to teach it to some but not to others. Or, you might maintain a different position based upon yet another ethical principle. You might hold, for example, that equals should be treated equally and that unequals should be treated unequally. Your argument might continue that since some children are by inheritance or family position better suited to be the technological leaders of society, they are the ones who should be taught the requisite mathematics and science. Other children, because they are not as well suited, need not be taught these subjects.

The point here is that reasoning from social outcomes to the matter of a person's education can be helpful in trying to make rational decisions concerning matter. However, in order for this strategy to result in a rational decision to teach some particular matter to a particular person, you must have reasons in addition to those that support the beliefs that certain social outcomes ought to occur and that teaching some matter to some people is necessary for this occurrence.

You should also realize that it may not be possible to identify a strong argument for believing that teaching some matter is both necessary and sufficient for the occurrence of a particular social outcome. If you determine that a social outcome ought to occur and that teaching someone some matter is sufficient but not necessary for the occurrence of the outcome, you have not established strong reasons for teaching that matter— and certainly not strong reasons for teaching that matter to a particular person. Additional reasons will be required if you are to make a rational decision to teach that matter to a particular person.

In addition, when you reason from social outcomes to decisions concerning the matter of a person's education, you must be careful to determine whether there are other probable consequences of teaching the matter you have in mind. Then, you should determine whether any of these side consequences ought not to occur (see Chapter 13); these side consequences may be either social outcomes or individual outcomes. Finally, you will have to determine whether, given the probability of some undesirable consequences, it is more rationally defensible to teach that matter or to not teach it.

We can summarize this strategy for making rational decisions concerning the matter of a person's education as follows:

1. Identify a social outcome of education that ought to occur.

2. If possible, identify a strong argument that shows that teaching someone some particular matter is both necessary and sufficient for the occurrence of that outcome.

    Remember that the most that such an argument can establish is that *some* members of the society ought to be taught that matter.

3. Identify good reasons for teaching that matter to a *particular* person (or group of persons).

    Consider whether teaching the person this matter has additional probable outcomes.

    ·If there would be additional outcomes, are there any good reasons for believing that some or all of them ought *not* to occur? If so, determine which is the more rationally defensible posi-

Many people believe that one of the primary social outcomes of education ought to be world peace:

> Preventing World War III is common cause today. Part of the effort is educational. Just as wars start in the minds of men, so might the creation of a peaceful world. Earlier generations of peace educators conceived of their task as one of rational persuasion, convincing the apathetic and uninformed that wars could be forever avoided by adopting some special plan for world government. Today peace education is shifting from salesmanship to enlightenment. Its new mission is to inform and enlighten the public about the problems of building a safe and just world order. . . .
>
> There is widespread, although not universal, agreement that the avoidance of World War III requires drastic revisions in the structure of international society. In particular, there is agreement on the need to transfer the control of military power from nations to international institutions. This outlook usually includes at least total national disarmament, an international police force, and some means by which to "legislate" changes in international life so as to be able to unfreeze the status quo from time to time. It usually assumes, as well, that despite these profound changes in the international environment, national governments will remain the dominant political and economic units in the world. . . .
>
> This search for politically relevant forms of peace education is the essence of the educational endeavor. Such political relevance is achieved, above all, by the adoption of an informed and rigorous set of intellectual tools for the analysis of international behavior. . . .
>
> Despite this new intellectual climate, relatively little is being done in the United States to educate the student generation about the problems of world order. (Richard A. Falk, "The Revolution in Peace Education," *Saturday Review,* 21 May 1966, pp. 59–60.)

Is "international order" something that we should strive to produce? Is it possible? Is it an educational outcome? What would people have to be taught in order for it to occur?

tion: to teach the person that matter and produce some (social and/or individual) outcomes that ought to occur and some that ought not to occur or to not teach the person the matter and forego the original outcome.

4. If you cannot identify any strong reasons for believing that teaching some particular matter is necessary for the occurrence of the social outcome identified in step 1, you cannot properly argue that it ought to be taught only on the grounds that it is sufficient for the outcome.

You must have reasons in addition to the fact that the outcome ought to occur and that teaching some matter is sufficient for its occurrence.

Moreover, even further reasons must be given to support the decision to teach that matter to a particular person.

Also, you must consider whether there are good reasons for believing that there will be additional outcomes that ought not to occur. If there are, you will have to take these arguments into consideration in determining the most rationally defensible position.

5. From time to time, you should reexamine your decisions and beliefs concerning the matter of a person's education by

   (a) reassessing your arguments and those of others in the light of new evidence;

   (b) reassessing the reasonableness of the ethical theory you hold.

ANOTHER STRATEGY: BEGINNING WITH THE MATTER

Instead of reasoning from beliefs concerning outcomes to a decision concerning the matter of a person's education, you can sometimes begin with a belief about the matter. That is, in considering what to teach a person, you might begin with a belief that some particular matter ought to be taught and then search for reasons to support that belief.

One version of this strategy involves arguing for teaching some particular matter to someone on the grounds that the person's acquiring certain beliefs, understandings, skills, or dispositions is worthwhile in itself. For example, you might reason that it would be good to teach John history, because having an understanding of history is valuable in itself. In other words, any additional outcomes of John's understanding history are not what makes his understanding history a good thing—even though those additional outcomes may themselves be good.

There are, of course, other kinds of arguments that contain no reference to additional outcomes. It might even be possible for you to offer a strong argument of this sort in some situations. But this fact does not mean that additional outcomes are irrelevant to your decision, only that no reference to them need be made in offering a strong argument. And while you may be able to offer a strong argument that makes no reference to additional outcomes, you should nevertheless *consider* those outcomes.

For example, suppose that you have some good reasons for believing that you ought to teach some particular matter to someone. And suppose that none of these reasons make reference to the outcomes of teaching the

The following excerpt contains an interesting argument in support of the belief that children should be taught "knowledge [that is: beliefs and understandings] in all its forms":

> To ask for a justification for the pursuit of knowledge is not at all the same thing as to ask for the justification for, say, teaching all children a foreign language or making them orderly and punctual in their behaviour. It is in fact a peculiar question asking for justification for any development of the rational mind at all. To ask for the justification of any form of activity is significant only if one is in fact committed already to seeking rational knowledge. To ask for a justification of the pursuit of rational knowledge itself therefore presupposes some form of commitment to what one is seeking to justify. Justification is possible only if what is being justified is both intelligible under publicly rooted concepts and is assessable according to accepted criteria. It assumes a commitment to these two principles. But these very principles are in fact fundamental to the pursuit of knowledge in all its forms, be it, for instance, empirical knowledge or understanding in the arts. The forms of knowledge are in a sense simply the working out of these general principles in particular ways. To give justification to any kind of knowledge therefore involves using the principles in one specific form to assess their use in another. Any particular activity can be examined for its rational character, for its adherence to these principles, and thus justified on the assumption of them. Indeed in so far as activities are rational this will be possible. It is commitment to them that characterizes any rational activity as such. But the principles themselves have no such assessable status, for justification outside the use of the principles is not logically possible. (Paul H. Hirst, "Liberal Education and the Nature of Knowledge," in *Philosophical Analysis and Education,* ed. R. D. Archambault [New York: Humanities Press, 1965], pp. 126–27.)

Assess the strength of this argument. Is there a stronger argument that could be offered *against* teaching children "knowledge in all its forms"? Explain your answer.

person that matter. Someone else may offer a counter-argument to the effect that the person ought not to be taught that matter on the grounds that doing so will produce outcomes that ought not to occur. As we have seen, you would have to seriously consider this counter-argument to determine whether it is stronger than your argument.

Proponents and opponents of uncensored reading materials for school children often disagree in this way. One group argues that any matter a child wants to read should be part of the matter of his or her education. And their reasons for this usually make no reference to the outcomes of reading the material. Rather, they stress a person's rights (both legal and moral) and the intrinsic value of knowledge. The opponents, on the other hand, argue that if children read certain things—usually those having to do with sex or violence or those advocating a different political system—certain individual or social consequences will occur that ought not to occur.

In general, you can begin with a belief that some matter ought to be taught to someone and develop a good argument without making any references to the outcomes for that person. However, you should always *consider* the probable outcomes (both individual and social) of teaching that matter to that person. In doing so, you should try to determine whether there are any strong arguments to support the claim that some or all of those outcomes ought not to occur. If there are such arguments, you will have to determine how much support they (along with some other reasons) afford the claim that the matter ought not to be taught to the person. And finally, you will have to compare the relative strengths of the opposing arguments concerning whether the matter should be taught to the person.

REASONING FROM DECISIONS OF MATTER TO OTHER DECISIONS OF MATTER

The final strategy we will consider involves reasoning from one decision concerning matter to another decision concerning matter. For example, suppose that you have determined that you have very good reasons for the decision to teach Deborah calculus. On the basis of this, you can easily justify the decision to teach her arithmetic. Your argument might be

> Deborah ought to be taught calculus.
>
> In order for her to acquire an understanding of calculus, she must have an understanding of arithmetic.
> _____
> Deborah ought to be taught arithmetic.

This reasoning is based upon certain relationships between different understandings, skills, and dispositions. Specifically, there are many cases in which the possession of one understanding, for example, is a necessary condition for acquiring another understanding. For instance, you would have to understand what taxation is before you could formulate any rational beliefs concerning how people should be taxed. Likewise, it is necessary to have acquired the skill of running before you can acquire the skill of being a wide-receiver in football. And in order to have the disposition to read good literature, you must have acquired the skill of being able to read.

If you can show that there are good reasons for teaching certain matter to someone *and* that teaching some other matter is *necessary* to accomplish this, then you have some good reasons for a decision to teach the person that other matter.

Of course, as in other cases we have considered, you should also examine the decision for possible side consequences. For even though teaching some other matter may be necessary, it may be that doing so will have outcomes that you have good reason to believe ought not to occur. In such a case, you will have to assess the strengths of the arguments in support of and opposed to the decision to teach that matter.

Another way of reasoning from a decision concerning matter to a different decision concerning matter involves showing that teaching a certain matter is sufficient but not necessary for teaching some other matter. For example, suppose that you have determined that there are good reasons for teaching your students that they should be wary of politicians who promise sudden economic improvement or denigrate a particular cultural group. Teaching certain things about Hitler and his rise to power might be sufficient for teaching them to be wary of such demagogues, but it certainly is not necessary. Nevertheless, you might argue that it would be good (or that you ought) to teach them about Hitler on the grounds that doing so would be sufficient for teaching them to be wary of demagogues.

Like other instances of trying to justify a decision on the grounds that it is sufficient for the occurrence of something else, your argument would not be a very strong argument. If you are to make a rational decision in such a case, you must have reasons in addition to the claim that teaching that matter is sufficient for teaching some other matter. Moreover, as we have also seen, you must consider whether there are any probable side consequences of teaching that matter and whether there are good reasons for believing that some or all of them ought not to occur. Such an examination might result in your identifying an even stronger argument against the original decision.

We can summarize the strategy of reasoning from one decision concerning the matter of a person's education to another decision concerning the matter of the person's education as follows:

1. You have already determined that someone ought to be taught certain matter.

2. Determine whether teaching some other matter is a necessary condition for teaching the person the matter identified in step 1.

    If it is, then you have some good initial reasons for teaching the person this other matter.

    You should also consider whether teaching the person this other matter has additional probable outcomes.

If there are additional outcomes, are there any good reasons for believing that some or all of them ought *not* to occur? If so, determine which is the more rationally defensible alternative: to teach the person that matter and produce some outcomes that ought to occur and some that ought not to occur or to not teach the person that matter and forego teaching the matter identified in step 1.

3. If you cannot determine that teaching some other matter is necessary for teaching the person the matter identified in step 1, you might nevertheless be able to identify some good reasons for thinking that teaching it is sufficient.

However, you would have a very weak argument if you claimed that the person ought to be taught this other matter on the sole

---

In recent years, many educators have emphasized the notion of "readiness." They believe that a teacher should not attempt to teach a child any matter until the child is "ready" to learn it. What should be taught at a given time, they reason, depends upon what the particular child is ready to learn. The following position takes exception to this view:

The "curriculum revolution" has made it plain even after only a decade that the idea of "readiness" is a mischievous half-truth. It is a half-truth largely because it turns out that one *teaches* readiness or provides opportunities for its nurture; one does not simply wait for it. Readiness, in these terms, consists of mastery of those simpler skills that permit one to reach higher skills. Readiness for Euclidian geometry can be gained by teaching intuitive geometry or by giving children an opportunity to build increasingly elaborate constructions with polygons. Or, to take the aim of the new, "second-generation" mathematics project, if you wish to teach the calculus in the eighth grade, then begin it in the first grade by teaching the kinds of ideas and skills necessary for its mastery later. Mathematics is no exception to the general rule, though admittedly it is the most easily understood from the point of view of what must be clear before something else can be grasped. Since most subjects can be translated into forms that place emphasis upon doing, or upon the development of appropriate imagery, or upon symbolic-verbal encoding, it is often possible to render the end result to be achieved in a simpler, more manageable form so that the child can move more easily and deeply to full mastery. (Jerome Bruner, "Education as Social Invention," *Saturday Review,* 19 February 1966, p. 72.)

Why do you agree (or disagree) with this position? Are there any relevant outcomes that need to be considered here? Explain.

ground that doing so is sufficient for teaching the matter identified in step 1.

In such a case, to make a rational decision to teach the person this other matter, you must have reasons in addition to the fact that teaching this other matter is sufficient for teaching some matter that ought to be taught.

You must also consider whether there are good reasons for believing that teaching the person this other matter will have additional outcomes.

If there are probable additional outcomes, are there any good reasons for believing that some or all of them ought *not* to occur? If so, determine which is the more rationally defensible alternative: to teach the person the other matter and produce some outcomes that ought to occur and some that ought not to occur or to not teach the person the matter.

4. From time to time, you should reexamine your decisions and beliefs concerning the matter of a person's education by

   (a) reassessing your arguments and the arguments of others in the light of new evidence;

   (b) reassessing the reasonableness of the ethical theory you hold.

MORAL AND NONMORAL WORTH OF DECISIONS CONCERNING THE MATTER OF EDUCATION

So far, we have considered decisions concerning matter primarily from the point of view of what morally ought to be taught. But as we have seen before, such decisions may also be considered with regard to their moral and nonmoral worth and whether they nonmorally ought to be made. These other points of view, however, are usually not especially relevant unless you have some strong reasons for believing that you are under no moral obligation to teach or not to teach a particular matter.

As a general rule, you should always consider possible decisions first from the point of view of your moral obligations. If the best available evidence indicates that you have no particular moral obligations with regard to the decision under consideration, you should next consider the alternatives in terms of their moral worth. If this does not result in your finding enough evidence for a rational decision, then you should consider the alternatives in terms of their nonmoral worth and what nonmorally ought to be done. Remember, however, that any nonmoral value scale or set of conditions that you employ must be relevant to the decisions under consideration.

Review

1. Define each of the following terms used in this chapter:

   Matter of education
   Matter of a person's education
   Side consequences

2. Explain why it is that having good reasons for believing that a certain individual outcome ought to occur and for believing that teaching some particular matter is both necessary and sufficient for producing that outcome amounts to having good reasons for believing that the matter ought to be taught to that person.
3. Discuss the problem of side consequences as it relates to reasoning from individual outcomes to a decision about the matter of a person's education.
4. Identify and discuss the strategy for making intelligent decisions concerning the matter of a person's education by reasoning from individual outcomes.
5. Identify and discuss some important differences between reasoning from individual outcomes to a decision concerning the matter of a person's education and reasoning from social outcomes to such a decision.
6. Identify and discuss the strategy for making intelligent decisions concerning the matter of a person's education by reasoning from social outcomes.
7. Identify and discuss the strategy that begins with a belief that some matter ought to be taught to a person and then searches for reasons to support the belief.
8. Explain how in many cases the possession of certain understandings, skills, or dispositions is a necessary condition for acquiring others.
9. Identify and discuss the strategy of reasoning from one decision concerning the matter of a person's education to another decision concerning the matter of that person's education.

Making Intelligent Decisions Concerning the Manner of Education

O nce it has been determined that there are good reasons for teaching some matter to someone, a decision must be made concerning *how* to teach it. In order to make such a decision intelligently, you will have to take into consideration the effectiveness of various alternatives and the morality of those alternatives.

This chapter will begin with an examination of the notion of the effectiveness of a manner of education, and it will consider how you can gather evidence for your beliefs concerning effectiveness. It will then consider the factors that influence the morality of a manner. Finally, the chapter will identify a strategy for making intelligent decisions concerning the manner of education.

PREREQUISITES FOR
DETERMINING EFFECTIVENESS

We have defined a manner of education as a way in which some matter could be taught. In order to make an intelligent decision to use a certain manner, you must have good reasons for believing that the manner in question is an actually possible way of teaching some particular matter to a particular person or group. That is, you must have some good reasons for believing that the manner is an *effective* one.

This notion of the effectiveness of a manner is not as simplistic as it may seem. One fact that needs to be recognized is that the effectiveness of a manner is usually a matter of degree. That is, a certain manner may be *more or less* effective. This is always the case when you are considering the effectiveness of a manner in teaching some matter to a group.

For example, suppose that you use a certain manner in trying to teach a group of children about the Franco-Prussian War. The effectiveness of this manner will depend in part upon how many of the children actually acquire the beliefs that you are trying to teach them. If most of them acquire those beliefs as a result of your using that manner, you have a good reason for thinking that the manner is quite effective. On the other hand, if only a small percentage of the children acquire the desired beliefs, clearly the manner used is not very effective.

There is a second way in which the effectiveness of a manner is a matter of degree. Suppose, for example, that you use a certain manner in trying to teach Carol how to row a boat. As a result of your using this manner, she may acquire this skill. But, as we have seen, one acquires a skill to a certain degree. Perhaps Carol can now row a boat, but maybe she cannot row very well. If the desired outcome was that Carol become an expert rower, then, given the actual outcome, the manner was not very effective.

In general, the effectiveness of a manner depends upon the degree to which the intended outcome is achieved. Clearly, certain individual outcomes are the sort that can be achieved with varying degrees of success. Believing, having a skill, and having a disposition are in themselves a matter of degree. Many social outcomes can also be achieved to greater or lesser degrees: an economic system can be more or less fair and equitable, a government can be more or less democratic, and so on. If an intended outcome can be achieved to varying degrees, the effectiveness of a manner depends upon the degree to which the outcome is actually achieved.

Determining how effective a certain manner is, then, requires that you have a clear understanding of the outcome the manner is intended to produce. It is possible for a certain manner to be quite effective in producing one outcome, moderately effective in producing another, and not at all effective in producing a third. Moreover, it may also be that a given manner is very effective in teaching some matter to one person and not effective in teaching that same matter to a different person.

So, in order to determine how effective a manner is, you must have a clear understanding of the outcome to be produced, the manner being considered, and the degree to which the outcome is achieved.

As we saw in Chapter 11, a manner of education usually involves more than just what a teacher does. And it may also exclude many (irrelevant) things a teacher does. Consequently, the clear identification of a particular manner requires that you specify both the relevant things the teacher does *and* the conditions under which they occur. For behaving in way B under conditions C, D, and E is a different manner from behaving in way B under conditions F, G, and H. Once you have a clear understanding of the manner under consideration, the outcomes to be produced, and the degree to which these are to occur, you are in a position to determine how effective that manner is likely to be.

Some research suggests that when teachers behave in certain ways under one set of conditions, outcomes occur that are different from those produced by the same behavior under other conditions. The following statement discusses this point as it relates to the "expository method" of teaching:

> Reception learning, where principles or higher abstractions are presented to the learner and not first "discovered" by him, is an instructional method that serves an important function in classroom learning. It is a method, however, that operates with certain important limitations in the elementary school. Ausubel, in his defense of verbal learning, demonstrates one of the restrictions: the limited power of children below the age of twelve to grasp directly presented, verbal constructs, or to relate those concepts to existing cognitive structure. Children require adequate and time-consuming opportunities to engage in direct operations with the instances, objects, or data from which those abstractions are derived. Reception learning in the elementary school can present children with those instances as examples of "presented" constructs or rules. It is necessary, however, to give adequate time to these presentations, to children's examination of object-examples of those rules or relationships, and to making appropriate transfer to those understandings to other (related) concept examples. (Charlotte A. Crabtree, "Inquiry Approaches: How New and How Valuable?" *Social Education,* November 1966, pp. 523–24.)

According to the statement, what are the relevant conditions under which expository teaching can be successful? Why do you agree (or disagree) with this position? How strong is your argument?

MILL'S METHODS

Like other beliefs, beliefs concerning the effectiveness of a manner in producing certain educational outcomes may be held more or less rationally. In this section, we will examine three methods that can be used for gathering evidence for such beliefs and for assessing the arguments offered in support of them. These methods—popularized by the nineteenth-century English economist and philosopher John Stuart Mill—are ways of gathering evidence for determining whether something is a necessary and/or sufficient condition for something else.

Mill's first method, *the method of agreement,* is a way of showing that one thing is a necessary condition for something else. It can be used in trying to determine whether a certain manner of education is necessary for the occurrence of a particular outcome—that is, in answering the question, "Does this outcome occur *only if* that manner is employed?" To see how the method of agreement works consider the following (greatly simplified) example. Suppose that Peter, Mildred, and Cheryl have become very good spellers. An examination of the different manners used in trying to teach them spelling skills reveals that

Peter was taught by a teacher who stressed phonics, assigned large amounts of homework, and required him to read the dictionary.

Mildred was taught by a teacher who stressed phonics, assigned large amounts of homework, but did not require her to read the dictionary.

Cheryl was taught by a teacher who stressed phonics, did not assign any homework but did require that she read the dictionary.

Now, if we assume that of the conditions—stressing phonics, assigning large amounts of homework, requiring the child to read the dictionary—one is in fact a necessary condition for the occurrence of the outcome that the children are very good spellers, there is good reason to believe that stressing phonics is necessary for producing children who are good spellers.

As indicated, this is an oversimplified example. But its function is not so much to show an actual use of the method of agreement as it is to illustrate the method's essential features. Based upon the principle that a necessary condition for an outcome must be present whenever the outcome occurs, the method of agreement involves the following basic steps:

1. Identify a particular outcome that has occurred in several students (for example, good spelling ability in three students),
2. In each case, identify the probable conditioning factors, that is, the different things that could reasonably be considered manners of education that are necessary for the occurrence of the outcome.

3. Assume that in each case one and only one of the possible conditioning factors is necessary for the occurrence of the outcome.
4. Using the assumption in step 3 and the facts in step 2, argue that the manner that is present in each case is the one necessary for the occurrence of the outcome.

In this way, the method of agreement can be employed to argue that the manner that was used in each case where the desired outcome occurred was the one necessary to produce that outcome.

Now consider a different situation. Suppose that Ramona has become a good speller but Michael and Margaret have not. An examination of ways in which their teachers intended to teach them how to spell reveals that

> Ramona was taught by a teacher who provided positive reinforcement whenever Ramona spelled a word correctly, assigned large amounts of homework, and required her to read the dictionary.
>
> Michael was taught by a teacher who did not provide positive reinforcement whenever Michael spelled a word correctly, did not assign large amounts of homework, but did require that he read the dictionary.
>
> Margaret was taught by a teacher who did not provide positive reinforcement whenever Margaret spelled a word correctly, did assign large amounts of homework, but did not require that she read the dictionary.

If you assume that the list of possible conditioning factors contains one and only one *sufficient* condition for Ramona's having become a good speller, you can use Mill's method of difference to determine which one it is.

The *method of difference* is based upon the principle that if a possible conditioning factor is present when the outcome did *not* occur, then it cannot be a sufficient condition for the occurrence of that outcome. In our example, Michael was required to read the dictionary, but he did not become a good speller. Similarly, Margaret was assigned a large amount of homework and she did not become a good speller. Hence, neither being required to read the dictionary nor being assigned a large amount of homework can be sufficient for making a person a good speller. And since this is so, by the process of elimination, we see that the factor that was actually sufficient for Ramona's becoming a good speller was that her teacher provided positive reinforcement whenever she spelled a word correctly.

The method of difference involves the following basic steps:

1. Identify a particular outcome that has occurred in one case but *not* in several other cases.
2. In the case in which the outcome did occur, identify each of the

probable conditioning factors that could reasonably be considered sufficient for the occurrence of the outcome.

3. Using the factors identified in step 2 as your base, identify other cases in which one or more of those factors occurred but the outcome identified in step 1 did *not* occur.
4. Assume that in the case in which the outcome did occur, one and only one of the possible conditioning factors is sufficient for the occurrence of the outcome.
5. Using the assumption in step 4 and the facts in step 3, determine through a process of elimination which factor identified in step 2 was present in the case in which the outcome did occur but absent in those cases in which the outcome did not occur.

The last of Mill's methods that we will consider is the *method of concomitant variation.* It is based on the principle that if one thing varies in relation to changes in another thing, the change in the one produces the change in the other. The more closely the variations in one thing are correlated with the variations in the other, the greater the probability that one produces the other.

For example, suppose that you are teaching the multiplication tables to two different classes. In teaching the first class, you use a good deal of oral and written drill. But in teaching the second class you use very little drill. In all other respects, you teach the two classes in the same way. However, you observe that the class that has had more drill has mastered the tables to a higher degree than the class that had less drill. Here the outcomes vary directly with the degree to which the manner (that is, drill) is employed. As more drill is used, the desired outcome is achieved more effectively.

The method of concomitant variation involves the following basic steps:

1. Identify several cases in which a particular outcome has occurred in varying degrees (for example, cases in which some children have learned more than others)
2. Identify the probable conditioning factors in those cases whose variations could reasonably be considered sufficient to produce the variations in the outcomes.
3. Assume that a variation in one of the factors identified in step 2 is sufficient to produce variations in the outcome identified in step 1.
4. Using the assumption in step 3, determine how highly the variations in one of the factors identified in step 2 correlate with the variations in the outcomes observed in step 1.

These methods, if used properly, can be very helpful in gathering evidence to support your beliefs concerning the effectiveness of a manner of education in producing a certain outcome. However, their proper use depends upon two considerations.

First, each of Mill's methods requires that you identify the probable conditioning factors of the outcomes. Consequently, you must have good

---

Many educators believe that how well (or how poorly) a child reads affects how well the child does in most academic areas. But why do some children read better than others? Some teachers attribute poor reading ability to a negative self-concept. Thus, they reason that, if you change the child's negative self-concept to a positive one, he or she will begin to read better. One procedure aimed at such a change is known as "self-directive dramatization":

> In recent times the failure of culturally disadvantaged children to make satisfactory progress in reading has come to be associated with the concept they have of themselves. . . .
>
> Self-directive dramatization was used . . . for the purpose of bringing about a change in the pupil's self-concept from a negative to a positive one and for the improvement of reading. . . .
>
> *Self-directive dramatization* of stories . . . refers to the pupil's original, imaginative, spontaneous interpretation of a character of his own choosing in a story which he selects and reads cooperatively with other pupils in a group which is formed only for the time being and for a particular story. It places emphasis upon what the child does instead of upon what the teacher does not do. It is not a new term used for an old activity such as "creative dramatics," although there may be a degree of similarity. Self-directive dramatization involves self-selection of stories, and for this purpose many books of many levels and varieties are available at all times in the classroom. . . .
>
> Significantly greater gains in reading were achieved . . . by groups of culturally disadvantaged elementary school children through the use of classroom self-directive dramatization of stories which pupils selected and read than through the use of methods involving the traditional techniques of the basal readers in small groups or in the whole class. There is also evidence to indicate that through the use of self-directive dramatization favorable changes occurred in the self-concept of the children. (Lessie Carlton and Robert H. Moore, "The Effects of Self-Directive Dramatization on Reading Achievement and Self-Concept of Culturally Disadvantaged Children," *The Reading Teacher,* November 1966, pp. 125, 127, 130.)

Design an experiment that uses Mill's method of difference to test the hypothesis that self-directive dramatization is sufficient for increasing reading skills. Then, design an experiment using Mill's method of agreement to test the hypothesis that self-directive dramatization is necessary for increasing reading skills.

reasons for believing that the factors you identify actually could be necessary or sufficient conditions for the occurrence of the outcome in question. If you do not have good reasons for this belief, it is not proper to use these methods.

For example, suppose that you determine that Bert's teacher always wore a blue suit and a green hat, and that Judy's teacher always wore a blue suit and a brown hat. Both Bert and Judy, you also determined, learned how to read well. Using this data and the method of agreement, you reason that Bert and Judy learned how to read well as a result of their teachers' wearing blue suits. Obviously, your conclusion is absurd: there are no good reasons for believing that the color of a teacher's suit or hat is a necessary condition for a student's learning how to read.

The second condition for the proper use of Mill's methods derives from the fact that with each method you must assume that one and only one of the probable conditioning factors is a necessary or a sufficient condition for the occurrence of the outcome. If this assumption is false, the use of any of these methods will not result in the identification of the manner that produces the outcome. Hence, to properly use Mill's methods, you must have some good reasons for believing that this assumption is true.

To see how this particular false assumption can lead to an erroneous conclusion, consider the following example. Suppose that you find that whenever a strict, authoritarian approach is used in teaching, students learn arithmetic much better than when a more liberal, non-authoritarian approach is used. Resorting to the method of concomitant variation, you argue that using a strict, authoritarian approach is more effective for teaching arithmetic than is a non-authoritarian approach.

At best, you would have a weak argument; there are other factors that may account for the increased learning. For instance, one group's parents may have helped their children with arithmetic at home, whereas the parents of the other group did not. Or, one group may have come to the grade-level with much better preparation for arithmetic than the second group had. The point here is that there are additional factors that need to be taken into consideration before these methods can be properly used to offer a strong argument for your conclusion.

EDUCATIONAL RESEARCH

We have said that Mill's methods can be used as a way of gathering evidence for beliefs concerning the effectiveness of a manner of education. However, there may be many cases in which it is either impossible or impractical for you to employ them. Teachers seldom have the time or the means to engage in the experimentation or systematic observation necessary for the proper use of these methods. But they should still have good reasons for thinking that the particular manner they use will actually result in the desired outcome.

You can overcome the difficulties involved in not being able to gather evidence yourself by consulting the reports of educational researchers. Today, many people are employing scientific methods in an attempt to determine what ways of teaching are effective in producing certain outcomes. Their research is published in scholarly journals and books and may be used as evidence for your beliefs concerning the effectiveness of various manners of education.

Whenever educators talk of the need to experiment in order to determine the rationality of beliefs concerning the effectiveness of manners of education, someone usually questions the morality of experimenting with children:

> Education is evaluated mostly by quasi experiments in which the experimental group is compared with some group that just happened not to get the treatment. These controls may be children whose parents did not enroll them in the compensatory program, or children in a community that did not establish one, or a national "norm group" whose training no one knows about. The important point is this: If the groups were not assigned at random, they may have differed at the outset, and any comparison of end-results is of uncertain meaning. The available statistical techniques cannot give unbiased results, and usually it is impossible to tell whether the bias works for or against the experimental treatment. . . . Decisions have to be made from the facts policy-makers can afford to collect, so quasi experiments are worthwhile. But their ambiguity accounts for a large part of the contention about whether "compensatory education has failed."
>
> Results become clear when groups have been assigned to treatments at random. Then (if everyone stays to the end) the post-test averages tell the story. But it is not easy to arrange for some children of a neighborhood to be helped while ignoring a randomly selected group of controls.
>
> . . . Is it ethical to provide compensatory treatment for a random fraction of children in a neighborhood and not others, in order to make a valid evaluation of the program? (Leo J. Cronbach, *Educational Psychology,* 3rd ed. [New York: Harcourt Brace Jovanovich, 1977], pp. 356–57.)

What is your answer to the excerpt's final question? Offer the strongest argument that you can in support of your answer. What ethical theory does your argument presuppose? Why is that theory reasonable?

Suppose that educators did not experiment. In what ways would acting on unsubstantiated empirical beliefs about the effectiveness of certain manners of education be different from experimenting? In what ways would it be similar? Why is it morally better (or worse) for teachers to act on partially substantiated beliefs about the effectiveness of a manner of education than it is for them to act on unsubstantiated beliefs?

However, before you rely on the research of others to support your beliefs, you must be careful to critically assess the arguments they offer in support of their conclusions. Too often, teachers accept the conclusions of a research article without giving serious consideration to whether the researchers have presented good reasons for them. To properly use the findings of someone else's research, *you* must have good reasons for believing that those findings are true. And this requires that you assess their arguments in the ways we discussed in Part Two.

When you assess the arguments of a researcher, you have to consider not only that person's arguments but any counter-arguments that may exist. As you will find, educational research often uncovers evidence for *and* against claims regarding the effectiveness of various manners of education. In such cases, you will have to determine which is the most reasonable conclusion in the light of the available evidence.

OUTCOMES AND THE MORALITY OF A MANNER OF EDUCATION

Suppose now that you have examined the research and that you have good reasons for believing that teaching some matter in a certain manner is quite effective for producing a particular educational outcome. Although your having determined this is necessary for making a rational decision to employ that manner to produce the outcome, it is not sufficient. In addition, you must have some good reasons for believing that the outcome ought to occur. If the outcome ought *not* to occur and if employing that manner results in the outcome, then you have good reasons to *not* use the manner. As we established earlier, decisions concerning outcomes are logically prior to decisions concerning manner.

But there is even more that must be done here. For even if you have good reasons for believing that a particular manner produces a certain outcome and that the outcome ought to occur, it is possible that using that manner has additional consequences that ought not to occur. And if this is the case, you have some good reasons to *not* employ that manner. Consequently, in trying to make a rational decision to use a particular manner, you need to investigate the probability of that manner's having undesirable consequences. If there are side consequences, and if you have good reasons for believing that some or all of them ought not to occur, you have to determine which is the more rationally defensible alternative: using that manner and producing some outcomes that ought not to occur or not using the manner.

Moreover, in such a case, you should also consider the possibility that there is a more acceptable manner, one that is effective in producing the outcome but which has no negative consequences or, at least, less undesirable ones. If an alternative manner of this sort is available, it would be more rational to use it.

MORAL PRINCIPLES AND
THE MORALITY OF A MANNER

Suppose that you have good reasons for believing each of the following:

Manner M is very effective for producing outcome O.

Outcome O ought to occur.

Manner M does not have any side consequences that ought not to occur.

Although these propositions are reasons for using manner M, they do not comprise good reasons for doing so. For it is possible that all of these propositions are true and that you still *ought not* to use manner M. The reason for this is that manner M may in itself be immoral.

Consider, for instance, the following (bizarre?) example. A teacher wants to act in such a manner as to produce an orderly, well-disciplined class. He or she has very good reasons to believe that an orderly class is an outcome that ought to occur. In addition, all available research shows that a very effective—indeed, the most effective—way to achieve it is to take the first child who misbehaves and hang him by the neck in front of his classmates. And suppose further that using this approach does not have any side consequences that ought not to occur. Even if all of these things were true, the teacher nevertheless ought not to use that manner, for it is clearly immoral.

This rather weird example serves to illustrate a most important point. Whether a manner of education ought to be used depends not only upon its potential for producing outcomes that ought to occur but also upon the morality of the manner itself and whether the use of that manner violates any moral principles.

In this respect, consider some manners of teaching that have actually been employed. For instance, many people advocate the hitting of students if they misbehave or fail to complete assignments properly. Leaving questions of effectiveness aside, is there anything immoral about doing this? Does it violate a moral principle of respect for children as persons, or the right of a person to fail? Does it deny principles of human worth and dignity? Or consider the rather common technique of belittling and demeaning students in front of their peers. Does this technique violate certain moral principles? Should teachers refrain from using it regardless of how effective it may be in achieving certain results?

The general point here is that a particular manner of teaching may be immoral because it violates certain moral principles. And if it is immoral, then *regardless* of its consequences and the desirability of those consequences, it ought not to be employed. So, in order to make an intelligent decision to use a particular manner, you must have some good reasons for believing that it is not immoral—that it does not violate any moral principles.

This requirement raises another important point. It is likely to happen that in many circumstances ethical constraints will make "effective" teaching quite difficult. That is, there may be many effective manners of teaching something to someone, but these may for one reason or another be immoral. And the remaining moral ways of teaching may all be much less effective than the immoral ways.

For instance, various forms of indoctrination such as brainwashing, hypnosis, and emotional manipulation may be very effective ways of teaching certain things. But at the same time, they may be immoral and hence ought not to be used. On the other hand, techniques that involve an appeal to the rationality of the learner, respect for the learner as a person, and a recognition of any person's right to be free to make choices may be moral, but far less effective, ways of teaching.

In recent years, there has been a great deal of emphasis on "setting" behavioral objectives, instructional objectives, individual plans for education, and so forth. For the most part, the advice to teachers has been to "set" your objectives and then "select" the most effective manner of achieving them. Such advice often seems to ignore the moral dimension of outcomes and of manner. Consider the following excerpt from a work intended to "examine the design elements of educational innovation":

> We must determine the most efficient and effective methods and then select materials to provide learning experiences that will utilize the content associated with each objective. . . .
>
> It is our purpose to offer some bases to help you make decisions when you are ready to select the teaching activities, student learning activities, and necessary instructional materials that will enable the largest possible number of students in your group to master the objectives at an acceptable level of achievement in a reasonable amount of time. This, we hope, will be the result of *effective* and *efficient* teaching and learning.
>
> Unfortunately, there is no formula for matching activities to objectives. What may work for one teacher or with one group of students can be unsatisfactory in another situation. You need to know the strengths and weaknesses of alternate methods and of various materials. Then, with that background, you can make your selections in terms of student characteristics and needs that will *best* serve the objectives that you have established.
>
> After pilot try-outs and full-scale use, you will be able to answer such questions as "Does the plan work?" and "How well does it work?" Then you can make up your own mind about which instructional methods and materials are most *effective* and *efficient*. (Jerrold E. Kemp, *Instructional Design: A Plan for Unit and Course Development* [Belmont, Calif.: Lear Siegler, Inc./Fearon Publishers, 1971], pp. 51–52.)

What significant moral issues does the excerpt seem to ignore? Explain.

So making an intelligent decision concerning what manner to use involves much more than just questions of effectiveness. Of greater importance than effectiveness are the ethical concerns having to do with the morality of the outcomes—both intended outcomes and side consequences—and the morality of the manner itself.

A STRATEGY FOR DECIDING
WHAT MANNER TO EMPLOY

The preceding discussion has shown that, in order to make a rational decision to use a particular manner of education, you must have good reasons for believing that

> The manner is an effective way of producing a certain outcome.
>
> That outcome ought to occur, or at least it is not the case that it ought not to occur.
>
> The manner has no side consequences that ought not to occur.
>
> The manner is not in itself immoral.

Given these requirements, the following is an effective strategy for making intelligent decisions concerning what manner to use in teaching something to someone:

1. Identify an educational outcome.

    This may be either a social outcome or an individual outcome.

    You should have good reasons for believing that this outcome ought to occur (or that it is not the case that it ought not to occur)—see Chapter 13.

2. Identify some particular matter that ought to be taught to some person (or group) so as to produce the outcome identified in step 1.

    You may want to use one or another of the strategies discussed in Chapter 14.

    In any event, you must have good reasons for your beliefs.

3. Consider whether there are alternative ways of teaching the matter to that person and identify some of the more effective ones.

    Remember that a manner usually involves more than just what the teacher does. Consequently, you should consider various aspects of the educational situation that might be conditioning factors affecting effectiveness (for example, curriculum design, books and materials, school structure, and so on). Would certain teacher behaviors be more effective if some of those factors were changed?

Your evidence for your beliefs here can be gathered through your own investigations or from the research of others. In either case, you must assess the strength of your evidence and be aware that conflicting evidence may exist. Eventually, you must determine the most reasonable conclusion in the light of available evidence.

4. Consider whether any of the effective manners identified in step 3 has side consequences that ought not to occur.

5. Determine whether any of the effective manners identified in step 3 is immoral.

6. Using the beliefs identified in steps 1 through 5, offer the strongest argument you can for believing that a certain manner ought to be used or that it is a good one.

7. Finally, from time to time, reexamine your decisions and beliefs concerning the manner of education by

(a) reassessing your arguments and the arguments of others in the light of new evidence;

(b) reassessing the reasonableness of the ethical theory you hold.

CONCLUSION

The quotation from Plato that begins this book raises the question of commitment—your commitment to people and their education. The intention throughout has been to provide you with the basic understandings you will need if you are to seriously devote yourself to "amending the false turns of education." But are you committed to this sort of enterprise? Are you seriously concerned about making the best possible educational decisions? Are you truly committed to "correcting" education? Are you really concerned about improving the quality of the education people receive and the ways of life they come to have as a consequence?

Commitment alone is not sufficient, however. It must be joined with an ability and willingness to base educational decisions on the best available evidence. Just as it is impractical and dangerous for the pilots of super jets to fly by the seats of their pants, educators cannot be expected to improve the quality of education, and through it, peoples' ways of life unless they act intelligently upon a knowledge and understanding of relevant information.

Education is vital to the lives of individuals and societies. As Plato says, when education "takes a false turn which permits of correction, we should, one and all, devote the energy of a lifetime to its amendment."

This book has been offered as a preliminary step in that effort. It should be clear that identifying false turns and making intelligent amendments will indeed take a lifetime of serious, sustained, systematic study by us all.

Review

1. Define each of the following terms used in this chapter:

   Manner of education
   Method of agreement
   Method of difference
   Method of concomitant variation

2. Explain how the effectiveness of a manner is usually a matter of degree.
3. Explain why determining the effectiveness of a certain manner requires a clear understanding of the outcome that manner is intended to produce.
4. Explain how a manner often includes both what a teacher does and certain other conditions.
5. Identify and discuss Mill's methods.
6. Show how Mill's methods may be used in gathering evidence for a belief that a certain manner is effective in teaching some particular matter to a person or group.
7. Discuss the role of educational research in providing evidence for beliefs concerning the effectiveness of different manners in producing certain outcomes.
8. Explain why it is necessary to make and justify moral judgments concerning the probable outcomes of a particular manner in order to make a rational decision to use it.
9. Show why knowing that a certain manner is effective in producing a certain outcome, that the outcome ought to occur, and that the manner does not have any side consequences that ought not to occur is not sufficient for making an intelligent decision to use that manner.
10. Show how whether a manner ought to be used depends upon the morality of the manner itself and whether the use of the manner violates any moral principles.
11. Explain how in many cases ethical constraints may make "effective" teaching quite difficult.
12. Identify and discuss the strategy for making rational decisions concerning manner in teaching something to someone.

Bandman, Bertram, and Guttchen, Robert, eds. *Philosophical Essays on Teaching.* New York: Lippincott, 1969.
> A collection of essays by contemporary philosophers that examines the concept of teaching and such related concepts as knowing and learning.

Dewey, John. *Democracy and Education.* New York: Macmillan, 1916.
> Dewey's statement of his philosophical beliefs concerning the matter, manner, and outcomes of education: a significant influence on the development of American education.

Green, Thomas F. *The Activities of Teaching.* New York: McGraw Hill, 1971.
> An in-depth analysis of the concept of teaching, with emphasis on the formation of beliefs, knowledge, truth and falsity, learning, and motivation.

Guttchen, Robert, and Bandman, Bertram, eds. *Philosophical Essays on Curriculum.* New York: Lippincott, 1969.
> A collection of essays by contemporary philosophers on various aspects of the matter of education, including mathematics, the physical and natural sciences, history, literature, the arts, and philosophy.

Hollins, T. H. B., ed. *Aims in Education: The Philosophic Approach.* Atlantic Highlands, N.J.: Humanities Press, 1966.
> A collection of essays concerned with what the outcomes of education ought to be.

Martin, Jane R., ed. *Readings in the Philosophy of Education: A Study of Curriculum.* Boston: Allyn and Bacon, 1970.
> A collection of essays on issues surrounding the matter and outcomes of education.

McClellan, James E. *Philosophy of Education.* Englewood Cliffs, N.J.: Prentice-Hall, 1976.
> An advanced examination of the nature of teaching.

Neill, A. S. *Summerhill: A Radical Approach to Child Rearing.* New York: Hart Publishing Company, 1960.
> An interesting position paper concerning the matter, manner, and outcomes of education.

Peters, R. S. *Ethics and Education.* Glenview, Ill.: Scott, Foresman, 1967.
> A good introductory study of the relationship between ethical theory and decisions concerning the matter and manner of education.

Plato. *The Republic.* (Available in various translations.)
> A classic that identifies some of the important philosophical issues surrounding the determination of matter, manner, and outcome in education, especially as they involve relationships between the individual and society.

Rogers, Carl R. *Freedom to Learn.* Columbus, Ohio: Charles E. Merrill Publishing Company, 1969.
> An alternative view concerning the matter, manner, and outcomes of education.

Troost, Cornelius J. *Radical School Reform: Critique and Alternatives.* Boston: Little, Brown, 1973.

   A collection of essays critical of some recent proposals concerning the matter, manner, and outcomes of education.

Whitehead, Alfred North. *The Aims of Education.* New York: Macmillan, 1929.

   A well-known work that identifies some possible outcomes of education and the matter that ought to be taught if they are to be achieved.

Index